The Bond of Grace and Duty

In the Soteriology of John Owen

The Bond of Grace and Duty

In the Soteriology of John Owen

By
Philip A. Craig

Founders Press

Cape Coral, Florida

Published by
Founders Press

P.O. Box 150931 • Cape Coral, FL 33915
Phone (239) 772-1400 • Fax: (239) 772-1140
Electronic Mail: officeadmin@founders.org
Website: http://www.founders.org

©2020 Founders Press

Printed in the United States of America

13 ISBN: 978–1–943539–16–1

Contents

Foreword

John Owen, the greatest biblical, systematic and spiritual theologian among the Puritans, named and profiled the people he wrote against as little as he well could. He was an expert controversialist when he had to be, but clearly he thought that solid exposition of biblical truth on each topic, elbowing error aside as he came to it and then leaving it behind, was under ordinary circumstances the most God-honoring and reader-edifying path to follow. That explains how it has been possible until now, amid the renaissance of Owen studies that recent years have seen, to miss the fact that the distorted version of Reformed Christianity that was then called Antinomianism was one of the targets at which Owen aimed his arrows when he wrote on the Christian life.

The present volume, however, goes far to fill this gap in our understanding of Owen's agenda. Philip Craig's analysis shows very clearly what was at issue here, and how completely and crushingly, without naming names, Owen outflanks and undercuts this widespread Puritan form of easy-believism. It is a thorough, painstaking and definitive piece of work that carries more of a message for the church of our time than doctoral theses usually do.

The link between grace and duty that Owen spells out with such consistency is the characteristic Puritan understanding of the Reformed conjunction of Word and Spirit as the twofold means whereby God imparts to sinful human beings the new life of knowing, serving and glorifying himself through the mediatorial ministry of Jesus Christ our Lord. Dr. Craig's elucidation of this central motif in Owen's thinking lets the great Puritan speak across the centuries to recall us all to the true roots of personal piety and pastoral reality—the things that, when all is said and done, always matter most for the people of God. Thoughtful persons who care about the renewing of God's church in these days will find what is written here an extremely valuable resource, and one calculated to lead them into the yet more fruitful exercise of reading and engaging with Owen for themselves.

What a privilege it is to introduce and commend such a worth-while book as this.

J. I. Packer

1

Owen's Doctrine of Preparation For Grace and Glory

John Owen and His Influence

John Owen (1616–1683), pastor, preacher to Parliament, chaplain to Oliver Cromwell, and Vice-Chancellor of Oxford University, is widely regarded as the greatest British theologian of all time, though his name recognition today among evangelical Christians falls far short of what he well deserves. While his theological works, ultimately comprising 24 volumes in William Goold's edition of 1850–53, exerted considerable influence in British and American church circles for roughly a century and three quarters following his death, their nineteenth-century shift from Reformed theology to Arminianism and even liberalism diminished his influence and effectively consigned his massive corpus of divinity, including his magisterial theology of the Holy Spirit, to the ash heap of history.

This regrettable state of affairs began to change, however, with the renewed interest in Reformed theology in English-speaking countries catalyzed by the ministries of Dr. Martyn Lloyd-Jones (1899–1981) and Dr. James Innell Packer (1926–) who founded in 1952 the Puritan Studies Conference, now known as the Westminster Conference.

The Banner of Truth Trust, a British publishing house founded in 1957, republished Goold's edition of Owen's collected works in 1968. Then followed Peter Toon's biography *God's Statesman: Life and Work of John Owen* (1971) and Sinclair B. Ferguson's *John Owen on the Christian Life* (1987). Packer's Puritan Conference addresses on Owen's theology, published in 1991 as *Among God's Giants* in the U.K. and *A Quest for Godliness* in the U.S., were also pivotal in exposing a wider audience to Owen's incredibly rich, comprehensive, and incisive theology. Since then, Owen scholarship has advanced with the publication of several published doctoral theses: Randall G. Gleason, *John Calvin and John Owen on Mortification* (1995), Carl R. Trueman, *The Claims of Truth: John Owen's Trinitarian Theology* (2002), and Sebastian Rehnman, *Divine Discourse: The Theological Methodology of John Owen* (2002).

Gleason entered the "Calvin vs. the Calvinists" fray started by R.T. Kendall's *Calvin and English Calvinism to 1649* (1979) by concluding that Owen's theology of mortification exhibited continuity with Calvin's by "maintain[ing] a tension between the unconditional and conditional dimensions of the covenant [of grace]."[1] Rehnman insisted that Owen's Protestant scholastic theology, though more Christ-centered and less metaphysical, resembled medieval scholasticism more than early Reformed theology. This study has found substantial solidarity regarding the doctrine of preparation for grace, however, between Owen and other mainstream Puritans with the teaching of Martin Luther and John Calvin.

John Owen's Theology

John Owen's theology, breath-taking in architectonic grandeur and scope, powerfully depicts the broad sweep of the interaction between gracious divine initiative and human responsibility in Christian salvation, conceived as preparation for both grace and glory. His treatment of the bond of the grace and duty fleshes out, with wonderful depth and clarity, the injunction given by Paul in Philippians 3:12–13 to "work out your own salvation with fear and trembling, for God is at work in you both to will and to perform His good pleasure."

Owen's holistic treatment of preparation for grace and glory carries an urgent message for today's church. Significantly, he clears up the modern confusion between the meritorious preparationism of late Roman Catholic medieval theology (nominalism) and the gracious preparation for grace

---

[1] Randall C. Gleason, *John Calvin and John Owen on Mortification of Sin: A Comparative Study in Reformed Spirituality* (New York: Peter Lang, 1995), 158. Similarly, this study will cast serious doubt on Gavin McGrath's assessment that Owen's theology regarding the conditionality of the covenant of grace was contradictory. Gavin McGrath, *Puritans and the Human Will: Voluntarism within Mid-Seventeenth Century English Puritanism in Richard Baxter and John Owen*, unpublished doctoral thesis, University of Durham, 1989.

championed by Luther, Calvin and the Puritans. The Puritans, including Owen (widely regarded as their best theologian), taught the Christian duty of putting oneself "in the way of salvation" while upholding the primacy of God's grace in drawing the seeker to Himself.

Highly instructive is Owen's distinction (one shared by John Bunyan) between absolute and conditional promises whereby, for example, God's absolute promise of preservation guarantees the Christian's fulfillment of the conditional promise of perseverance. Owen also highlighted the vital importance of the preparatory work of the law in Christian conversion, because he considers conviction of sin necessary to conversion. By recovering these three crucial emphases of historic Reformed theology, Owen rescues the modern-day Reformed pastor and Christian from the false dilemma, observed by Packer, of pursuing evangelism either Arminian-style or not at all:

> [There is] a widespread uncertainty about the evangelistic implications of the Reformed faith. Many today …see the scripturalness of the doctrine of grace…but do not see how … one can preach evangelistically. If the doctrines of total inability, unconditional election and effectual calling are true—if, that is, sinners cannot of themselves turn to God, and faith and repentance are graces given only to the elect—what sense does it make to command all men indiscriminately to repent and believe?[2]

Equally important, Owen's comprehensive treatment of salvation stresses the importance of using the means of grace (including Christian obedience) for Christian sanctification (preparation for glory). His theology is a clarion call to the modern church to escape from its pervasive cocoon of the cheap-grace (antinomian) theology that is destroying its spiritual power and evangelistic witness.

The Puritan Doctrine of Preparation For Grace

The Puritan doctrine of preparation for grace is often misrepresented by modern scholars, and even modern Reformed theologians, as preparationism or crypto-Arminianism. Preparationism, a product of late medieval Roman Catholic nominalism, is the view that man is able to prepare himself for grace and that God becomes obligated to confer further grace upon whoever has done his best to prepare.[3] The Puritan view of prepara-

---

[2] J. I. Packer, *A Quest for Godliness: The Puritan Vision of the Christian Life* (Westchester, IL.: Crossway, 1990), 165.

[3] Jaroslav Pelikan, *The Christian Tradition: Reformation of Church and Dogma (1300–1700)* (Chicago: University of Chicago Press, 1984), 380–81.

tion denies any meritorious or self- preparation that God has to reward with regeneration. Jonathan Edwards (1703–1758), for example, declared that his sermons most blessed with conversions during the Great Awakening were those insisting that God in His absolute sovereignty was not obligated to save unregenerate seekers.[4] Conversely, the Puritan concept of preparation is that a person must usually take certain steps, in diligent exercise of God's appointed means of grace, to prepare himself for grace and glory. As the Puritans put it, a person was to put himself "in the way of" salvation because God's normal (though not invariable) method was to graciously reward those with salvation who diligently sought him through the means of grace.

Preparation for grace is not a Puritan innovation but can be traced back to Martin Luther (1583–1646), who considers that the "emphatically necessary and serious" preparatory work of the law enlightens the unregenerate to face up to their delusion of spiritual freedom, the stark reality of their bondage to sin, and their desperate need for Christ:

> But the Scripture sets before us a man who is not only bound, wretched, captive and sick but who, through the operation of Satan, his lord, adds to his miseries that of blindness, so that he believes himself to be free, happy, possessed of liberty, whole and alive… Christ was sent 'to preach the gospel to the poor, and to heal the broken-hearted.' Hence the work of Satan is to hold men so that they do not recognize their own wretchedness. But the work of Moses the lawgiver is the opposite of this—namely, through the law to lay open to man his own wretchedness, so that, by thus breaking him down, and confounding him in his self-knowledge, he may make him ready for grace, and send him to Christ to be saved. Therefore, the function prepared by the law is nothing to laugh at, but is most emphatically necessary and serious.[5]

Richard A. Muller, when defining the Reformed understanding of *praeparatio ad conversionem*, notes the prevalence of a very similar concept in Lutheran theology, that of the terrified conscience:

---

[4] "No discourses have been more remarkably blessed than those in which the doctrine of God's absolute sovereignty with regard to the salvation of sinners, and his just liberty with regard to answering prayers, or succeeding the pains of natural men, continuing such, have been insisted on. Romans 3:19 shows that it would be just with God for ever to reject and cast off mere natural men" (Jonathan Edwards, "The Great Awakening," in *Works of Jonathan Edwards*, ed. C. C. Goen [New Haven: Yale University Press, 1972], 4:168).

[5] Martin Luther, *The Bondage of the Will*, trans. James I. Packer and O.R. Johnston (Old Tappan, New Jersey: Revell, 1957), 162.

A term used in Reformed dogmatics, particularly by the English, to in-
dicate the terror of heart, the deep remorse, and the fear of hell brought
on by the elenctical [pedagogical] use of the law that precede conversion
and can be viewed as a preparatory work of the Spirit, which subdues
pride and opens the will for grace. The Reformed are anxious to preserve
their doctrine from synergism and argue that *praeparatio* is itself a work
of grace, an *actus praeparatorius*, or preparatory work, an *actus praeceda-
neus*, or work preceding, that involves the inward life of sinners but does
not constitute a human merit. Among the Lutherans this *praeparatio* is
referred to under the terms *terrores conscientiae*.[6]

Despite ample precedent established by Luther and John Calvin
(1509–1564), as discussed below, the doctrine of preparation for grace,
though deeply developed and evangelistically potent during the Puritan
era, has fallen into modern obscurity and found little, if any, place in modern Reformed theology. Several historical reasons seem to account for this
ominous neglect, which has arguably stunted true conversion growth in
American and British Commonwealth churches.

(1) Arminianism, ascendant in modern evangelical theology, has no
place for preparation for grace because the latter concept implies that conversion is usually a more gradual process.[7] Arminian theology stresses the
freedom of the will and a merely persuasive role of the Holy Spirit in conversion, whereas Reformed theology, as reflected in the Westminster Confession, stresses the bondage of the will and transformative power of the
Holy Spirit renewing human faculties in conversion.[8] In short, Reformed
theology views conversion as a more "violent" event in which the unbeliever is weaned from his natural love affair with sin.[9] Modern evangelical

---

[6] Richard A. Muller, *Dictionary of Latin and Greek Theological Terms* (Grand
Rapids: Baker, 1985), 237.

[7] John H. Gerstner and John N. Gerstner, "Edwardsean Preparation for Salvation," *Westminster Theological Journal* 42 (1979): 67.

[8] Westminster Confession section 9.4 (Of Free Will) states in part, "When
God converts a sinner, and translates him into the state of grace, he frees him
from his natural bondage under sin, and by his grace alone enables him freely to
will and to do that which is spiritually good." Section10.1. (Of Effectual Calling)
declares in part: "All those whom God has predestined to life, and those only, he
is pleased, in his appointed and accepted time, effectually to call, by his word and
Spirit, out of that state of sin and death…, enlightening their minds;…giving
unto them an heart of flesh; renewing their wills.…."

[9] J. I. Packer, *Quest*, 40–41: "The occasionally voiced suggestion that there
was something legalistic in their stress on the need for a 'preparatory work' of
contrition and humbling for sin before men can close with Christ is false; the only
point they were making… was that, because fallen man is naturally in love with

theology considers conversion a relatively easy work, whereas the Puritans marked the difficulty of conversion.[10] An Arminian believes that anyone can be saved at any time, whereas the Reformed view, again as represented by the Westminster Confession, is that God saves only His elect and does so in His "due season" or "appointed and accepted time."[11] Consequently, Reformed evangelists have a sense of urgency about encouraging conversion to take place during seasons of grace when God may be wooing the sinner.

(2) There is widespread confusion between the Puritan doctrine of preparation for grace and the concept of preparationism espoused by medieval Roman Catholic nominalists. William of Ockham (1285–1349) and Gregory Biel (ca.1425–1495) believed that, "In accordance with God's gracious goodness, he who does his best in a state of nature receives grace as a fitting reward."[12] As Harvard historian Steven Ozment analyzes it, nominalism held to a four-stage process of salvation:

1. Moral effort: doing the best one can on the basis of natural moral ability;

2. Infusion of grace as an appropriate reward;

3. Moral cooperation: doing the best one can with the aid of grace; and

4. Reward of eternal life as a just due.[13]

The Protestant Reformers and mainstream Puritans objected to the medieval nominalist concept of preparationism because it made preparation for grace meritorious, thereby placing God in man's debt.

---

sin, it is psychologically impossible for him to embrace Christ whole-heartedly as a Saviour, not just from sin's penalty but from sinning itself, until he has come to hate sin and long for deliverance from it. The 'preparatory work' is simply the creating of this state of mind."

[10] Thomas Hooker's treatise, *The Sincere Convert* (1643), is subtitled in part "The Great Difficulty of Saving Conversion." Owen observes that many, upon "beginning a serious closing with Christ find it a work of difficulty and tediousness to flesh and blood" (*Works*, 9:28). Thomas Watson (ca.1620–1686) declares, "The fourth bar in the way to salvation is an [erroneous] view of the easiness of salvation. Is regeneration easy? Are not there pangs in the new birth? Is self-denial easy?" (*Select Works of Thomas Watson* [Morgantown, PA: Soli Deo Gloria, 1990 reprint], 1:378).

[11] Westminster Confession sections 3.6 and 10.1.

[12] Steven Ozment, *The Age of Reform* (1250–1550) (Yale University Press: New Haven (1980), 234. For more background, see Pelikan, *Christian Tradition*, 374–85.

[13] Ibid.

(3) There is a prevalent fear in Reformed circles that the doctrine of preparation betrays crypto-Arminianism. Harvard scholar Perry Miller led the charge by asserting that "It was but a short step from such thinking to an open reliance upon human exertions and to a belief that conversion is worked entirely by rational argument and moral persuasion."[14] Yet this study will argue that preparation is simply the acknowledgment that God in His Providence almost always utilizes means—including the preparatory work of the law—in the salvation of His people; to quote the John Gerstners: "All Reformed theology always maintained that God himself prepares the elect [who are still] unregenerate for regeneration through his providential disposition of the means of grace."[15]

Calvin versus the Calvinists?

The doctrine of conversion occupied a central place in Puritan piety. As Packer observed, "The elaborate practical 'handling' of the subject of conversion in Puritan books was regarded by the rest of the seventeenth-century Protestant world as something of unique value."[16] The work of an entire generation of Puritan scholars centered on the Puritan doctrine of conversion and its continuity or discontinuity with Calvinism. David D. Hall observed in 1987 that, "Certain issues, especially the role and nature of conversion and the relationship between Calvinism and Puritanism, remain the vital center of Puritan studies."[17] In 1979, R. T. Kendall asserted, given Calvin's sudden conversion,[18] that Calvin denied the necessity of preparation and any preparatory work of the law. Kendall writes:

> Calvin's position... rules out any preparation for faith on man's part....
> But not only that; there is nothing in Calvin's doctrine that suggests, even

---

[14] Perry Miller, "Preparation for Salvation in Seventeenth-Century New England," *Journal of the History of Ideas* 4 (1943): 286. R. T. Kendall, discussed below, has adopted Miller's view.

[15] Gerstner and Gerstner, "Edwardsean Preparation," 6.

[16] Packer, *Quest*, 292, quoting the contemporary observations of Thomas Goodwin (1600–1680) and Philip Nye (ca.1596–1672) to this effect.

[17] David D. Hall, "On Common Ground: The Coherence of American Puritan Studies," *William and Mary Quarterly* 44 (1987): 195.

[18] R. T. Kendall, *Calvin and English Calvinism until 1649* (Oxford: Oxford University Press, 1979), 21. Kendall's conclusions have been controversial and disputed. See Paul Helm, *Calvin and the Calvinists* (Edinburgh: Banner of Truth Trust, 1982), 60. Helm concludes that Calvin, the Puritan divines and the Westminster Confession all teach "preparation for faith, but not self-preparation."

in the process of regeneration, that man must be prepared at all—including by the work of the Law prior to faith.[19]

To determine whether Kendall has misconstrued Calvin's position, this study will examine briefly Calvin's two most relevant works: *Institutes of the Christian Religion* and recently translated *The Bondage and Liberation of the Will.*

Calvin's Rejection of the Nominalist View of Preparation

In *Institutes of the Christian Religion*, Calvin denied self- or meritorious preparation (preparationism). Because human seeking is always preceded "by the impulsion of the Holy Spirit," Calvin exclaims, "Away then with all that 'preparation'!" Here we ought to guard against two things: (1) not to say that lawful use of the first grace is rewarded by later graces, as if man by his own effort rendered God's grace effective; or (2) so to think of the reward as to cease to consider it from God's free grace.[20]

Further development of Calvin's thought about preparation for grace found expression in *The Bondage and Liberation of the Will* (1543), his reply to Roman Catholic theologian Albert Pighius (c. 1490–1542), who apparently (His treatise has still not been translated.) held a semi-Pelagian view of conversion:

> He thinks that God does stretch out his hand to fallen humanity to raise them up, but only to those who long to be raised up and do not neglect the grace which is available to help them, but rather lay hold of it, try with its help to return to God, desire to be saved by him, and hope for this—those who deliver themselves to him to be healed, enlightened and saved.[21]

Calvin argues, like Luther, that owing to the bondage of the will, "man cannot prepare himself by his natural powers to receive the grace of God."[22]

---

[19] Ibid., 26. Kendall hedges his statement by admitting that Calvin states that the law can prepare men "to seek what previously they did not realize they had." But Kendall minimizes the value of this preparation by calling it merely "an accidental effect of the law."

[20] John Calvin, *Institutes of the Christian Religion*, ed. John T. McNeill and trans. Ford Lewis Battles (Philadelphia: Westminster Press, 1960), II.ii.26—27 and II.iii.11.

[21] John Calvin, *The Bondage and Liberation of the Will: A Defense of the Orthodox Doctrine of Human Choice against Pighius* (Grand Rapids: Baker, 1996), 187–88.

[22] Ibid., 26.

Accordingly, man "cannot seek anything but evil"[23] and brings to the salvation equation only his sin, total depravity[24] and "crooked will."[25] Following Augustine, Calvin interprets John 6:44 to mean that God's drawing prepares the will prior to any human preparation.[26] He insists that "God is not induced by our preparation to bestow his grace upon us, but in every way he goes before us."[27] In a comment denying self-preparation, Calvin gleans from Romans chapter 3:

> But who cannot see that … it is not in man's power to prepare himself to receive the grace of God, but his whole conversion is the gift of God? … For when the Lord promises that he will give us a heart of flesh in place of our heart of stone, what room is left for preparation? How shall he who is made willing instead of unwilling, ready to obey instead of rebellious and obstinate, claim for himself the praise for his preparation? This is no less declared in the following words: 'I was found by those who did not seek me.' For even though the prophet is speaking about the calling of the Gentiles, yet in it he exhibits the universal pattern of the calling of all of us.[28]

The Importance of Preparation for Grace in Calvin's Theology

If then, as Calvin asserted, the will is passive in conversion, does it automatically follow that human activity has no place? Surprisingly, it does not. In the *Institutes*, Book 2, Chapter 1, Calvin developed, in tandem with certain related doctrines, the doctrine of seeking or preparation for grace. The first related doctrine is that of original sin: a comparison of human nature before and after the Fall should "truly overwhelm us and fill us with shame" and thereby "kindle a new zeal to seek God, in whom each of us may recover those good things which we have utterly and completely lost."[29] The second related doctrine is that of the bondage of the will. Calvin advocates self-examination, not self-complacency: "God's truth requires us to seek in examining ourselves…the kind of knowledge that will strip off all confidence in our own ability, deprive us of all occasion for

---

[23] Ibid., 69.

[24] Ibid., 49, quoting Augustine. Total depravity means that the noetic effects of sin, stemming from the Fall, extend to every human faculty (including reason), not that man is as bad as he can possibly be (ibid., 213).

[25] Ibid., 108.

[26] Ibid., 110, 131–32, 153, 176.

[27] Ibid., 135.

[28] Ibid., 173–74.

[29] *Institutes*, II.i.1.

boasting, and lead us to submission.[30] Only self-examination according to the "standard of divine judgment" will lead to salutary self-despair."[31] In language echoing Romans chapter 8, Calvin stresses that a before-and-after comparison of human nature relative to the Fall should compel us, by recognizing our unworthiness, to seek God:

> Yet God would not have us forget our original nobility, which ... ought truly to arouse in us a zeal for righteousness and goodness. For we cannot think upon either our first condition or ... purpose ...without being prompted to meditate upon immortality, and to yearn after the Kingdom of God. ...It is that from which we have been completely estranged, so that sick of our miserable lot we groan, and in groaning we sigh for that lost worthiness.[32]

This emphasis on the importance of seeking God, even by the unregenerate, continues apace in *The Bondage and Liberation of the Will*. According to Calvin, God's commandments, far from implying human ability, demand the impossible "with the very intention that we should know what we ought to seek from him. For it is faith which obtains by prayer what the law commands."[33] Commenting on Hebrews 11:6, he emphasizes that human seeking of God should be an all-consuming activity:

> Nor do we deny that the struggle ... involve[s] the utmost difficulty and ... require[s] the greatest ... dedication. The question is only whether we fight for God with our own strength, or He supplies from heaven the strength. It is not that we ourselves do nothing or that we without any movement of our will are driven to act by pressure from him, but that we act while being acted upon by him. We will as he guides the heart, we endeavor as he rouses us, we succeed in endeavor as he gives us strength, so that we are animate and living tools, while he is the leader and finisher of the work.[34]

God's Benevolent Blessing of Human Seeking

Calvin also mentions that God's propensity to reward seeking operates on the ground of grace, not merit. "I grant that believers are to expect this blessing of God: that the better use they have made of the prior graces, the more may the following graces be increased. But I say also this reward

[30] *Institutes*, II.i.2.
[31] *Institutes*, II.i.3.
[32] Ibid.
[33] *Bondage and Liberation*, 142.
[34] Ibid., 152.

arises from his free benevolence."[35] Calvin developed his treatment of this theme more thoroughly in *The Bondage and Liberation of the Will*. Though against preparationism, he still points out that God graciously—and not meritoriously—rewards the improvement of grace:

> On the basis of the [parable of the talents] repaid with interest, [Pighius] claims that God rewards the right use of earlier ones by [the gift of] later ones. But I have never denied this absolutely; I have only added this qualification, that a twofold danger must be avoided: God should not be believed to reward the right use of his grace as if man, by his own efforts, rendered the grace which is offered to him effective; and the rewarding should not be thought of in such a way that the grace is no longer gratuitous. On the contrary, the parable should be interpreted [as saying] that God constantly follows up his earlier gifts in us with new and greater ones.[36]

The Preparatory Work of the Law

Contrary to Kendall's claim, Calvin did insist that conversion normally requires a preparatory work of the law. In Book 2, Chapter 5 of the *Institutes*, Calvin counters Pighius' objection that the doctrine of the bondage of the will removes the need for Scriptural exhortations, warnings and precepts by pointing Luther-like to the preparatory work of the law:

> If exhortations and reproofs profit the godly nothing except to convince them of sin, these ought not for this reason to be accounted utterly useless. Now, who would dare since, with the Spirit acting within, they are perfectly able to kindle in us the desire for the good, to shake off sluggishness, to remove the lust for iniquity and its envenomed sweetness— on the contrary, to engender hatred and loathing toward it?[37]

In fact, knowledge of the law drives man to pray for the power to obey, and Scripture promises are added to precepts to motivate even more fervent seeking: "Because our sluggishness is not sufficiently aroused by precepts, promises are added in order... to entice us to love the precepts. The greater our desire for righteousness, the more fervent we become to seek God's grace."[38]

The condemnation of the law, then, is designed to make the unconverted flee to God's mercy. God also uses the law to restrain them from

---

[35] *Institutes*, II.iii.11.

[36] *Bondage and Liberation*, 234–35.

[37] *Institutes*, II.v.5.

[38] *Institutes*, II.v.8.

committing conscience-searing sins prior to the "time of his visitation."[39]
Calvin reinforces his message by painting a vivid picture: "the law is to the
flesh like a whip to an idle and balky ass, to arouse it to work ...to [attain]
the goal [of moral purity]."[40]

Far from entertaining "thunderbolt theology,"[41] Calvin notices God's
frequent utilization of an ordered sequence of steps (a morphology of conversion):

> There is not the least reason for us to be afraid of coming where the Holy
> Spirit distinctly calls [us] to come. For this sequence and these steps of
> God's mercy are described for us, so that he may glorify those whom he
> has justified, justify those whom he has called, and call those whom he
> has chosen.[42]

In the same vein, he observes that God "bestows his favors in stages, so
that the one is a preparation for the other."[43]

Rejection of Preparation by Prominent
Modern Reformed Theologians

Nevertheless, the Puritan doctrine of preparation for grace continues
to be tragically misunderstood today, even by eminent modern Reformed
divines. One example is Scottish church historian Thomas M'Crie, who
objects to any preaching that "teaches that repentance and new obedience
are necessary as prerequisite qualifications, in order to warrant our coming
to the Saviour.[44] M'Crie is right to object to Baxter's erroneous insistence
on the "priority of repentance to faith"[45] and to his teaching (summarized

---

[39] *Institutes*, II.v.11.

[40] *Institutes*, II.v.12.

[41] William K. B. Stoever remarks that "the doctrine of divine sovereignty as
held by sixteenth- and seventeenth century Reformed divines, Continental and
English, does not appear to have required an understanding of conversion as an
instantaneous, lightening-bolt-on-the-road-to-Damascus sort of experience. This
conception seems more reminiscent of a Cane Ridge meeting than of a Swiss or
early Puritan congregation" (*'A Faire and Easye Way to Heaven': Covenant Theology
and Antinomianism in Early Massachusetts* [Middleton, Conn.: Wesleyan University Press, 1978], 219 n.16).

[42] *Bondage and Liberation*, 153.

[43] Ibid., 225.

[44] Thomas M'Crie, *The Story of the Scottish Church* (Glasgow: Bell and Bain,
1874), 453.

[45] Ibid.

by Packer) that, "repentance and faith, being obedient to this new law [of the gospel] are the believer's saving righteousness,"[46] which makes "new obedience" an added condition of the sinner's justification.

But M'Crie does not stop while he is ahead. He goes on to complain of a "legal" strain of preaching, exemplified by David Dickson (1583–1663) in his *Sum of Saving Knowledge* (a small book appended since 1650 to the Scottish version of the Westminster Confession) and contrasts the "very different … evangelical strain of Hugh Binning, Samuel Rutherford and Archbishop Leighton. The two lines of antagonistic sentiments now came [in the Marrow Controversy] into open and violent collision.[47]

M'Crie's argument against preaching the need for repentance seems motivated by his fear that the unregenerate might take his repentance (or new obedience) to be a work meriting salvation. Yet none of the three divines cited by M'Crie appear on closer examination to share his objection to the preaching of repentance. Hugh Binning, the first cited authority, writes:

> I know it is not possible that a lost soul can receive Christ till there be some preparatory convincing work of the law to discover sin and misery; but I hold to look for any such preparation and fetch an encouragement or motive therefrom to believe in Christ is really to give him a price for his free waters and wine. It is to mix in Christ and the law in the point of our acceptation. He must examine himself not to find himself a *sensible humble* sinner, that so he may have ground of believing, but that he find himself a *lost perishing* sinner, void of all grace and goodness, that he may find the more necessity of Christ.[48]

Note well that Binning qualifies his opinion by first acknowledging the absolute necessity of the preparatory work of the law. Binning's concern seems to be not that preaching repentance should be avoided but that a "sensible" or "qualified" sinner might fail to realize his "lostness."

Likewise, the second cited authority, Samuel Rutherford in *Trial and Triumph of Faith* (1645) insisted on the necessity of preparation for grace through conviction of sin. Rutherford declares:

> Those at whose salvation Christ has a special aim, and whom he actually converts, are first sinners and lost in their own eyes. Hence Christ actually calls and saves but [only] those who are prepared. There is a prepara-

---

[46] Packer, *Quest*, 108.
[47] M'Crie, ibid., 454.
[48] Ibid.

tion of order. God's ordinary way is to bring men to Christ [who first realize that they are] lost and condemned. [49]

Finally, Robert Leighton, the third authority relied on by M'Crie, expects "faith, and inseparable repentance and leaving off sin" for a seeker to come to Christ[50] and enforces the necessity of the preparatory work of the law:

> The gospel is not a doctrine of licentiousness... but of new life in Christ, ...though in the notion of repentance, there is ... the law convincing of sin and death, and working a sense of misery and sorrow. [Yet] nothing is so powerful as the doctrine of free grace to convert a soul, not excluding convincements [convictions of sin] by the law, but including them.[51]

Owen, in common with other Puritans, never equates conviction of sin with conversion from sin. In fact, he depicts several ways in which conviction of sin could miscarry without reaching the point of conversion (see chapter 7). What is more, the usual Puritan sequence of conversion insists on self-despair. As J. I. Packer points out, "The themes of man's natural inability to believe, of God's free election being the ultimate cause of salvation, and of Christ's dying specifically for his sheep [are meant through preaching to] drive sinners to despair, by suggesting to them that it is not in their own power to be saved through Christ."[52] Owen, though of a different persuasion from M'Crie, still would have sympathized with his concern, observing that:

> [Gospel] promises will sufficiently warrant a perplexed soul to close with Christ, even when it can find in itself no other qualifications or conditions, but only such as render it every way unworthy to be accepted. At [the] least, a man's sense and acknowledgement of his [lost] condition is needful to precede his closing with the promise.[53]

In other words, to answer Binning's expressed concern, it is not the qualified sinner but the lost one who feels his need to come to Christ.

---

[49] Samuel Rutherford, *The Trial and Triumph of Faith* (Edinburgh: Banner of Truth, 2001), 148–49. Rutherford also subscribed to the difficulty of salvation (ibid., 285–86).

[50] Robert Leighton, "Lectures on the First Nine Chapters of Matthew" in *The Whole Works of Robert Leighton*, Vol. 3:16.

[51] Ibid., Vol. 3:21–22.

[52] Packer, *Quest for Godliness*, 126.

[53] Owen, *Works*, 9:48.

Abraham Kuyper (1837–1920), a second example, repudiates the idea that preparatory grace can be a material cause of regeneration.[54] Wresting a metaphor originally used by Owen and other Puritans[55] to explain the doctrine of preparation for grace (see Chapter 9), Kuyper interprets it so as to deny this doctrine altogether. In *The Work of the Holy Spirit*, he asserts:

> Even the representation, still maintained by some of our best theologians, that preparatory grace is like the drying of wet wood, so that the spark can more readily ignite it, we cannot adopt. Wet wood will not take the spark. It *must* be dried before it *can* be kindled. And this does not apply to the work of grace. This disposition of our souls is immaterial.[56]

Kuyper provocatively maintains that, "Neither slothfulness nor neglect can ever hinder an elect person from passing from death to life at the appointed time."[57] Owen begs to differ, unwilling to encourage any despite of God's appointed means of grace: "It is brutish ignorance in any to argue in things of God, from the effectual operations of the Spirit, unto a sloth and negligence of our own duty.... God hath promised to 'work in us' in a way of grace what He requires from us in a way of duty."[58]

Yet a third example of this misunderstanding surfaced in 1995 in a published debate between Robert Letham and Donald Macleod. Macleod takes the same road traveled earlier by M'Crie:

> Long before it became fashionable to denigrate the scholasticism of 17th Century Calvinism, voices within Evangelicalism itself were commenting on the marked differences between the Christianity represented by David Dickson's *Sum of Saving Knowledge* and that represented by the sermons of Samuel Rutherford.[59]

[54] He and Owen would both agree that preparation can never serve as a formal or efficient cause of regeneration. Aristotle posited four types of causes: (1) An efficient cause is that by which some change is wrought; (2) A final cause is the end or purpose for which the change is produced; (3) A material cause is that out of which a change is wrought; and (4) A formal cause is that into which something is changed (Richard Taylor, "Causation," *The Encyclopedia of Philosophy*, ed. Paul Edwards [New York: Macmillan, 1967], 2:56).

[55] See for example, Iain H. Murray, "Antinomianism: New England's First Controversy," *Banner of Truth* 179–180 (August 1978): 45, quoting similar metaphors for preparation from David Dickson and John Cotton (1584–1652).

[56] Abraham Kuyper, *The Work of the Holy Spirit*, trans. Henri De Vries (New York: Funk and Wagnalls, 1900), 307 (emphasis his).

[57] Ibid., 371.

[58] Owen, *Works*, 3:204.

[59] Robert Letham and Donald Macleod, "Is Evangelicalism Christian?" *Evangelical Quarterly* 67 (1995): 17.

Like M'Crie before him, Macleod criticizes Dickson as a "legal" preacher and mistakes Rutherford to be an opponent of preparation for grace. Macleod claims that in Dickson's work "disproportionate attention is given to the processes by which men are convicted of sin, righteousness and judgment"[60] and, somewhat surprisingly, goes far beyond M'Crie in approving the wording of the Auchterarder Creed that had sparked the Marrow Controversy.[61] M'Crie had conceded that, "The proposition was unhappily worded; for the duty of every sinner must, no doubt, be to forsake sin."[62]

In Kuyper's case, his opposition to preparation for grace is most readily explained by hyper-Calvinism. The most obvious exhibition of this strain in his theology, besides his failure to discourage slothfulness, is his view that covenant children (i.e., those with Christian parentage who have undergone infant baptism and remained under the means of grace) are presumptively regenerate. As for M'Crie and Macleod, their opposition stems primarily from their "Marrow" theology, a theology that arose in early Eighteenth-Century Scotland when Thomas Boston (1677–1732) rediscovered *The Marrow of Modern Divinity* (1645), a book whose theological tenets bear several striking affinities with those of Seventeenth-Century English antinomian theology.

First, both Marrowmen and Seventeenth-Century English antinomians object to the conditionality of the covenant of grace, as when the Westminster Larger Catechism question and answer 153 insists that both faith and repentance are conditions of salvation and Westminster Confession section 15.1 declares that, "repentance unto life is an evangelical grace,

---

[60] Ibid., 18. Macleod's criticism of Dickson of a "legal" preacher seems somewhat unfair. Dickson acknowledges that faith and repentance are gifts from God. (The Westminster Confession of Faith, 325.) Dickson's treatment suggests matter of conviction of sin, righteousness and judgment from not only the law but also the gospel (Ibid., 326–330). He also insisted that, "The true end of the law, preached unto the people, is that they, by the law being made to see their deserved condemnation, should flee to Christ unfeignedly, to be justified by faith in Christ (Ibid., 341). Though he does provide a model sinner's prayer, Dickson insists only that God "may" answer it (Ibid., 330).

[61] The Auchterarder Creed provided, "I believe it is not sound and orthodox to teach that we must forsake sin in order to our coming with Christ, and instating us in covenant with God" (cited in McCrie, 452). Formulated by the Auchterarder Presbytery, this creed contradicts Proverbs 28:13 which declares that "He who covers his sins will not prosper, but whoever confesses and forsakes his sins will have mercy." It was probably a well-intentioned, but not well-executed, attempt to correct Richard Baxter's error of placing repentance before faith in the order of salvation.

[62] Ibid.

the doctrine whereof is to be preached by every minister of the gospel, as well as that of faith in Christ" and section 15.3, that "repentance is of such necessity to sinners, that none may expect pardon without it." In a fairly recent article on Thomas Boston, A. T. B. McGowan shockingly suggested that the Church of Scotland churchmen who condemned the Marrowmen "were guilty of a perversion of covenant theology. They made repentance a condition of salvation."[63]

Most importantly, as discussed at length in Chapter 4, John Owen's theology cuts the ground out from anyone like McGowan who objects to the conditionality of the convenant of grace: Owen demonstrates that because the bond of grace and duty is indissoluble, any perceived contradiction between absolute and conditional promises in the covenant of grace is only apparent and not real. In his treatise *Justification* (1678), Owen reconciled these two types of gospel promises:

> That those who were to be taken into this covenant [of grace] should receive grace enabling them to comply with the terms of it, fulfills its conditions, [and] yield the obedience which God required therein; for, by the ordination of God, [Jesus Christ] did merit and procure for them, the Holy Spirit and all needful supplies of grace, to make them new creatures, and enable them to yield obedience from a new principle of spiritual life faithfully to the end.[64]

Secondly, both groups at large object to preaching the law as preparation for grace. Thirdly, neither group accepts fear of hell, or hope of heaven and reward as legitimate gospel motives. Fourthly, both groups tend to downplay obedience because of their shared view that it flows almost automatically from regeneration.[65]

---

[63] A. T. B. McGowan, "Thomas Boston," in *New Dictionary of Theology*, ed. Sinclair B. Ferguson and David F. Wright (Downers Grove: InterVarsity Press, 1988), 109.

[64] Owen, *Works*, 5:188. Owen also affirms later in this same treatise that "all the good things... promised in the covenant [of grace] were all procured for us by the obedience and death of Christ" (*Works*, 5:194). See also Bunyan's statement in *Come and Welcome to Jesus Christ*: "There is a blessed harmony between [absolute and conditional promises]. The conditional promise calls for repentance, the absolute promise gives it (Acts 5:31). The conditional promise calls for faith, the absolute promise gives it (Zeph. 3:12; Rom. 15:12). The conditional promise calls for a new heart, the absolute promise gives it (Ezek. 36:25–26). The conditional promise calls for holy obedience, the absolute promise gives it, or causes it (Ezek. 36:27)" (*Works*, 1:255).

[65] Thomas Boston seems to be a notable exception to this generalization, at least as applied to preparation for glory. See A. W. Pink, *Exposition of the Ser-*

Though understandably sympathetic to the Marrowmen as the evangelical party in the Church of Scotland during the controversy, W. G. Blaikie, professor of theology at New College, Edinburgh for almost 30 years, powerfully captures semi-antinomian tendencies of their theological tenets and is worth quoting in full:

> The [General] Assembly laid stress on the obligation of obedience to the moral law, as revealed under the covenant of works, and to the fear of punishment and hope of reward as still being considerations that ought to influence believers in their life; while the [Marrowmen] held the believer to be free from the obligation of the law as a covenant and maintained that, under the new covenant of grace, gratitude, filial love and delight in God were the [only] true motives to obedience. But the [real] drift [of the Marrow school] was to maintain and magnify the glorious grace of God, and sometimes, through fear of an undue place being given to personal obedience, to speak of it somewhat disparagingly. Not that the evangelical school failed to maintain the necessity of obedience; not that they failed to urge that a faith not followed by works was no living faith but only a dead pretender; but somehow they failed to expend their strength on this department of truth; they regarded [Christian obedience] as something that in a large degree might take care of itself: if they were successful in procuring the right kind of faith, good works would certainly follow. But to preach good works before faith [i.e., the preparatory work of the law] was to try to reap a harvest where no right seed had been sown.[66]

Professor Blaikie observes, then, four striking resemblances between Marrow theology and Seventeenth-Century antinomianism, namely shared objections to (1) treating repentance as a condition of justification; (2) preaching the law as preparation for grace; (3) embracing fear of eternal punishments or hopes of heavenly reward as motives for obedience; and (4) emphasizing the importance of obedience.

A fourth prominent example is furnished by the theology of Norman Shepherd, who resurrects Richard Baxter's neonomianism by claiming the conditions of justification are not only faith and repentance but "new obedience" too.[67] In rejecting traditional "regeneration-evangelism", Shepherd

mon on the Mount (Grand Rapids: Michigan, Baker Book House,1982 repr.) 353 quoting Boston's *View of the Covenant of Grace*: "[God] gives the rewards of the covenant in the course of their obedience."

[66] W. G. Blaikie, *The Preachers of Scotland* (Glasgow: T. & T. Clark, 1888), 193–94.

[67] Norman Shepherd, *The Call of Grace: How the Covenant Illuminates Salvation and Evangelism* (Phillipsburg, NJ: Presbyterian and Reformed, 2000), 98.

jettisons the preparatory use of the law and even preaching for conversion. Given that "the climax of the gospel appeal is reached when the hearer is urged to ask God for a new heart with which to lay hold of the grace of Christ,"[68] Shepherd objects to a supposed inconsistency between natural inability and any sort of preparation for grace:[69]

> The serious tension between the demand for faith and repentance and denial of any ability to do what is demanded... is all too familiar to any Reformed [evangelist]. Even the exhortation to ask for a new heart does not square with the doctrine of total inability. There is *nothing* the unregenerate person can do or will to do to move toward conversion.[70]

Shepherd 's counsel of human inactivity is very similar to that of Abraham Kuyper.

Vast Importance of Preparation For Grace in Puritan Evangelism

In marked contrast to its prevalent neglect in modern Reformed theology, the doctrine of preparation loomed large in Puritan theology and evangelism. Edwards' grandfather Solomon Stoddard (1639–1729) wrote the standard guide to evangelism for New England pastors entitled *A Guide to Christ* (1714). In his foreword, Increase Mather (1639–1723), another leading Puritan pastor in New England, signals the urgency of preparation for grace.

> That preparation for grace is necessary before the soul can be united by Him to faith is an undoubted truth. *He came not to call the righteous, but sinners to repentance.* Men must be convinced of their being sinners or they will not be in bitterness for it. Sin must be bitter to them or they will not forsake it. As long as they love their sins, it is impossible that they should believe on Christ (John 5:44), nor will they come to Christ for righteousness and life unless they have a humbling sense of their own unrighteousness (Romans 10:3).[71]

---

[68] Ibid., 97.

[69] Guy Prentiss Waters, in criticizing Shepherd's view of justification, aptly cites the Westminster Larger Catechism question and answer 32 which declares "holy obedience" to be "the way... appointed... to salvation" but not the way to justification. *Justification and the New Perspective on Paul* [Phillipsburg, NJ: Presbyterian and Reformed, 2004], 210).

[70] Ibid., 98 (emphasis his).

[71] Solomon Stoddard, *A Guide to Christ* (Ligonier, Pa.: Soli Deo Gloria, 1993 reprint), ix.

Stoddard likewise insists on the necessity of a 'work of preparation.' He even predicts that catastrophic consequences for the church would ensue from neglect of this doctrine.

> There are some who deny any necessity of the preparatory work of the Spirit of God in order to a closing with Christ. This is a very dark cloud, both as it is an evidence that men do not have the experience of this work in their own souls, and as it is a sign that such men are utterly unskillful in guiding others who are under this work. If this opinion should prevail in the land, it would give a deadly wound to religion. It would expose men to think of themselves as converted when they are not.[72]

Nor were these New England Puritan pastors unrepresentative of English Puritans. Scholars have discovered a prominent doctrine of preparation for grace in the sermons of Richard Greenham (1540–1594),[73] Thomas Hooker (1586–1647)[74] and Richard Sibbes (1577–1635).[75]

Moreover, mainstream Puritan pastors even gave directions toward 'getting' faith and repentance (as the instrumental means of conversion). Thomas Watson (ca.1620–1686) prescribes six means of repentance. These include (1) a serious consideration of sin, God's mercies, affliction and final judgment; (2) comparison of conditions now and later for the penitent as opposed to the impenitent; (3) a settled determination to forsake sin; (4) earnest supplication for the gift of repentance; (5) a comparison of God's holiness with one's own sinfulness; and (6) labor for faith.[76] Similarly, John Flavel (ca.1630–1691) gives out ten directions toward receiving faith. Among these are counting the cost, engaging in petitionary prayer, parting with any "darling" sin and making covenant to accept Christ as Prophet, Priest and King.[77]

[72] Ibid., xv.

[73] John H. Primus, *Richard Greenham: The Portrait of an Elizabethan Pastor* (Macon, Ga.: Mercer University Press, 1998), see especially chapter 6, "The Doctrine of Means."

[74] Sargent H. Bush, Jr., *The Writings of Thomas Hooker: Spiritual Adventure in Two Worlds* (Madison: University of Wisconsin Press, 1980). Though Hooker immigrated to New England, he began his pastoral ministry in England.

[75] Mark E. Dever, *Richard Sibbes: Puritanism and Calvinism in Late Elizabethan and Early Stuart England* (Macon, Ga.: Mercer University Press, 2000).

[76] Thomas Watson, *The Doctrine of Repentance* (Edinburgh: Banner of Truth, 1987 reprint), 106–22.

[77] John Flavel, *Works of John Flavel* (Edinburgh: Banner of Truth, 1982), 4:137–42.

The Puritan View of Conversion and Preparation for Grace and Glory

The doctrine of conversion occupied a central place in Puritan piety. As Packer observes, "The elaborate practical 'handling' of the subject of conversion in Puritan books was regarded by the rest of the seventeenth-century Protestant world as something of unique value."[78] Pride of place for modern study of the Puritan view of conversion goes to Perry Miller, the Harvard professor who revived academic interest in Puritan theology. Miller popularized involuntary conversion as "the rape of the surprised will."[79] In *The New England Mind* he writes: "Supernatural grace, a work peculiar to the elect, comes upon them with irresistible force and depends upon no antecedent conditions and preparations. This conception is the very heart of Puritanism. This [force] is free, unpredictable and lawless."[80]

Miller's view of Puritan conversion, though criticized by Norman Pettit (see chapter 3) has been widely influential, which is unfortunate for several reasons. The Puritans never limited the subject of conversion to the will, as Miller does, because all human faculties are renewed in regeneration. Nor did the Puritans view the will as unwilling in conversion. In fact, the Westminster Confession declares that those whom God has effectually called "out of a state of sin and death... come most freely, being made willing by his grace."[81] Miller even contradicted himself by admitting that the Puritans did not view conversion as involuntary and voluntaristic. In a chapter "The Means of Conversion", Miller in full-scale retreat mode admits that the Puritans understood regeneration to be voluntary and to involve the mind and not just the will:

> In regeneration God deals with men as rational creatures, converts them by an influence of grace and yet also by a rational enlightenment. The will is not forced, but led. We come to faith voluntarily. Because grace does not destroy but rectifies nature, conversion must come through the reason.

> Though grace is a cataclysm, a sudden revelation, a burst of light, though it is above [nature], it is not entirely unrelated to efficient causes. A naturalistic account can be given of the supernatural, even though in many

---

[78] J I Packer, *Quest for Godliness*, 292, quoting the contemporary observations of Thomas Goodwin (1600–1680) and Philip Nye (ca.1596–1672) to this effect.

[79] Miller, "Preparation for Salvation," 261.

[80] Perry Miller, *The New England Mind* (Boston: Beacon Press, 1961), 34.

[81] Westminster Confession section 10.1. See Psalm 110:3.

instances the same natural causes produce no regeneration. There is a logic and a preparation, a conception and a gestation. In orthodox Puritan theory, grace is not thrust upon the soul unexpectedly and abruptly, but is insinuated according to the laws of psychology through means.[82]

In fact, the Puritans did not view conversion as a merely one-time event, but as an ongoing course of sanctification involving repetition of the same basic pattern of conversion. Charles Hambrick-Stowe notices that:

> Scholars have commonly limited their discussion of Puritan religious life to the issue of conversion. New Englanders, admittedly, made much of this experience as a personal milestone and credential, but it marked only the beginning of the journey. The spiritual dynamics of preparation and implantation [union with Christ]—death and resurrection, repentance for sin and subsequent salvation—described the actual experience of individuals over the course of their lives.[83]

In other words, preparation for grace (though monergistic) and preparation for glory (though synergistic) both nevertheless follow the same prescribed steps such as conviction, faith, and repentance. Hambrick-Stowe, citing William Perkins (1558–1602) and Thomas Shepard (1605–1649),[84] states that "Shepard referred to his own progress in grace with a startling phrase 'renewed conversions.' The stages of these deeper experiences followed the original conversion pattern."[85]

As appears in chapters 2 and 3, many antinomians such as John Everarde and Anne Hutchinson (1615–1643) decried the doctrine of preparation as a supposed infringement on free grace. But both Owen and Edwards, probably the two greatest Puritan theologians, believed that preparation for grace was sound and important for powerful evangelistic preaching. Edwards highlights the importance of preaching with a morphology of conversion kept firmly in mind:

> Many persons seem to be prejudiced against affections and experiences, that come in such a method as has been insisted on by many divines: first, awakenings, fears and awful apprehensions, followed with such legal humblings in a sense of total sinfulness and helplessness, and [only] then light and comfort.... But such prejudices and objections are without rea-

[82] Miller, *The New England Mind*, 288–89.

[83] Charles Hambrick-Stowe, *The Practice of Piety: Puritan Devotional Disciplines in Seventeenth-Century New England* (Chapel Hill: University of North Carolina Press, 1982), 21.

[84] Ibid., 78. Perkins, as quoted by Hambrick-Stowe, acknowledges the monergism-synergism distinction between the two.

[85] Ibid., 199.

son or Scripture.... It is God's manner of dealing with men to lead them into a wilderness, before he speaks comfortably to them and so to order it, that they shall be brought into distress, and made to see their own helplessness and absolute dependence on his power and grace, before he appears to work any great deliverance for them is abundantly manifest by the Scripture.[86]

Owen and Edwards did believe, nevertheless, that some Puritan divines had prescribed too much detail and uniformity in their published morphologies of conversion. Edwards writes that, "Some have gone too far toward directing the Spirit of the Lord, and marking out His footsteps for Him, and limiting Him to certain steps and methods."[87] In *The Real Christian* (1670) Puritan pastor Giles Firmin (1615–1697), who had resided in England and New England, identifies Thomas Hooker and Thomas Shepard.

Surprisingly, however, Owen does not figure among Puritans whose view of preparation has been studied in-depth. Why should Owen's views of preparation for grace and glory repay study? First, he is widely considered the "prince of the Puritan divines," both doctrinally and experientially. As Ferguson remarks, "There is widespread agreement that John Owen was *the* theologian of the Puritan movement."[88] His stature as a theologian may be grasped by the nearly unprecedented public response to Goold's release of his 24-volume collected works in 1853 when nearly 300 libraries ordered the full set.[89] Owen regularly preached to a congregation numbering nearly 2,000 and frequently to Parliament. Vice-Chancellor of Oxford University from 1652–1657, Owen even with a Doctorate of Divinity awarded by Oxford in 1653, remained self-effacing enough to attend the preaching of John Bunyan (1628–1688). Seeking Bunyan's release from prison, Owen's self-deprecating remark to King Charles II about his own preaching should not be taken at face value. Owen's preaching combined theological incisiveness with searching application. In 1839 under the preaching of young William Chalmers Burns revival broke out in Dundee and Kilsyth, Scotland, ultimately leading to the founding of the Free Church of Scotland. Burns' preaching drew mainly from Owen's *Exposition of Psalm 130* (1688)[90] about personal appropriation of God's forgiveness.

[86] Jonathan Edwards, *The Religious Affections*, in *Works of Jonathan Edwards*, ed. John E. Smith (New Haven: Yale University Press, 1959), 2:151–52.

[87] Ibid., 89.

[88] Sinclair B. Ferguson, *John Owen on the Christian Life* (Edinburgh: Banner of Truth, 1987), 19 (emphasis his).

[89] *Works*, 1:xii.

[90] Michael McMullen, *God's Polished Arrow: William Chalmers Burns* (Rosshire, UK: Christian Focus Publications, 2000), 32.

Owen wrote a large number of treatises relevant to preparation for grace and glory. *Pneumatologia* (1674) is a systematic theology expounding the person and work of the Holy Spirit and spelling out the bond of grace and duty in the Christian life. *On the Mortification of Sin* (1656) lays out a Scriptural approach to putting to death the principle of indwelling sin. *Of Temptation* (1658) counsels strategies of avoidance and conquest. *On Indwelling Sin in Believers* (1668) equips the Christian to withstand the formidable power of indwelling sin. *The Nature and Causes of Apostasy* (1676) surveys total and partial apostasy in church history and Christian living. *On Spiritual-Mindedness* (1681) demonstrates that the transforming reality of regeneration can be known primarily by the spiritual transformation of the mind. *On the Dominion of Sin and Grace* (1688) gives directions toward securing the throne of grace in the believer's heart against the usurpation of sin. His massive seven- volume *Exposition of Hebrews* (1668–1684) sets out the importance of sounding gospel warnings, even to Christians.

Secondly, often called the English Calvin and known for exhaustive treatment of every subject tackled, Owen's thorough views on preparation for grace and glory should set the benchmark for mainstream Puritan theology while demonstrating the basic continuity between Puritan and Reformed theology. As Packer observes,

> By common consent the greatest among Puritan theologians, no one can touch him for solidity, profundity, massiveness and majesty in exhibiting from Scripture God's ways with sinful mankind. He stands in the centre of the Puritan mainstream.... In his own day he was seen as England's foremost bastion and champion of Reformed evangelical orthodoxy. For method and substance [of his theology] Owen reminds one frequently of Calvin; he is constantly near the centre of seventeenth-century Reformed thought throughout.[91]

Thirdly, though Owen wrote in far less detail on preparation for grace and the morphology of conversion than Hooker or Shepard, he wrote correspondingly more on preparation for glory. A study of Owen should give a greater sense of the symmetry between preparation for grace and preparation for glory in the overall scheme of the Christian life. Though Owen acknowledged with Perkins that the former is monergistic and the latter synergistic, he still regarded the Christian life as the ongoing repetition of the basic pattern of conversion.

Fourthly, Owen himself, in discussing mortification of sin in *On the Dominion of Sin and Grace* (1688), clearly differentiates between preparation for grace and preparation for glory.

[91] Packer, *Quest for Godliness*, 81, 193 (conflated and paraphrased slightly).

It is true, in our first conversion to God, we are as it were surprised by a mighty act of sovereign grace, changing our hearts, renewing our minds, and quickening us with a principle of spiritual life. Ordinarily, many things are required of us in a way of duty in order thereunto; and many previous operations of grace in our minds, in illumination and the sense of sin, do materially and passively dispose us thereunto, as wood when it is dried is disposed to firing; but the work itself is performed by an immediate act of divine power, without any active cooperation on our part. But this is not the law or rule of the communication or operation of actual grace for the subduing of sin. It is given in a way of concurrence with us in the discharge of our duties; and when we are sedulous in them, we may be sure that we shall not fail of divine assistance, according to the established rule of the administration of gospel grace.[92]

Note that preparation for grace does not involve "any active cooperation on our part." By contrast, as Owen puts it, God hath promised to 'work in us' in a way of grace what He requires from us in a way of duty.

Fifthly, and most importantly, as fully discussed in Chapter 4, John Owen and John Bunyan will not only make a very important theological distinction between absolute and conditional promises of the covenant of grace. Owen and Bunyan will demonstrate how the absolute promise secures the full covenantal performance of the conditional promise, thereby removing the ground out from under any who would object to the conditionality of the covenant of grace.

Recovering the doctrine of preparation for grace and glory should make a dramatic difference in the effectiveness of evangelism and the pursuit of holiness. The doctrine of preparation for grace greatly influences the way the gospel is preached. Does a preparatory work of the law, for example, normally precede conversion? Stoddard believes that neglect of the doctrine of preparation produces false conversions and gives religion a "deadly wound." Owen likewise affirms that it is "a duty incumbent on all ministers of the gospel to acquaint themselves with the normal morphology of conversion that they may be able to comply with the will of God and grace of the Spirit in the effecting and accomplishment of it [conversion] upon the souls of them unto whom they dispense the word."[93] Owen

---

[92] *Works*, 7:549. On the doctrine of divine concurrence, see Louis Berkhof, *Systematic Theology* (Grand Rapids: Eerdmans, 1941), 171–75.

[93] *Works*, 3:227. A morphology of conversion describes the work of the Holy Spirit in bringing a sinner to a place of repentance and faith in Christ and the steps normally involved in the process. See Samuel T. Logan, "Jonathan Edwards and the Northampton Awakening," in *Preaching and Revival* (London: Westminster Conference, 1984), 69.

even attributes pastoral ignorance of the morphology of conversion and the "want [lack] of an experience of the power of this work in their own souls" as "one great cause of that lifeless and unprofitable ministry" among Reformed pastors.[94]

The doctrine of preparation for glory is no less crucial. Owen, by tracing out bond of grace and duty throughout the whole spectrum of the Christian life, has given the church the spiritual weapon to identify and escape from the cheap-grace theology that enervates the power of its holiness and witness to the watching world.

Methodology

Earlier Owen scholars generally recognized that Owen's theological output targeted clearly identified opponents: Arminians, Socinians, Roman Catholics, Anglican moralists, and Quakers. His first published theological work, *A Display of Arminianism* (1642), attacked the resurgent Arminianism of Laudian Anglicanism; and both *The Death of Death in the Death of Christ* (1647) and *The Doctrine of Perseverance* (1674) challenged the Arminian denial of particular redemption and perseverance. His sustained attack on Socinianism [Unitarianism] appeared in *Vindication of the Doctrine of the Trinity* (1669) and *Vindiciae Evangelicae, or the Mystery of the Gospel Vindicated* (1655). Volume 14 of his Works collects a number of his treatises written against Roman Catholic theology and practice. *Pneumatologia* (1674) insisted on the reality of regeneration over against Anglican moralists; and his *Pro Sacris Scripturis Exercitationes adversus Fanaticos* (1659) rebutted the main tenets of Quakerism.

Yet this study will argue that Owen wrote against a more subtle and pernicious theological opponent that has yet to become a central focus of Owen scholarship, namely, Seventeenth-Century antinomians. This battleground has remained largely out of sight for two reasons. First, while earlier Owen scholars recognized the presence of named theological opponents and mentioned the antinomian threat occasionally, studies by David Como[95] and Theodore Bozeman[96] documenting the vitality and growth of the antinomian underground in both England and New England even in

---

[94] *Works*, 3:227–28.

[95] David R. Como, *Blown by the Spirit: Puritanism and the Emergence of an Antinomian Underground in Pre-Civil-War England* (Stanford, Calif.: Stanford University Press, 2004).

[96] Theodore Dwight Bozeman, *The Precisianist Strain: Disciplinary Religion and Antinomian Backlash in Puritanism to 1638* (Chapel Hill: University of North Carolina Press, 2004).

early decades of the 1600's did not appear in print until 2004. Secondly, for undisclosed reasons, Owen took a stealth tack in opposing his antinomian adversaries. While he often named or even quoted his recognized theological opponents, Owen never quoted antinomians directly, much less mentioned them by name.[97] Although it was a convention of Seventeenth-Century authors not to quote their contemporaries when more ancient authorities would serve,[98] this convention does fully explain his mysterious reticence.

To demonstrate that Seventeenth-Century antinomians served as one of Owen's more prominent theological opponents, three strands of evidence will be marshaled. The first body of evidence comes from Owen's treatises and prefaces wherein he bemoans the prevailing apostasy of his era and its doctrinal and practical antinomianism. For example, *The Glory of Christ Applied to Unconverted Sinners and Saints under Spiritual Decays* (1692), as its title implies, addresses a time of "public apostasy" involving the "notorious" neglect of public worship and private devotion.[99] It was antinomian preachers and their doctrinal antinomianism that were blamed by Owen for this sorry state of affairs. He lambasts their hypocritical coupling of moral laxity with claims to Christian perfection, "Cursed be the man who encourages you to come to Christ with hopes of indulgence for even one sin. I do not speak this as though you could at once absolutely and perfectly leave all sin, in the roots and branches of it."[100] Any lingering doubt that Owen is addressing perfectionist antinomians (see chapter 2) should vanish as he by all accounts seems to make a direct allusion to Rutherford's statement made only a few years earlier: "Antinomians will have the justified to be so quiet in spirit, as if Christ had removed sin root and branch."[101]

The treatise *On Indwelling Sin* (1658) reveals Owen's awareness of practical antinomianism too. In explaining how indwelling sin undermines Christian obedience, Owen points out that the antinomian ruse of excusing sin works "by a horrible abuse of gospel grace."[102] "The deceit of sin

---

[97] He does mention "antinomianism" by name twice in *The Doctrine of Justification by Faith* (*Works*, 5:73, 145).

[98] Rehnman, *Divine Discourse*, 22.

[99] *Works*, 1:455.

[100] *Works*, 1:431.

[101] Rutherford, *The Trial and Triumph of Faith*, 245. Owen's writings show him to be fully aware of Rutherford, especially on the disputed issue of satisfaction, though Owen otherwise admired him. For background on the dispute, see Trueman, *Claims of Truth*, 28.

[102] *Works*, 6:218.

interposes itself. It separates between the doctrine of grace and its [proper] use. From the doctrine of the assured pardon of sin, it insinuates a regardlessness [heedlessness] of sin."[103] Citing Romans 6:4 ("ungodly men turning the grace of God into lasciviousness"), Owen had witnessed "dreadful" moral lapses.[104]

The second type of evidence, and probably the most conclusive, is Owen's own identification in his preface to *Pneumatologia* of "enthusiasts" (in addition to Socinians and Anglican moralists) as major theological opponents. His Nineteenth-Century biographer Andrew Thomson noticed Owen's crucial identification of enthusiasts.[105] Owen was responding to the charge, most likely made by Anglican moralists, that "by the operations we ascribe to the Holy Spirit, we expose men to be deceived by *satanical delusions*, and open a door to enthusiasms, directing them to the guidance of unaccountable impulses and revelations."[106] They accused Owen of illuminism, irrationalism and immediatism, which are presuppositions usually associated with antinomian authors, as chapter 2 will demonstrate.

In self-defense Owen left no doubt that *Pneumatologica* targeted antinomian errors. First, he attacks "foul enthusiasm" taking the form of receiving supposedly divine guidance from "impulses."

> Foul enthusiasm ha[s] pretended to proceed from the Spirit of God and to have a divine original [origin]. So far [am I] from affirming any operation of the Holy Spirit to consist in enthusiasms of any kind, I do not pretend to regard the two as consistent. By impulses, some men do not mean the promised supplies of grace we are supposed to pray for but irrational impressions or violent inclinations toward duties [nowhere described in Scripture].[107]

Exactly what is this "foul enthusiasm"? Packer identified the essence of "enthusiasm" as a "different doctrine of the Spirit's work."[108] He continues,

> The *enthusiasts* held, that over and above what [God] may do through the means [of grace], the Spirit works in the saints immediately, going beyond Scripture both in revelation of truth and in direct impulses to action. Man's duty, therefore, was to forego religious routine and to wait

[103] *Works*, 6:219.
[104] Ibid.
[105] *Works*, 1:xciv.
[106] *Works*, 3:12–13.
[107] *Works*, 3:13.
[108] J. I. Packer, *The Redemption and Restoration of Man in the Thought of Richard Baxter* (Vancouver, B.C.: Regent University Press, 2003 reprint), 324.

passively before God until the Spirit spoke. He must not tie himself to the means, for the Spirit was now working above and without means.[109]

Packer found that both Seventeenth-Century antinomians and Quakers had come under the spell of enthusiasm and mentions that the former "owed some of their own peculiarities to the influence of *enthusiastic* thought."[110]

After rejecting "enthusiastic" guidance because false to the *modus operandi* of the Holy Spirit, Owen blasts "enthusiastic" claims to direct and new revelation. He wrote,

> The same [claim of enmity to the true operations of the Holy Spirit] may be said concerning revelations. They are of two sorts: objective and subjective. Those of the former sort, whether they contain doctrines contrary to that of the Scripture, or additional thereto, or seeming confirmatory thereof, they are all universally to be rejected, the former being absolutely false, the latter useless. Neither have the operations of the Spirit pleaded for the least respect to them; for he having finished the whole work of external revelation, and closed it in the Scripture, his whole internal work [of spiritual illumination whereby we are enable to discern and understand the mind of God in Scripture] is suited and commensurate to [the closed canon of Scripture].[111]

Owen argues that new revelation either confirmed or falsified Scripture. In the former case, it was useless; in the latter, dangerous.

The third type of evidence will consist of a reasoned attempt, using relevant primary and secondary sources, to identify Seventeenth-Century antinomians as Owen's theological opponents in many relevant contexts despite his restraint in "naming names." Both convergence and divergence among Owen's theological opponents will be seen. Sometimes Owen simultaneously answered convergent theological opponents or, at other times, singled out antinomian adversaries for special rebuke. Where convergence exists, Owen's theological arguments are often of a "one-size-fits-all" variety. For example, as he mentioned in the preface to *Pneumatologia*, Socinians rejected the person of the Holy Spirit, Anglican moralists denied His work, and the enthusiasts falsified His work. Thus Owen's predications regarding the true *modus operandi* of the Holy Spirit in the application of redemption will sometimes correct multiple opponents simultaneously.

---

[109] Ibid. (emphasis his).
[110] Packer, *Redemption and Restoration*, 325 (emphasis his).
[111] *Works*, 3:13.

On the other hand, two key areas of divergence between Socinians and Anglican moralists, on the one hand, and antinomians, on the other, should not escape notice. First, Socinians and Anglican moralists elevate the role of reason and reduce Scriptural truths to the rule of reason, whereas antinomians downplay the importance of reason and adopt irrationalism as their approach to divine guidance. Secondly, although Owen thought that Socinians and Anglican moralists built morality on the wrong foundation by dispensing with the necessity of regeneration, both remained moralists at heart. Not so the antinomians. They were constantly seeking to sever the bond of grace and duty and to eliminate the significance of the moral law. Confirmation of the thesis that Owen is frequently targeting antinomian opponents is suggested by the fact that Owen's *Pneumatologia*, expressly directed against "enthusiasts," is quoted with great relevance no fewer than 16 times in a crucial chapter of this study, namely Chapter 4, "The Bond of Grace and Duty."

Conclusion

The Puritan doctrine of seeking is the view that man must generally undertake certain steps, in the diligent use of God's appointed means of grace, to prepare for grace and for glory. Though this Puritan doctrine built on a foundation laid by Luther and Calvin, it has fallen from favor in modern Reformed theology as the victim of widespread misunderstanding. While modern Arminian soteriology, with its revivalist emphasis on instantaneous conversion, has no place for a doctrine of preparation, defenders of Reformed orthodoxy are ironically inclined to characterize the doctrine of preparation as crypto-Arminianism. This misunderstanding stems from failure to recognize that God in His providence normally makes use of natural means, though supernaturally charged, in the conversion of the elect.

The doctrine of conversion was a central theme in Puritan theology and accordingly has been a dominant preoccupation in modern Puritan scholarship. Miller's influential involuntary and voluntaristic understanding of the Puritan model of conversion was misbegotten. The Puritans, by contrast, viewed conversion as requiring voluntary consent and involving grace perfecting nature. In addition, they viewed the pattern of conversion as something repeated throughout the entire Christian pilgrimage.

The Puritan doctrine of preparation, which acknowledges the necessity and priority of God's grace in the entire salvation process, is not related to meritorious medieval nominalism. The Puritans, like Luther and Calvin and unlike the nominalists, emphasized that preparation for grace in no way indebted God to give further supplies of grace to the sinner, even though God normally rewards those who seek Him through the appointed means of grace (Hebrews 11:6). In fact, preparation for grace is actually designed to bring the sinner to a place of "salutary self-despair"[112] whereby he, recognizing his own powerlessness and unworthiness, is drawn to Christ.

Calvin and mainstream Puritans see the great importance to the church of the doctrine of preparation for grace and glory. Though rejecting the meritorious preparationism of Ockham and Biel and asserting the passivity of the human will in conversion, Calvin embraced the doctrine of preparation for grace. Even the unregenerate, drawn by grace and impelled by self-examination, should seek God as an all-consuming passion, particularly since God's usual method of grace is to reward the full use of grace with further grace. Just as biblical exhortations and reproofs convince of sin, so biblical promises and precepts motivate a more fervent seeking of God's grace. The preparatory work of the law is not only an essential prelude to conversion, but part of an even larger process whereby the Holy Spirit leads one through a "sequence of steps" to effectual calling, justification, and ultimately glorification.

In upholding the doctrine of preparation, Owen forged an indissoluble bond between Christian duty and grace. In direct opposition to Kuyper, Owen demonstrates that effectual grace should encourage diligence, not sloth, because "God has promised to work in us in a way of grace what He requires from us in a way of duty."[113] This linkage between grace and duty would seem to explain why Puritan pastors like Watson, Flavel, Owen and Baxter felt comfortable in giving "directions" for conversion, though never attaching any efficacy to the directions *per se*. Owen's indissoluble bond between grace and duty and reconciliation of absolute and conditional promises in the covenant of grace, such that the absolute promises guarantee the covenantal fulfillment of the conditional ones, obviates the objections of theologians who mistake making repentance a condition of conversion for legalism.

The doctrine of preparation for grace played an indispensable and pivotal role in Puritan evangelism. Leading Puritan pastors, such as Stoddard, Mather and even Owen himself, predicted disaster would befall the Christian church if this teaching ever fell into abeyance, as it indeed has done. Neglect of this doctrine casts serious doubt on whether pastors understand the depths of their own Christian conversion well enough to lead others to Christ and would also lead people to consider themselves converted when

---

[112] Calvin, *Institutes*, II.i.3.
[113] *Works*, 3:204.

they were not. The Puritan doctrine of preparation for glory can also play a vital role in Christian spiritual growth and maturity. The bond of grace and duty properly understood reinforces Paul's injunction to work out one's salvation "with fear and trembling."

2

Seventeenth-Century
English Antinomianism

Introduction

Antinomianism was a term first coined in the early 1530's by Luther during his conflict with Johann Agricola (1494–1566).[1] This compound word derives from two Greek words: the preposition *anti* meaning "against" and the noun *nomos* meaning "law." In short, an antinomian is a professing Christian who denies the ongoing application of the Old Testament moral law as a rule of life. It is ironic that Luther coined the term, as many seventeenth-century antinomians claimed, somewhat disingenuously and selectively, to have derived their theology from him. Luther was certainly not an antinomian. Although he rediscovered the Scriptural truth of justification by faith alone, he balanced his teaching by making it clear that justifying faith is never alone but always accompanied by good works. Luther never recognized, however, the so-called "third use" of the law, and neither did Lutheranism until the Formula of Concord (1577).

The antinomian controversies in England and New England developed, at least in part, from several unfortunate overreactions. Antinomianism emerged within—and as a reaction to—mainstream Puritanism, not (as one might expect) Anglican Arminianism. Baxter attributed its rise "among us from our obscure preaching of evangelical grace, and insisting

---

[1] Como, *Blown by the Spirit*, 113.

too much on terrors and tears."[2] Secondly, though seeking to erect a holy commonwealth, New England received several prominent antinomians by immigration: Anne Hutchinson, John Wheelwright and, chameleon-like John Cotton.[3] Ironically, Hutchinson's father, Puritan pastor Frances Marbury (ca. 1592–1679), had written a preface endorsing John Rogers' *Seven Treatises*, an early masterwork of Puritan practical divinity, which prescribed a regimen of Christian diligence, duty, and self-examination that would prove distasteful to Mrs. Hutchinson, who though an adult seemed to be the classic rebellious preacher's kid.

When Parliament in 1643 had instructed Westminster Assembly delegates to confront the antinomian challenge, the volatility of antinomian sectaries, particularly those in the New Model Army, complicated the task of reconstituting lawful government.[4] Scottish delegates, like Robert Baillie (1602–1662) and Samuel Rutherford (1600–1661), thought England a veritable hotbed of antinomian sentiment; yet, in still another ironic twist, an English treatise *The Marrow of Modern Divinity* (1645) would ignite the Marrow Controversy (1718–23), which rent the Church of Scotland asunder. In 1692, posthumous republication in London of sermons authored by Tobias Crisp (1600–1643), widely considered an antinomian, wrecked the proposed plan of union for Presbyterians and Independents. Even during the Great Awakening (1734–1742) antinomian theology reared its ugly head through the raucous preaching and protesting of extreme New Lights, like Andrew Croswell (1709–1785), who entertained themselves royally by setting a bonfire for classic Puritan works of divinity.[5]

In general, the stream of seventeenth-century English antinomianism flowed from two main tributaries. The first tributary was that of familism (or the Family of Love), a perfectionistic communitarian sect founded and removed to England by Hendrik Nichlaes (ca. 1502–1580). The second and less noticed tributary was that of "high" or hyper-Calvinism as per the theologies of William Pemble (ca. 1592–1623), William Twisse (1578–1646), and Edward Fisher (1627–1655), author of the aforementioned *The*

---

[2] Richard Baxter, *Apology for the Nonconformists Ministry*, 226 cited in Packer, *Redemption and Restoration*, 37.

[3] John Cotton's theology will be evaluated in depth in Chapter 3.

[4] Gertrude Huehns, *Antinomianism in English History: With Special Reference to the Period 1640–1660* (London: Cresset Press, 1951), 81.

[5] See Leigh Eric Schmidt, "A Second and Glorious Reformation: The New Light Extremism of Andrew Croswell," *William and Mary Quarterly* 43 (1986): 214–44. The extreme New Lights reduced faith to assurance by the direct witness of the Holy Spirit, believed in justification by faith without repentance and salvation without any subsequent evidence of good works, and rejected the concept of preparation for grace.

Marrow of Modern Divinity.[6] Pemble and Twisse, prolocutor of the West-minster Assembly, taught the doctrine of justification from eternity, which minimized the importance of using the means of grace in real time and space. From the inflow of hyper-Calvinism, antinomianism can fairly be characterized as an example of intra-Puritan conflict.[7]

Como observes that, "Antinomianism emerged as a threatening trend within the godly community at the exact moment (1625–1630) that the [Arminian] controversies sparked by Richard Montagu (1573–1645) reached their peak."[8] With the party of Archbishop William Laud (1573–1645) already suspecting Puritans of antinomianism because of their belief in predestination, an outburst of antinomian fervor threatened to undermine the Puritan program of national, ecclesiastical, and personal reform. Mainstream Puritans were caught in a pincer movement, assaulted on one flank by the Laudians, and on the other by the antinomians who suspected them of crypto-Arminianism.[9] In London between 1629 and 1631, there were no fewer than nine active antinomian ministers.[10] The gravity of the crisis inspired five Puritan ministers, including Thomas Taylor (1579–1632) and Edward Reynolds, (1599–1676) to publish treatises against antinomianism in the brief period from 1630 to 1632.[11]

Two Basic Types of English Antinomians

Como cites two basic types and eight common theological and/or sociological characteristics of seventeenth-century English antinomianism. The two basic types are perfectionist and imputative. The former derived from familism with its basic elements being "a deeply allegorical mode of biblical interpretation, the claim that believers were already resurrected in this life, and most emphatically, the belief that true believers had somehow merged with God himself—a belief captured most succinctly by the notorious formula that the faithful had been 'Christed with Christ and Godded with God.'"[12] One such perfectionist, John Traske (1585–1636) declared that "[T]he new creature is not any renovation of the old man. This understanding, will, affections, memory and rest are gifts from heaven, and

---

[6] Como, *Blown by the Spirit*, 1–2, 4, 6.

[7] Ibid., 23. Como does so by defining Puritanism as a cultural, rather than purely doctrinal or ecclesiological, phenomenon (Ibid., 29).

[8] Ibid., 37.

[9] Ibid., 46, 81.

[10] Ibid., 59.

[11] Ibid., 99–100.

[12] Ibid., 38–39.

must of necessity be perfect."[13] Owen's treatise *On Indwelling Sin* (1668), discussed in depth in chapter 11, serves as a fairly comprehensive rebuttal of the anthropology of perfectionist antinomianism.

Though the two types tended to converge over time, the second type, imputative antinomianism, may have appeared to be less outlandish. "Imputative antinomians tended to argue that although humans remained sinful throughout their earthly lives, by virtue of Christ's sacrifice, the faithful appeared before God as perfect, just and sinless."[14] This was the "more influential" strain and more dangerous in the sense that it hewed more closely to the mainstream Reformed doctrine of justification, though still drawing dangerously false inferences from it.

John Eaton (1575–1631), an imputative antinomian often considered the godfather of seventeenth-century English antinomianism, authored two main works, both published posthumously: *The Honeycombe of Free Justification* (1642) and *The Discovery of the Most Dangerous Dead Faith* (1642).[15] He declares that by free justification, "we have all our sins that we feel daily dwelling in us quite taken away from God and so utterly abolished out of his sight, that we might not have one spot or wrinkle of sin in the sight of God."[16] Eaton admits that Christians feel the presence of indwelling sin and their imperfect sanctification but insisted that these feelings were illusory and could be dispelled by faith: "It is no matter that we feel sin and death still in us, as if Christ had not taken them away: because God thus establishes the faith [in] His power: and therefore that there may be place for [the exercise of] faith."[17]

These two strains of English antinomianism took contrary approaches to the issue of preparation for grace. Perfectionist antinomians tended to dismiss the preparatory work of the law as much-ado-about-nothing.[18] On the other hand, imputative antinomians generally affirmed its necessity.[19] Eaton describes those who qualify for free justification "such as truly feel what lost creatures they are in themselves, and in all their works: this is all

---

[13] Ibid., 357, citing quotation of Traske appearing in Edward Norice, *The New Gospel, Not the Gospel* (London, 1638).

[14] Ibid., 40.

[15] Ibid., 177.

[16] John Eaton, *The Honeycombe of Free Justification by Christ Alone* (London: Robert Lancaster, 1642), 24.

[17] Ibid., 25.

[18] Ibid., 351, 354. Como speculates that in response, the Puritans may have made their teaching on "preparationism" more formal and detailed.

[19] Ibid., 180, 213.

the preparative condition that God requires on our part to this high and heavenly work; for hereby is a man truly humbled for sin."[20]

The eight common sociological and/or theological characteristics of seventeenth century English antinomianism began with their shared belief that the new covenant repealed the Ten Commandments as a moral rule of life. A second characteristic was the insistence that they, not the Puritans, were true proponents of "free grace and justification by faith."[21] A third tendency was "the propensity to use images and motifs common to Puritanism [like legalism and dead faith] to attack mainstream Puritanism itself."[22] The fourth hallmark was undue stress on the "total passivity of the believer" in regeneration, assurance, and sanctification and on the all-sufficient impact of Christ's death to fill the void.[23] Eaton claims that Christ's atonement blotted out even original sin: "God gave his own Son to death for us, that he might both from this [original] sin and from all sins flowing from this original sin, free us by his blood, and so make us clean."[24] A fifth trait of English antinomianism, which seems closely related to the fourth, was "a paradoxical claim that [regenerate Christians] were transformed [by union with Christ] into exalted, or even divine, supernatural beings."[25] Como thought this claim paradoxical in the sense that these same writers simultaneously disparaged human activity and will.[26] Como comments,

> Each of the antinomian thinkers examined [here] maintained that no act of human effort or will could do anything to earn salvation or assurance, both of which come solely from the overwhelming power of Christ's life and death [or the indwelling of the Holy Spirit]. One and all, [they] showed a marked tendency to emphasize the utter sinfulness and inability of naked human effort, while celebrating and emphasizing the raw and irresistible power of the divine will.[27]

Perfectionist John Everarde (ca. 1585–1650) held that Christians must re-enact the crucifixion of Christ. Of his recommended six steps, step two

[20] Eaton, *Honeycombe*, 7.

[21] Como, *Blown by the Spirit*, 34. See Eaton, 6-7, presumably warning his readers off the Puritans' "dead faith" despite largely affirming their holiness of life and great zeal for God's glory in a left-handed compliment.

[22] Ibid., 35.

[23] Ibid.

[24] Eaton, *Honeycombe*, 27.

[25] Como, *Blown by the Spirit*, 34.

[26] Ibid.

[27] Como cites Robert Towne as holding the same view as Eaton on the eradication of original sin (*Blown by the Spirit*, 200).

is self-annihilation and step six "deiformity" meaning "when we act no longer ourselves, but God acts in us; that if we do anything, yet we see and feel, and confess it is God that doth it."[28] Similarly, John Traske denies all human agency in sanctification.

> Sanctification is by the Spirit only... so that the sanctified person is no further forth sanctified than he is in union with the Lord Jesus Christ; and it is not he that hath any habit of grace in his flesh: but the Lord Jesus dwelling in him, doth put forth the bright beams of his glory in such virtues [good works] as do best fit the time and place in which he lives.[29]

A sixth characteristic belief was that because Christians are free from the tutelage of the moral law, God is blind to their sin. Hence, the mainstream Puritan regimen of daily self-examination, repentance, and working out one's salvation with fear and trembling (Philippians 2:13) was considered misguided.[30] Eaton undermines sanctification by elevating as the preeminent means of grace meditation on "free justification", which supposedly proves "mighty for the working of faith, and true prayer and all godly conversation [behavior],"[31] and by using meditation on free justification to replace daily repentance. He writes, "This meditation [is] an effectual means to apprehend [free justification] deeper and deeper, and to create in you knowledge [of] and faith in [free justification], especially when you feel your conscience pricked and troubled with sin."[32]

The seventh characteristic was the prominence of teaching of full assurance of salvation, unwavering and free of doubt because coming directly and immediately from the Holy Spirit.[33] The antinomians rejected using the practical syllogism (discerning marks of grace to confirm assurance). The eighth, and final, characteristic was practical libertinism, or loose living, stemming from their belief that Christians would obey God's moral law (for imputative antinomians)– or the more amorphous "law of love" (for perfectionist antinomians)– automatically. Obedience was expected to flow effortlessly "not out of external compulsion [such as fear of punish-

[28] Ibid., 252 citing Everarde, *Gospel-Treasures* (1653), 128–31.
[29] Ibid., 358 citing Traske, *True Gospel*, 21–23.
[30] Ibid., 35–36.
[31] Eaton, *Honeycombe*, 9.
[32] Como, *Blown by the Spirit*, 18. See also his unusual interpretation of 1 John 1:7, which serves to discourage holy living: "Your walking in the light is not the cause of your fellowship with God; but only shows that you are in the light or righteousness of free justification" (Ibid., 28).
[33] Ibid., 36, 193.

ment or hope of reward] but by virtue of [regeneration]."[34] Eaton insists that out of Christ's death arose "good and holy desires and affection such as humility, purity and gentleness, and then all good works are practiced, and that with a willing heart."[35]

Mainstream Puritans took the continuing appeal and spread of antinomianism to be a serious threat, and a second generation of Puritan writers, including Owen, Baxter, Rutherford, and John Flavel (1627–1691), arose in opposition. Rutherford refuted many antinomian errors in *The Trial and Triumph of Faith* (1645) and *The Spiritual Antichrist* (1645). In a second appendix to *A Blow at the Root*, John Flavel lists ten antinomian errors:

1. The elect are justified before faith.

2. Justifying faith is merely the persuasion that Christ died for you.

3. One ought never to doubt his faith.

4. Christians need not confess sin or pray for forgiveness.

5. God sees no sin in believers.

6. God never chastises believers on account of their sins.

7. By the atonement, Christ became as sinful as the believer, and the believer as righteous as he.

8. No sin can harm a believer; nor need he perform any duties in connection with his own salvation.

9. The covenant of grace lacks conditions on the believer's part; and Christ fulfills the conditions for him by repenting, believing and obeying.

10. Sanctification should never be used as evidence of justification.[36]

Baxter published an enumeration of 100 antinomian errors in 1691.

Thus far two approaches to analyzing Commonwealth antinomianism have been presented. The first approach (that of Como) focused on general theological and sociological characteristics of antinomian thought. The second approach (that of Rutherford, Flavel and Baxter) dealt with specific enumerated antinomian tenets.

---

[34] Ibid., 36. Of course, the radical fringe went further and claimed to be able to obey the law through possessing the "mind of Christ."

[35] Eaton, *Honeycombe*, 27.

[36] John Flavel, *Works* (Edinburgh: Banner of Truth, 1968 reprint), 3:551–91.

This study suggests that a third complementary approach may have more power as a principle of understanding and unifying antinomian theology in its various forms. According to this proposed model, antinomianism can be more easily identified by its five overarching presuppositions. These are: (1) illuminism; (2) irrationalism; (3) immediatism; (4) essentialism; and (5) hyper-supernaturalism.

Overarching Presuppositions of 17th Century English Antinomian Theology

1. Illuminism

The first overarching presupposition of Seventeenth-Century antinomian theology is illuminism, defined here as belief in ongoing direct or immediate inspiration from the Holy Spirit. It is based on an assumption of primitivism that the Holy Spirit operates the same now in every respect as in apostolic times. Illuminism is also marked by a strong tendency to dispense with the necessity of the means of grace and to base assurance solely on the direct revelation of the Holy Spirit. Direct revelation differs markedly from Owen's concept of illumination, as discussed in chapter 6. Illumination is an operation of the Holy Spirit working in, by and through the word of God, whereas direct revelation is basically new revelation independent of Scripture.

Owen's response to illuminism was threefold. First, as discussed in chapters 4 though 6, he reaffirmed the traditional Puritan emphases on the means of grace and the Spirit's operation in, by, and through the word of God. Secondly, following Calvin, he put forward a robust doctrine of cessationism. Cessationism is the view that the revelatory 'sign gifts' such as prophecy ceased with the early church.[37] Owen developed the Reformed and Puritan understanding of the cessation of prophecy (defined by Calvin as 'particular revelation') in *A Discourse on Spiritual Gifts* (1693). Considering prophecy or direct revelation to be an extraordinary and temporary office in the early church, Owen defines prophecy as "immediate revelation from Christ by the Holy Ghost."[38] "Prophets... had a *temporary* and *extraordinary ministry* in the Church."[39]

Owen makes a crucial distinction between three biblical usages of "prophesy," with the first two extraordinary and temporary, and the third

---

[37] Philip A. Craig, "'And Prophecy Shall Cease': Jonathan Edwards on the Cessation of Prophecy," *Westminster Theological Journal* 64 (2002): 164–67.

[38] *Works*, 4:446.

[39] *Works*, 4:450 (emphasis his).

ordinary and permanent. The two extraordinary usages have to do with "receiv[ing] immediate revelations and directions from the Holy Ghost" regarding church administration, as in setting apart Saul and Barnabas, or "foretelling things to come, by the inspiration of the Holy Ghost," as in Agabus's prediction of Paul's imprisonment. The ordinary usage, mentioned in Romans 12:6, relates to 'nothing but teaching or preaching, in the exposition of the word."[40] Owen comments:

> [A]s in these extraordinary officers and their gifts did consist the original glory and honour of the churches in an especial manner, and by them was their edification carried on and perfected; so by an *empty pretense* unto their *power*, without their order and spirit, the churches have been stained, deformed and brought to destruction.[41]

Owen goes on to say that no pretense to prophetic gifts is any longer asserted "unless by some persons *phrenetical* and *enthusiastical*, whose madness is manifest to all."[42] He was probably aware that claims to prophetic gifts had been staked by antinomians Heinrik Nichlaes,[43] Hutchinson,[44] and Everarde.[45] Claiming that more ordinary spiritual gifts are now operative in the church, Owen points out that even for the apostles, preaching served as the preeminent means of conversion.[46]

The third aspect of Owen's response to illuminism was his denial that full assurance of salvation exists in a vacuum independently of vigorously exercised graces.[47] Owen insists that holy violence in using the means of grace is indispensable to attaining assurance:

> Get up, watch, pray, fast, meditate, offer violence to your lusts and corruptions; fear not, startle not at their crying or importunities to be spared; press unto the throne of grace by prayers, supplications, importunities, restless requests, This is the way to take the kingdom of heaven. These things are not peace, they are not assurance; but they are part of the means that God has appointed for the attainment of them.[48]

---

[40] *Works*, 4:451–52.

[41] *Works*, 4:453.

[42] *Works*, 4:472 (emphasis his).

[43] Primus, *Richard Greenham*, 71.

[44] David D. Hall, *The Antinomian Controversy, 1636–1638: A Documentary History*, second edition (Durham: Duke University Press, 1990), 337.

[45] Como, *Blown by the Spirit*, 265.

[46] *Works*, 4:483.

[47] *Works*, 5:439.

[48] *Works*, 6:567–68. Similarly, Edwards insists that "A true assurance is not upheld but by the soul's being kept in a holy frame and grace maintained in lively

Owen's elevation of the means of grace is answered by antinomians like John Everarde who denigrate the means of grace as a dead-end street:

> Here is a misery of all miseries and the height of all aggravations, for a man to go to hell by his Religion, by his hearing of sermons, by receiving the communion, by praying, by preaching, by abstinence and overcoming of vice, by resisting of sin, giving of alms, etc.[49]

Owen counters that progress in sanctification is essential to assurance and that assurance is not directly mediated by the Holy Spirit. "No man can have the least ground of assurance that he has seen Christ and his glory by faith, without some effects of it in him changing him into his likeness."[50] Antinomian Error 31 makes the totally opposite point: "Such as see any grace in themselves, before they have assurance of God's love sealed to them, are not to be received [as] members of churches."[51]

2. Irrationalism

A second presupposition of Seventeenth-Century English antinomianism flowing logically from illuminism and essentialism is irrationalism. Essentialism is the belief that regeneration implants the divine essence rather than created graces in the believer. Irrationalism holds that regeneration does not renew the faculties of understanding, will, and affections and thus bypasses the intellect. Packer observes this characteristic among Seventeenth-Century antinomians.

> Quakers, Ranters, [and] Antinomians... were all 'enthusiasts' in this sense, all sure that sometimes Christ spoke and moved them apart from His written word and in a way that by-passed the intellect altogether. They claimed that revelation thus given was more certain than the conclusions of rational exegesis: that action thus prompted by imperious inner constraint was more certainly God's will than that done according to the dictates of rational conscience. Its very immediacy proved that it was wholly and purely Divine.[52]

exercise" (Edwards, *The Religious Affections*, *Works*, 2:174). For a much fuller account of Owen's view of assurance, see Joel R. Beeke, *Assurance of Faith: Calvin, English Puritanism, and the Dutch Second Reformation* (New York: Peter Lang, 1991), 213–80.

[49] Como, *Blown by the Spirit*, 245, citing Everarde, *Gospel-Treasures Opened* (1653), 158–59.

[50] Works, 1:413.

[51] Hall, *The Antinomian Controversy*, 227.

[52] Packer, *Redemption and Restoration*, 297.

Owen, like Baxter, rejected irrationalism outright. Owen stresses the vital, even indispensable, role played in Christian spirituality and sanctification by spiritually renewed human faculties.

> If we are spiritually renewed, all the faculties of our souls are enabled to exert their respective powers.... This must be done in various duties, by the exercise of various graces, as they are to be acted by the distinct powers of the faculties of our minds.... All the distinct powers of our souls are to be acted by distinct grace and duties in cleaving to God by love.[53]

Owen's view of grace acting through spiritually renewed human faculties stood in stark contrast to Cotton's view, discussed at length in chapter 3, that God through regeneration grants "gifts of grace" that operate independently of human faculties.

3. Immediatism

Professor Nuttall views the broad Puritan movement as a "movement toward immediacy in relation to God," especially given its abandonment of mediation from the Roman Catholic sacramental system.[54] Antinomians, though less so than Quakers, stressed immediacy significantly more than Puritans did because of their hyper-supernatural severance of the orders of creation and redemption.[55]

Immediatism, the third overarching presupposition of Seventeenth-Century English antinomianism, is defined here as the belief that all operations of the Holy Spirit are immediately efficacious. The antinomian believes that the Holy Spirit always accomplishes His designs directly and immediately and not over process of time or indirectly through created means. Immediatism, with its tendency to collapse any process of time into instantaneity, seems to explain several antinomian tenets: (1) the doctrine of justification from eternity (i.e., before coming to faith); (2) the disallowance of faith and repentance as "conditions" of the covenant of grace,

[53] *Works*, 1:320. In other words, graces and duties "act" our faculties in our loving God.

[54] Geoffrey F. Nuttall, *The Holy Spirit in Puritan Faith and Practice*, second edition (Chicago: University of Chicago Press, 1992), 134. Nuttall recognizes a dialectical tension in Puritan thought between direct communion with God and the necessity of the means of grace (Ibid., 91–92).

[55] See T. L. Underwood, *Primitivism, Radicalism and the Lamb's War: The Baptist-Quaker Conflict in Seventeenth-Century England* (Oxford: Oxford University Press, 1997), 26: "Quakers insisted on the centrality of immediacy like that enjoyed in New Testament Christianity."

denying any place for the application of redemption to occur in real time-and-space; and (3) the denial of preparation for grace and any morphology of conversion by more radical antinomians such as Hutchinson.

How does Owen respond to these antinomian tenets? Though Owen concurred with the Westminster Confession in his outright rejection of justification from eternity and insistence on faith and repentance as "conditions" of justification,[56] some scholars claim that contradiction mars his theology here. Gavin McGrath writes,

> There was, however, a modicum of contradiction in Owen's thought: on the one hand, he insisted that the death of Christ merited *ipso facto* the justification of the elect, his death was a cause independent from the faith of the believer; on the other hand, Owen stressed the necessity of faith and repentance, for in the truest sense a person was not justified before personal faith.[57]

Though a fuller rejoinder awaits in Chapter 4, "The Bond of Grace and Duty," this tension (rather than "contradiction") in Owen's thought appears to derive mainly from his view of limited atonement, that Christ's death actually secures the salvation of the elect, but the personal appropriation of their salvation must takes place through God's giving them faith and repentance in real time and space, usually in response to their seeking God.

The antinomians denied that the covenant of grace could ever be conditional and yet continue to be gracious. As Stoever points out, "The more radical element tended to absorb the covenant of grace into the [covenant of redemption], lest the gratuity of redemption be compromised by a transaction involving human consent."[58]

4. Essentialism

A fourth overarching presupposition of Seventeenth-Century English antinomianism is essentialism. Thomas Watson, tracing it back to Servetus and Osiander,[59] describes essentialism as the view that regeneration infuses the divine essence into the Christian's soul.[60] Essentialism was a dualistic

[56] See e.g., *Works* 5:193 and *Works* 12:592, 602 ; cp. Westminster Confession of Faith section 11.4.

[57] Cited in Hans Boersma, *A Hot Pepper Corn: Richard Baxter's Doctrine of Justification in Its Seventeenth-Century Context of Controversy* (Uitgeverij: Boekencentrum Zoetermeer, 1993), 105.

[58] Stoever, *'A Faire and Easye Way to Heaven,'* 187.

[59] According to Baxter, Osiander taught justification by communication, not imputation (Boersma, *A Hot Pepper Corn*, 223).

view that in regeneration, the divine essence was infused in the regenerate soul while remaining distinct and separate from the unregenerate soul. Essentialism explains why antinomians denied that sanctification must be progressive and that God sees and punishes sin in His children. It may also explain their strange view that Christ became a sinner by His death on the cross whilst the Christian becomes pure as the driven snow. It also fosters antinomian denial of human agency, such that Christ is said to "believe, repent and obey" for the believer, and promotes a carefree "once-saved-always-saved" attitude.

Packer sheds light on the practical implications of essentialism. Quoting John Saltmarsh, he writes,

> The covenant of grace, he tells us, is 'free without all condition.' Faith is not its condition; faith, defined as 'a being perswaded more or lesse of Christ's love,' is a state of mind, whose function is merely to assure men that the covenanted blessings are theirs.... None need question their interest in the covenant through doubts as to the sincerity of their own repentance; for 'Christ hath believed perfectly, he hath repented perfectly, he hath sorrowed for sin perfectly, he hath perfectly obeyed.... We are to believe our repentance true in him, who hath repented for us.' Nor need daily shortcomings, however grievous, worry the believer: 'that soul can never fall away that can believe; and no sin can damn it, if it will but believe the pardon of that sin.'[61]

In response, Owen maintains the progressive nature of sanctification. In *Pneumatologia* he highlights the need to strengthen the principle of sanctification through exercise and duty.

> That although this habit and principle is not acquired by any or many acts of duty or obedience, yet it is, in a way of duty, preserved, increased, strengthened and improved thereby. God hath appointed that we should live in the exercise of it; and in and by the multiplication of duties is it kept alive and stirred up, without which it will be weakened and decayed.[62]

This necessity explains the importance of the frequently repeated Puritan maxim to "improve" grace. Grace is not steady-state but subject to ebb and flow as it is nurtured or neglected. Owen also affirms, in *Commentary on Hebrews*, God's chastisement of His elect. God sees sin in them and disciplines them accordingly. Opening Hebrews 12:5, Owen defines

---

[60] Watson, *Select Works of Thomas Watson*, 27.
[61] Packer, *Redemption and Restoration*, 203.
[62] *Works*, 3:476.

"despising" God's discipline as heedlessness of sin and its consequences. It involves overlooking God's "displeasure against our sins" and refusing "sedulous [thorough] reformation."[63]

Owen knew a faulty view of imputation when he saw one. In *The Doctrine of Justification by Faith* (1677), he dismisses on three grounds the notion, which antinomians like Tobias Crisp apparently borrowed from Cardinal Bellarmine (1542–1621) and Socinian writers, that imputation makes the Christian as righteous as Christ, and Christ as sinful as the Christian.[64] First, writes Owen, imputation is a transfer of guilt, not a transference of essence. Secondly, the antinomian view of imputation contradicts Scriptural testimonies of Christ's sinlessness. Thirdly, "sin" in 2 Corinthians 5:21 should be interpreted as "sin offering," a position within the lexical range of meaning of the Greek word *hamartia*. Owen, as further discussed in chapter 4, makes short work of the antinomian denial of free agency. He writes that "The Holy Spirit works in us by us, and what he does in us is done by us."[65]

Finally, Owen's treatise *On Apostasy* (1676) rebutted Saltmarsh's claim, quoted above, that no one can fall from grace through sin. Though Owen in his treatise *The Doctrine of the Saints' Perseverance Explained and Confirmed* (1654) upholds traditional Reformed teaching of divine preservation, he balances such reassurance with the warning that the glib professor can apostasize through a careless, devil-may-care attitude to sinning. Chief among Owen's directions for avoiding apostasy are "self-distrust" and deliberate avoidance of temptations:

> A bold, hazardous, careless frame of spirit, venturing on all companies and temptations, complying with vanities and profane communications, offering itself with a fearless confidence to ways of seduction through the 'cunning sleights of men that lie in wait to deceive' is that which has ruined innumerable professors. Self-distrust, humility, fear of offending, with the like soul-preserving graces, will be kept in exercise only where men are awake to the consideration of the deceitfulness of their own hearts.[66]

Owen's striking image of a "bold, hazardous, careless" frame of spirit fits to a tee the "once-saved-always-saved" antinomians. Because they believed that they partook of the divine essence and that God was blind to their sins, their motto could have been "anything goes."

---

[63] *Works*, 23:257.
[64] *Works*, 5:54–55.
[65] *Works*, 3:83.
[66] *Works*, 7:247.

5. Hyper-Supernaturalism

The fifth and final overarching presupposition of Seventeenth-Century antinomian theology, hyper-supernaturalism, is akin to what Packer called super-supernaturalism in assessing the charismatic movement.[67] Hyper-supernaturalism assumes a guaranteed sanctification without diligent use of the means, warring with sin or otherwise working out one's salvation with fear and trembling, and consequently begets practical libertinism. Gertrude Huehns notices this trait in her seminal study of English antinomianism:

> The issue now turned mainly on the share occupied by nature and by grace, respectively, in the work of salvation. Antinomianism holds the extremist position on one side of the question. It contends that there neither is, nor possibly can be, any limitation to the exercise of the divine grace in and through men. Thus man's reformation 'once begun is never intermitted again till all be perfected. For as long as God's nature dwells in ours, it will ever be reforming our nature to itself, till it be altogether like it.'[68]

This particular presupposition of antinomian theology bulked large in the New England Antinomian Controversy. After identifying two related types of New England antinomianism, Stoever describes their shared feature of hyper-supernaturalism:

> Both forms of the syndrome exalted the unconditioned, unmediated operation of the Spirit in the application of redemption to the point of seriously minimizing, if not altogether overruling, the Christian's continuing rootedness in the ontological and moral orders of creation. Reformed orthodox theologians conceived of regeneration as the infusion into man of supernatural principles, empowering him to new understanding and new obedience, but without altering his condition as a creature or freeing him from earnest struggle with the remnants of sinfulness in himself. Antinomians, in contrast, tended to regard regeneration as a spiritual transformation, elevating the individual above the moral ambiguities of creaturely existence and freeing him from the canons of 'common,' 'earthly,' merely 'legal' morality.[69]

In contrast to the antinomian denigration of the means of grace, Owen reiterates that diligent application of the means of grace is abso-

[67] J. I. Packer, *Keep in Step with the Spirit* (Old Tappan, N.J.: Revell, 1994), 193.
[68] Huehns, *Antinomianism in English History*, 38 citing William Dell.
[69] Stoever, *'A Faire and Easye Way to Heaven,'* 161–62.

lutely essential not only for Christian growth but also for perseverance. He declares:

> There is not any thing in the whole course of our obedience wherein the continual exercise of faith and spiritual wisdom is more indispensably required than the due improvement of gospel privileges and ordinances: for there is no other part of our duty whereon our giving glory to God and the eternal concern of our own souls does more eminently depend. Gospel institutions of worship are the only ordinary outward means whereby the Lord Christ communicates his grace to us, and whereby we immediately return love, praise, thanks and obedience to him, on which spiritual intercourse, our spiritual growth does depend. It is therefore certain that our growth or decay in holiness [and] our steadfastness in, or apostasy from, profession, are greatly influenced by the use or abuse of those privileges.[70]

Beyond this, Owen's grand strategy for rebutting hyper-supernaturalism appears to be his full-fledged development of the theme of the intricate and indissoluble bond of grace and duty. He fully develops this theme of the bond of grace and duty in two contexts: preparation for grace and preparation for glory. Chapter 4, "The Bond of Grace and Duty," will unfold Owen's master strategy for turning back the antinomian challenge.

Summary

Antinomianism, a doctrinal deviation from Christian orthodoxy, denies that Old Testament moral law furnishes a binding rule of life for the Christian. Antinomianism first erupted in London, England (1625–1630) and shortly thereafter in New England (1636–1638).

Seventeenth-Century English antinomianism seems to have been inspired by familism and hyper-Calvinism, the latter tributary emerging from within Puritanism itself. An example of hyper-Calvinism is the doctrine of justification from eternity held by William Pemble (1591–1623) and prolocutor of the Westminster Assembly, William Twisse (1578–1646). Contra Twisse, Westminster Confession Section 11, subsection 4, repudiates justification from eternity in no uncertain terms by stating that "the elect... are not justified until the Holy Spirit doth in due time actually apply Christ to them."[71]

David Como distinguishes between two types of seventeenth-century antinomians: the perfectionist antinomians (from familism) and the im-

---

[70] *Works*, 7:250.
[71] Westminster Confession, 59.

putative antinomians (from hyper-Calvinism). Perfectionist antinomians believed that the new birth eradicates sin and renders the new Christian perfect. Imputative antinomians, though holding that indwelling sin survives regeneration, still took it "by faith" that believers appeared faultless and perfect before God, who cannot see their sin.

There are three approaches to analyzing seventeenth-century English antinomianism. The first approach (that of Como) focuses on general theological and sociological characteristics of antinomianism. The second approach (those of Rutherford, Flavel and Baxter) dealt with specific enumerated antinomian tenets. This study suggests that a third complementary approach may possess more explanatory power as a unifying principle of antinomian theology in its various guises. Accordingly, the suggestion is made that antinomianism can be more readily identified by its five overarching presuppositions:

(1) Illuminism: new revelation and direct assurance;

(2) Irrationalism: the intellect bypassed by regeneration;

(3) Immediatism: immediately efficacious operations of the Holy Spirit;

(4) Essentialism: infusion of the divine essence by regeneration; and

(5) Hyper-Supernaturalism: operation of divine grace not dependent on means.

Against illuminism, John Owen rejected its disjunction of the word and Spirit and upheld cessationism and self-examination. Against irrationalism, Owen assigned a leading role to sanctified reason that meditates on Scripture and declared that grace entered through the understanding. Against immediatism, he insisted on faith and repentance as conditions of conversion and preaching for regeneration based on a sound morphology of conversion. Against essentialism, Owen affirmed the necessity of fresh communications of grace for exercising created graces and spiritual gifts. Against hyper-supernaturalism, Owen declared that conditional promises respecting growth in sanctification require the actual performance of Christian duties including diligence in utilizing the means (including obedience) of grace.

Now we will cross the Atlantic to view the strange events that occurred in the "holy commonwealth" of New England during its own antinomian controversy and included an unthinkable full-scale assault on preparation for grace and the concept of Christian duty.

3

The New England Antinomian Controversy

A Chronology of the Controversy

In the late 1630's, a controversy erupted in New England that shattered the unity of the Congregationalist church and largely molded the future of American Puritan orthodoxy for the next hundred years. The most recent historiography correctly views the New England Antinomian Controversy (1636–1638) as a continuation of the antinomian controversies beginning in the mid–1620's that rocked London, England. From his detailed survey of British antinomianism prior to the English Civil War, Como concludes,

> In the light of the evidence presented in this study, there can be little question that the so-called Antinomian Controversy, which gripped the Bay Colony between 1636 and 1638, had ample and clear precedents. It was, in some ways, a replay of the earlier controversies that had plagued London in 1628–31.... [I]n large part, New England's Antinomian Controversy progressed and was prosecuted according to just such well-established stereotypical categories of interpretation, categories that had been elaborated [in England] and disseminated above all in the ten years preceding the conflicts in Boston.[1]

[1] Como, *Blown by the Spirit*, 441, 443–44. He also writes that "Massachusetts' Controversy was, in many crucial ways, a reprise of earlier battles that had been fought in London" (Ibid., 27). See also Bozeman, *The Precisianist Strain*, 234.

The chronology of the New England Antinomian Controversy is virtually the only aspect of the controversy, however, simple enough to command general acceptance among scholars and historians. Anne Hutchinson, the daughter of a Puritan minister in England, began a series of meetings for women in which she "expounded" the sermons of their minister John Cotton. Before long she expanded her meetings to include men and began criticizing "legalistic" ministers in the colony who, by insisting on sanctification as evidence of assurance, preached what she termed a "covenant of works."

Her like-minded brother-in-law John Wheelwright (1592–1679), also a recent English immigrant, sought in late 1636 to be ordained as a teacher to the First Church of Boston where John Wilson (1588–1667) served as pastor and Cotton as teacher. Although Cotton supported Wheelwright's candidacy, Wilson and Governor John Winthrop (1588–1649) successfully opposed his call. On January 17, 1637, at a public fast proclaimed by the civil authorities in the hope of avoiding further division, Wheelwright used his bully pulpit as preacher of the Fast Day sermon to "bitterly attack the doctrine of preparation"[2] and to call for a holy war against "legal" preachers. Both he and Hutchinson seemed to include in this category every New England minister except himself and Cotton.

Cotton's initial instinct was to defend both Hutchinson and Wheelwright against a growing chorus of complaints that both taught dangerous familist tenets.[3] Despite Cotton's advocacy, the civil authorities banished Wheelwright following his conviction for sedition. In August of 1637, the Newtown (Cambridge, Massachusetts) Synod convened to consider a list of 82 errors of which the antinomians were allegedly guilty. Hutchinson, when examined by the Synod, deftly side-stepped her cross-examiners and might have escaped with only admonition had she not claimed a gift of prophecy and threatened God's imminent judgment on New England. Cotton, forced to re-evaluate his position, changed his stance and ultimately took the lead as special prosecutor in her eventual excommunication from First Church of Boston.

Thomas Weld (1595–1660), the colony's London agent, left posterity an excellent summary of Hutchinson's antinomian theology, which he memorably called "a faire and easye way to heaven." In a preface to Gover-

---

[2] Norman Pettit, *The Heart Prepared: Grace and Conversion in Puritan Spiritual Life* (New Haven: Yale University Press, 1966), 146.

[3] The adjective is used to describe the faith and practice of the Family of Love, a Dutch sect that had immigrated to England in the late 1500's and was thoroughly antinomian in outlook.

nor Winthrop's account of what had happened, he wrote,

> For if a man need not be troubled by the law, before faith, but may step to
> Christ so easily; and then, if his faith be no going out of himself to take
> Christ, but only a discerning that Christ is his own already, and is only
> an act of the Spirit upon him, no act of his own being done by him; and
> if he, for his part, must see nothing in himself, have nothing, do nothing,
> only he is to stand still and wait for Christ to do all for him. And then if
> after faith, the law no rule to walk by, no sorrow or repentance for sin; he
> must not be pressed to duties; and need never pray, unless moved by the
> Spirit; and if he falls into sin, he is never the more disliked by God, nor
> his condition never the worse. And for his assurance, it being given him
> by the Spirit, he must never let it go; but abide in the height of comfort,
> though he falls into the grossest sins that he can. Then is their way to life
> made so easy; if so, no marvel that so many like it.[4]

Divergent Views of the Primary Theological Issue

Traditional historiography has seen the primary theological issue
sparking the Controversy as that of preparation for grace. Perry Miller,
for example, influenced the course of treatment for the next generation of
historians by claiming that the Puritan doctrine of preparation of grace
represented "crypto-Arminian" degeneration from the pure Reformed theology of Calvin. Miller conceived of conversion vulgarly as a "rape of the
surprised will."[5] Norman Pettit and Janice Knight largely follow Miller's
lead. Pettit, for example, exaggerates when he suggests that most of the 82
errors charged to the New England antinomians had to do directly or indirectly with the doctrine of preparation.[6] Pettit did, however, attack Miller's
view of conversion and Calvinism.

> [Calvin] did not deny preparation as such. Nor did he dismiss the biblical
> exhortations to preparation as useless. Calvin saw grace as a seizure, but
> [one] conceived in terms of gradual constraint, not sudden disruption.
> Thus he could and did allow for a time of preparation in the external call,
> when God prepares man for effectual conversion.[7]

---

[4] Cited in Stoever, 'A Faire and Easye Way to Heaven', 11–12.

[5] Miller, The New England Mind, 56.

[6] Pettit, The Heart Prepared, 149. Compare the very different and more accurate categorization of the 82 errors, with 22 having to do with assurance, in
Michael Winship, Making Heretics: Militant Protestantism and Free Grace in Massachusetts, 1636–1641 (Princeton: Princeton University Press, 2002), 82.

[7] Ibid., 40 n.39.

Although recognizing that the controversy involved other theological issues, Knight gives a fairly central place to the doctrine of preparation. She attempts to lump Cotton, Sibbes, and John Preston (1587–1628) together in a group dubbed the "Spiritual Brethren" who supposedly stood against the teaching on preparation for grace put forward by the "Intellectual Fathers," mainly Hooker, Thomas Shepard, William Ames (1576–1633), and William Perkins (1588–1642). She writes,

> More emotional and even mystical, their theology stressed divine benevolence over power. Emphasizing the love of God, they converted biblical metaphors of kingship into ones of kinship. They substituted a free testament or voluntary bequeathing of grace for the conditional covenant described by the [Intellectual Fathers]. Such a view argues against a doctrine of preparation by refusing human performance as a sign of salvation and pastoral discipline as a mode of social order. They preached that grace was immediately infused into the passive saint by God alone. For the Spiritual Brethren the transformation of the soul was neither incremental nor dependent on exercises of spiritual discipline. In this piety there are no steps to the altar.[8]

Though accorded the Thomas J. Wilson Prize of Harvard University Press, her thesis is riddled with faulty analysis. Sibbes, for example, firmly believed in the doctrine of preparation for grace, as demonstrated by Mark Dever. Responding to Pettit who, in sharp contrast to Knight considered Sibbes the "most extreme" of preparationists, Dever writes,

> Pettit seems to have assumed that an adherence to a theology of predestination would also necessitate a belief in both an immediate conversion, and in a conversion that was, by its violence, inconsistent with natural human faculties. However, Sibbes said that, 'God usually prepares those that he means to convert, as we plough before we sow.'[9]

Hence, Sibbes regularly exhorted his parishioners to conversion.[10] Further, Knight's claim that the Spiritual Brethren anticipated the theology of Edwards is far-fetched.[11] In *The Religious Affections* (1746), his masterwork delineating the true marks of conversion, it is Shepard, the architect of

---

[8] Janice Knight, *Orthodoxies in Massachusetts: Rereading Puritanism* (Cambridge, MA: Harvard University Press, 1994), 3–4. She paraphrases Cotton.

[9] Mark Dever, *Richard Sibbes: Puritanism and Calvinism in Late Elizabethan and Early Stuart England* (Macon, GA.: Mercer University Press, 2000), 127–28.

[10] Ibid., 121–24.

[11] Knight, *Orthodoxies in Massachusetts*, 4.

New England Puritan orthodoxy and staunch defender of preparation for grace, and not Cotton, whom Edwards unflaggingly quotes.[12]

William K. B. Stoever subjects the Miller-Pettit view to a withering critique in his thorough study *'A Faire and Easye Way to Heaven': Covenant Theology and Antinomianism in Early Massachusetts*. He points out four flaws in their thesis that preparation for grace was the "hidden issue" underlying the controversy. The first flaw is that preparation for grace, far from being "censored," was a topic openly debated by Seventeenth-Century Puritans in four distinct contexts.[13] Stoever points out that none of these issues about preparation figured at all in the debates between Cotton and fellow ministers. The second flaw was that Cotton himself believed in preparation for grace and even described preparatory states such as the "spirit of bondage" and the "spirit of burning" in his sermon series *The New Covenant* delivered in 1636 during the height of the New England Antinomian Controversy.[14] In fairness to Miller and Petit, Cotton's view of preparation did vacillate and often minimize the importance of human activity,[15] while Hutchinson's opposition to preparation for grace was more thoroughgoing.[16] A third flaw was their overlooking the fact that the Pu-

---

[12] See William K. B. Stoever, "The Godly Will's Discerning," in *Jonathan Edwards' Writings: Text, Context, Interpretation*, ed. Stephen J. Stein (Bloomington: Indiana University Press, 1996), 85–99.

[13] Stoever, *'A Faire and Easye Way to Heaven'*, 193–94, mentions these widely debated issues: "(1) whether the preparatory states of compunction are themselves evidences of election, such that if God has wrought them, he will shortly and surely work vocation; (2) whether such states are evidence of effectual calling and may be resorted to by a person who doubts his calling because of imperfect sanctification; (3) whether such states are qualitatively saving or common works of the Spirit; and (4) whether works of preparation are proper conditions of vocation, which, when men perform them by their own efforts or common grace, God must accept and reward."

[14] Ibid., 194.

[15] Compare for example the quotations from Cotton culled by Bozeman and Murray.

[16] As noted in David D. Hall, *Puritans in the New World: A Critical Anthology* (Princeton: Princeton University Press, 2004), 211: "Hutchinson and her admirers regarded any minister who emphasized 'duties' as preaching a 'covenant of works', not free grace. She insisted that the right way of 'building a good estate' (assurance of salvation) was to rely on the 'immediate witness of the Holy Spirit', an argument that implicitly eliminated the intervening steps and stages [i.e., the morphology of conversion], the 'means of grace', the self-examination prompted by 'the law' that candidates so often cited in their [conversion accounts made in application for church membership]."

ritans regularly distinguished, as Owen certainly did, between preparation for grace and preparation for glory.[17] The fourth and most serious flaw of all is that the Puritan approach to preparation for grace involved neither "crypto-Arminianism" nor "thunderbolt theology." In a passage worth quoting extensively, Stoever writes,

> [T]he Reformed doctrine of divine sovereignty was not regarded in the orthodox period as excluding human activity from regeneration. That a person was predestined to a certain end, and saved by grace alone, did not affect his nature as a rational, willing agent, nor did it mean that he could 'do nothing' morally significant in daily life, but only that he was impotent to effect his own salvation. Denial of such efficacy to individuals, however, was not regarded as inconsistent with the assertion that human activity, in the context of the ordained means for dispensing grace, is instrumental in the application of redemption. The command to believe, Puritan divines believed, is incumbent upon everyone, and though only the elect receive the ability to fulfill it, everyone is obligated to consider himself susceptible of regeneration and to attend diligently upon the means. The utility of these conclusions for promoting exertion in religious duties is obvious. They do not necessarily, however, indicate an 'Arminian' drift, unless it is also concluded that the fallen will, of its own power, is able to consent to God's offer of forgiveness, and that this consent is the effective condition of justification–conclusions that were roundly rejected by Puritans on both sides of the Atlantic.[18]

More recent historiography has generally viewed assurance as the most central issue in the New England Antinomian Controversy. Hall observes that, "The collapse of the [1633] revival engendered a mood of acute religious anxiety. The revival and the new requirement [of giving a conversion testimony] for church membership were forcing everyone to ask himself, am I saved?"[19] Winship similarly declares that, "The doctrinal 'great question' of the free grace controversy was assurance of salvation."[20] Bozeman also notes that "spiritual desertion and failed assurance [had been] widespread complaints during the spiritual depression of 1635–6"[21] and that "the 'new Gospellers' [antinomians] bragged of satisfactions unknown to the pietist [Puritan] rank and file, and among them assurance sealed by the spirit [sic] ranked foremost."[22] Stoever sees the central issue as the

[17] Stoever, *'A Faire and Easye Way to Heaven'*, 196.
[18] Ibid., 195.
[19] Hall, *Puritans in the New World*, 15.
[20] Winship, *Making Heretics*, 13.
[21] Bozeman, *The Precisianist Strain*, 246.
[22] Ibid., 318.

relationship between nature and grace with ramifications for a host of related issues including "the nature and relationship of faith, justification and
sanctification in the order of regeneration and the means to the knowledge
of all three."[23]

The Controversial Theology of John Cotton

The strong theological links forged between British antinomianism
(see chapter 2) and New England antinomianism come into sharper focus
in the theology of Cotton, the major theologian supporting the radical
sectaries in New England. A well-established Puritan pastor who had emi-
grated from Lincolnshire, England, Cotton's theology, sound in England,
flirted with antinomianism in New England. In England, Cotton had upheld the abiding validity of the moral law, the necessity of preparation
for grace, and the evidential role of sanctification in assurance.[24] In his
commentary on 1 John, for instance, he had proposed no fewer than 40
behavioral signs for evidential assurance.[25] The only clue to any antinomian
leanings before his departure from England had been his acquisition of the
unpublished writings of Richard Rothwel, a leading English antinomian.[26]

Traditionally historians, like Larzer Ziff and Iain Murray, have pic-
tured Cotton as a misunderstood defender of traditional Puritan orthodoxy.[27] More recent historians, with the notable exception of Knight, have
concentrated their attention more on his antinomian or "semi-antinomian"
tendencies.[28] On the one hand, he upheld Reformed orthodoxy by insisting on the abiding validity of the moral law and God's taking cognizance
of the sins of His elect.[29] At times he also affirmed the importance of
preparation for grace and the evidential value of sanctification for assurance.[30] On the other hand, his theology clearly and decidedly exhibited the
five overarching presuppositions of seventeenth century English antino-

[23] Stoever, 'A Faire and Easye Way to Heaven', 194.
[24] Bozeman, The Precisianist Strain, 212, 221.
[25] Ibid., 219.
[26] Como, Blown by the Spirit, 207.
[27] Larzer Ziff, Puritanism in America (New York: Viking, 1973) and Murray,
"Antinomianism: New England's First Controversy." Banner of Truth 179–180
(August 1978), 1–75.
[28] Bozeman, The Precisianist Strain, 229–30; Como, Blown by the Spirit, 442.
Como confusingly takes the view that Cotton was not an antinomian but nevertheless replicated antinomian arguments. Bozeman observes his "intriguingly
eclectic and ambivalent state of mind" (ibid., 211).
[29] Ibid., 212.
[30] Ibid., 213, 219.

mianism identified in chapter 2: illuminism, irrationalism, immediatism, essentialism, and hyper-supernaturalism. Cotton's illuminism came out in his "unusually strong formulation of the Protestant principle of private judgment"[31] bringing about doctrinal changes based on further light from the Holy Spirit and his embrace of the gift of prophecy.[32] His irrational-ism appeared in his denigration of the importance of preaching, thought by other Puritans to be the preeminent means of grace.[33] His theological ally, Wheelwright, insisted that regeneration destroyed human faculties.[34] Stoever points out that Cotton's view of regeneration similarly stemmed from his belief that the covenant of grace excluded "creaturely works."

> Justifying faith [for Cotton] can only be the infused capacity passively to receive Christ, and not an active consent to the terms of justification. Cotton tended to disregard entirely human capacity as a rational agent and to that extent he abandoned the conditionality of the covenant of grace.[35]

Antinomian Errors 1 and 2 as compiled by the Newtown [Cambridge, Massachusetts] Synod of 1638 claim that conversion destroyed human faculties, such that the Holy Spirit does their work for them.[36] Cotton's immediatism surfaced in his treatment of the role in assurance which he accorded to the "seal of the Spirit." Cotton believed that the Holy Spirit sealed a believer such that his assurance of salvation was put beyond doubt. The seal also dispensed with the need to make diligent use of the means of grace or to look to sanctification as evidence of justification. Bozeman comments, "In the blink of an eye, the seal made superfluous all obedi-ence to the divine commands, any increase in graces, the passion to be diligent in the use of ordinances and spiritual exercises, the deep sorrow for sin, and other signs of a gracious state."[37] Antinomian Errors 32 and 42 are consistent with Cotton's view. These claim, respectively, that "After the revelation of the spirit, neither devil nor sin can make the soul to doubt" and that "There is no assurance true or right, unless it be without fear or doubting."[38] Cotton similarly denied that gross sin could lessen assurance

---

[31] Ibid., 223, 244.
[32] Ibid., 228.
[33] Ibid., 229–30.
[34] Ibid., 302, 304.
[35] Stoever, 'A Faire and Easye Way to Heaven', 79.
[36] Hall, The Antinomian Controversy, 219–20.
[37] Bozeman, The Precisianist Strain, 318.
[38] Hall, The Antinomian Controversy, 227, 230.

because assurance was directly given by the Holy Spirit.[39] Antinomian Error 20 had a similar thrust: "That to call into question whether God be my dear Father, after or upon the commission of some heinous sin (as murder, incest, etc.) doth prove a man to be in the covenant of works."[40]

The essentialist presupposition in Cotton was distinct and unmistakable. "*Covenant of God's Free Grace*," a frequently reprinted and influential sermon of his, reveals his unusual pneumatology and anthropology. Cotton created what Owen and other mainstream Puritans would consider to be a false dichotomy with regard to the Holy Spirit's communications to believers. According to Cotton, the Holy Spirit communicates either "His increated life" or "His gifts of spiritual graces created in them." Since the former cannot hold true short of the believer's deification, Cotton affirmed the latter as the only genuine possibility.

> If the members of Christ's body be living members and living stones, then they live either by some gifts of spiritual grace created in them, or else they live the uncreated life of the Holy Ghost communicated to them. But they do not live the uncreated life of the Holy Ghost communicated to them; therefore they live by the gifts of spiritual grace in them. There is no middle way.[41]

By the "middle way" Owen and other mainstream Puritans would have meant the Holy Spirit's communication of grace to the believer to be exercised by him through his spiritually renewed faculties and affections.

Cotton explicitly defined "gifts of spiritual grace" as "holy qualities or good dispositions whereby the [corrupt] faculties and affections are sanctified and made alive to God."[42] So far, so good: at first impression, this definition seemed to suggest the very middle way that Cotton has denied. But such is not the case as a closer reading of Cotton demonstrates. His departure from mainstream Puritan theology could not be clearer than in his handling of 2 Peter 1:5–8. For Cotton here insisted that the graces which the believer is exhorted to add one to another, such as faith, patience, and love, are "all wrought, increated and perfected by the Holy Ghost."[43] What Cotton's concept of "increated and perfected" spiritual gifts of grace means practically is that the believer need not be exhorted to do anything to promote these supposedly preexistent graces. His stress on union with Christ led to quietism and a virtual denial of free human agency. He preached,

[39] Ibid., 271.
[40] Ibid., 224.
[41] John Cotton, *The Covenant of God's Free Grace* (London: n.p., 1645), 30.
[42] Ibid., 28.
[43] Ibid.

"Nor are they (faith, virtue, etc.) the actions of the Holy Spirit proceeding from us; for the things are in us, and abounding in us, and consequently abiding in us; and they cause us to bring forth actions actions meet for Christian perfection."[44]

Thus Cotton turned 2 Peter 1:5–8 on its head. Far from exhorting a believer to exercise his Christian graces for an abundant entrance into heaven, Cotton instead claimed that it is the believer's preexistent graces that are abundant. Like Hutchinson who disliked the expression "grow in grace,"[45] Cotton treated sanctification, or Christian obedience, as a *fait accompli*. He declared that it is by these "spiritual gifts of grace whereby we are fitted and enabled (through [the Spirit's] leading) to walk in the law of God and keep it."[46] He also held that both faith and assurance could derive only from absolute promises as opposed to conditional ones, since the latter involved human activity.[47]

Finally, his hyper-supernaturalism took a strong turn. As Bozeman points out, "Cotton complemented his lowered estimate of human behavior (and disparagement of duties, conditions and qualifications) with a greatly magnified interest in divine agency explained in terms of divine concurrence."[48] This hyper-supernaturalism strongly shaped his view of preparation. Bozeman rightly notes, "Nowhere was the reactive [quietistic] ideal more evident than in Cotton's American treatment of the doctrine of preparation."[49] How so? For Cotton faith was "totally passive," whereas in Reformed and Puritan theology faith was both "gift and embrace."[50] In Cotton's view, then, faith was the empty, but not outstretched, hand.

---

[44] Ibid. Bozeman noticed the same phenomenon: "Cotton took [directions to union with Christ] to unusual lengths. He could so press the need to 'rely upon Christ, to lean on him, to rowl towards him' as, momentarily, to shrink the human element almost to null. Declaring that 'a living Christian lives not himself, but Christ in him' or that 'the life of a Christian is not his own life, but the life of Jesus Christ, he made the bond to deity so close that the normal sense of human presence and agency (a sense well manifest elsewhere in his work) began to blur. The tendency was carried further in portraits of the Christian in action, who seeks 'that Christ and his life in him might work all his works for him' and who, 'as a Mill moved by the breath of the wind,' has 'no further motion except as Christ moves him'" (Bozeman, *The Precisianist Strain*, 224).

[45] Murray, "*Antinomianism*," 37.

[46] Cotton, *The Covenant of God's Free Grace*, 32.

[47] Stoever, '*A Faire and Easye Way to Heaven*', 254–55.

[48] Bozeman, *The Precisianist Strain*, 257–61.

[49] Ibid., 263.

[50] Ibid., 264–65. Bozeman's take on Cotton's thrust is that, "The prepared soul is stunned into inaction" (ibid., 266–67).

Summary

The New England Antinomian Controversy (1636–1638) replicated antinomian controversies that had reverberated through London, England in 1628–1631. Virtually no aspect of the controversy commands general scholarly assent except the chronology of events. Anne Hutchinson and her brother-in-law John Wheelwright, supported at first by her pastor John Cotton, protested that pastors in New England were "legal" preachers pushing a "covenant of works". Cotton changed sides and became Hutchinson's special prosecutor after she claimed a gift of prophecy and pronounced doom on Massachusetts Bay Colony.

Historians have expressed divergent opinions as to the primary theological issue igniting the controversy. Perry Miller, Norman Petit and Janice Knight come down on the side of preparation for grace; David Hall, Michael Winship and Theodore Bozeman say repentance; and William Stoever opts for multiple issues of faith, justification and sanctification as influenced by the nature-grace continuum.

Preparation for grace played a prominent, though not exclusive role in the controversy: assurance according to Michael Winship's analysis was involved in 22 of the 82 Antinomian Errors cited by Newtown (Cambridge, MA) Synod. Janice Knight's meta-narrative of the controversy as a battle between the "Spiritual Brethren" (John Preston, Richard Sibbes and John Cotton) who dislike preparation for grace and the "Intellectual Fathers" (Hooker, Shepard, Ames and Perkins) is seriously flawed, largely because, as Iain Murray and Mark Dever have shown, preparation for grace figures in the theology of both John Cotton and Richard Sibbes. Further, her claim that the Spiritual Brethren anticipated Jonathan Edwards' theology does not hold water when one considers that it is Shepard, and not Cotton, whom Edwards quotes consistently throughout *The Religious Affections* (1746), his masterwork depicting the true marks of conversion.

It has been hard for historians to know what to make of John Cotton because of his chameleon-like volatility. Later in his American ministry, he seems to have taken the doctrine of union with Christ to extreme lengths in denying any role for human activity in faith, assurance (the practical syllogism), and even sanctification. Though he defended Puritan orthodoxy at key points, such as the binding authority of the moral law, still his theology was clearly marked by illuminism, irrationalism, immediatism, essentialism, and hyper-supernaturalism, which are all telling presuppositions of seventeenth-century English antinomianism (see Chapter 2). His frequently republished sermon *Covenant of God's Free Grace* marked a serious departure from mainstream Puritan theology. Owing to his pronounced hyper-supernaturalism, Cotton demurred at the expression "grow in grace" because in his view union with Christ had given the believer "increated and perfected graces" that work like an airplane on autopilot and make the believer a passive passenger on the flight of sanctification.

4

The Bond of Grace and Duty

A highly distinctive feature of Owen's soteriology is the intricate and indissoluble bond of grace and duty. Exhibiting the dialectical balance of Puritan theology, Owen's soteriology reconciles seeming opposites: in God's method of grace, grace is actualized through duty, faith works through obedience, and holy boldness in worship coexists with reverential fear of God.[1]

Many early English Reformers who influenced Puritan theology "found it hard to believe that, if consciences were consoled and reoriented through the grant of forgiveness, spontaneous love and gratitude would take over and morality in effect would take care of itself."[2] Their skepticism led to two related theological emphases among the English Puritans: teaching on preparation for grace, and the forging of the bond of grace and duty in covenant theology. Regarding early covenant theology in the English Reformed tradition, Bozeman writes, "Freely lavished grace was at its core, and its notion of a divinely guaranteed pact provided a firm basis for assurance. But its fuller work was to link and coordinate *sola fides* with duty."[3] In antinomian theology, by contrast, any linkage between grace and

---

[1] Owen distinguished, in common with other Reformed theologians between, *actual grace*, which did not preexist its exercise in Christian duty, and *habitual grace*, which resides in the Christian and makes him "meet" or suitable for the exercise of Christian duty. See *Works*, 2:172, 200–201, 206.

[2] Bozeman, *The Precisianist Strain*, 21.

[3] Ibid., 27.

duty was weak and tenuous. Eaton, for example, thought that Christian morality would flow automatically from the new creature.[4] Mainstream Puritan theologians strongly disagreed with the essentialism and hyper-supernaturalism presupposed by his view. Instead, they believed that grace perfects nature and works through the renewal of human faculties created by God. Packer comments on this emphasis, which the Puritans took over from the Reformers:

> The Reformation had brought back into theology an emphasis, foreign to scholasticism, on the noetic effects of the Fall. Grace elevates and per-fects human reason, not merely by supplying information, but primarily by renovating the instrument: grace frees the reason from bondage to a vicious will, which refuses knowledge of God.[5]

Antinomians also viewed, as a new legalism, the strong emphasis placed on the fulfillment of Christian duty by Puritan theologians like Owen. The Puritans countered by pointing out that sin marred even the best Christian performances and that salvation, which is all of grace, comes through justification by faith and the imputed righteousness of Christ. In this vein of thought, Owen repeats a refrain that runs through his treatises: "We cannot come to a practical compliance with [biblical truths] instruct-ing us in duty, obedience and gratitude but by grace from Christ, through whom alone [our performance of spiritual duties] is acceptable to God."[6] Owen's stress on the importance of receiving divine communication of fresh supplies of grace ran afoul of antinomian essentialism. Antinomian Error 51 proposes that, "The soul need not go out to Christ for fresh sup-ply, but is acted by the Spirit inhabiting."[7]

In a sermon entitled *The Nature and Beauty of Gospel Worship*, Owen explains that the Holy Spirit enables the saint's performance of all duties because of the bond of grace and duty and the coordinate bond of the word and Spirit:

> The Lord Jesus has promised to send his Spirit to believers, to enable them, both for matter and manner, in the performance of every duty required in the word (Isa 59:21). He will give his word and Spirit. The promise of the one and the other is of equal extent and latitude. What-ever God proposes in his word to be believed, or required to be done—that he gives his Spirit to enable to believe and do accordingly. There is

---

[4] Como, *Blown by the Spirit*, 195.
[5] Packer, *Redemption and Restoration*, 65.
[6] *Works*, 1:82.
[7] Hall, *The Antinomian Controversy*, 233.

neither promise nor precept but the Spirit is given to enable believers to answer the mind of God in them; nor is the Spirit given to enable [them] to any duty but what is in the word required. The Spirit and the word have an equal latitude; the one as a moral rule, the other as a real principle of efficiency.[8]

A number of general principles follow from Owen's statement. First, the word of God reveals both the content of Christian faith and the parameters of Christian duty. Antinomian Error 40 denies Owen's proposition by insisting on the validity of extra-biblical revelation: "There is a testimony of the Spirit, and voice unto the soul, merely immediate, without respect unto, or concurrence with the word."[9] Antinomian Error 61 also runs contrary: "All doctrines, revelations and spirits must be tried by Christ the word [i.e., the indwelling Spirit], rather than by the word of Christ [i.e., Scripture].[10]

Secondly, the Holy Spirit is given to believers to engender faith and obedience in harmony with Scriptural propositions, promises, and precepts. Thirdly, and most importantly, the Holy Spirit and the Scriptures possess "an equal latitude" in that Scripture regulates all Christian duty in "both matter and manner" and the Holy Spirit gives the grace necessary for the fulfillment of all Scriptural duties.

Owen sets forth three basic requirements of true spiritual worship: (1) knowledge of Scriptural duties; (2) grace in the heart enabling communion with God in "faith, love, delight and obedience"; and (3) spiritual ability to perform Scriptural duties.[11] How does the Holy Spirit enable the believer to fulfill these requirements? First, He leads him to search the Scriptures and "ordinarily" reveals the mind of God therein.[12] Owen rebuts the irrationalism governing antinomian theology.

Supposed in this expression of teaching [by the Holy Spirit in John 6:45, etc.] is a mind capable of instruction, leading and conduct. The nature

[8] *Works*, 9:69–70.
[9] Hall, *The Antinomian Controversy*, 230.
[10] Ibid., 235.
[11] *Works*, 9:70. Owen hints at a "mystery" of grace: grace is proportioned not to ability, but to need (*Works*, 9:81–82). In *Temptation* (1658), he clarifies his meaning: "The duties that God [ordinarily] requires at our hands are not proportioned to what strength we have in ourselves, but to what help and relief is laid up for us in Christ; and we are to address ourselves to the greatest performances with the settled persuasion that we [lack] ability for the least. When any required duty is extraordinary, this law of grace is a secret not often discovered." (*Works*, 6:94).
[12] *Works*, 9:71.

must be rational and [capable of being] taught. *Wherefore, we do not only grant herein the use of the rational faculties of the soul, but require their exercise and utmost improvement.* If God teaches, we are to learn, and we cannot learn but in the exercise of our minds. And it is vainly pretended that God's communication of a supernatural ability to our minds and our exercise of them in a way of duty, are inconsistent, whereas indeed they are inseparable in all that we are taught of God; for at the same time he infuses a gracious ability into our minds, he proposes the truth to us concerning which that ability is to be exercised. And if these things are inconsistent, the whole real efficacy of God in the souls of men must be denied; which is to despoil him of his sovereignty.[13]

Indeed, his hyperbole that irrationalism "despoils [God] of his sovereignty," means that it short-circuits the Holy Spirit's efficacious use of means to empower the performance of Christian duty and the accomplishment of God's decrees. Secondly, as the Spirit of grace and supplication (Zechariah 12:10–11), He discloses the believer's spiritual needs and God's relevant gospel promises and works in him suitable spiritual affections for intercessory prayer and communion with God.[14] Thirdly, the Holy Spirit bestows spiritual gifts needed by the minister to glorify God and edify the saints.[15] Owen concludes,

One and the same Spirit discovers the will and worship of God to them all; one and the same Spirit works the same graces for their kind in the hearts of them all; one and the same Spirit bestows [to ministers] the gifts necessary for the carrying on of gospel worship in the public assemblies.[16]

Contemporary antinomians had denied that the Holy Spirit operated in believers through created graces or spiritual gifts. Antinomian Error 15, similarly to the thrust of Cotton's "*Covenant of God's Free Grace*" sermon suggests, "There is no inherent righteousness in the saints, or grace, and graces are not in the souls of believers, but in Christ only."[17] Antinomian Error 18 goes even farther by maintaining that, "The Spirit doth work in hypocrites by gifts and graces but in God's children immediately."[18]

The bond of grace and duty is tight. Owen declares many aspects of Christian conversion and sanctification to be both a grace and a duty. These

[13] *Works*, 4:167 (emphasis mine).
[14] *Works*, 9:73.
[15] *Works*, 9:74–77.
[16] *Works*, 9:77.
[17] Hall, *The Antinomian Controversy*, 223.
[18] Ibid.

include, for example, obtaining a sense of Christ's love,[19] faith,[20] purification,[21] spiritual-mindedness,[22] and mortification of sin.[23] Such examples could be easily multiplied. Owen also gives detailed directions for fulfillment of a considerable number of Christian duties (without attributing efficacy to the directions *per se*): retaining a sense of Christ's love,[24] dying well,[25] meditation on Christ's glory,[26] recovery from backsliding,[27] seeking regeneration,[28] distinct communion with persons of the Trinity,[29] cleansing,[30] sanctification,[31] faith in Scripture,[32] prayer,[33] worship,[34] mortification of sin,[35] faith in Christ,[36] avoidance of temptation,[37] watchfulness,[38] waiting on God,[39] assurance,[40] and avoiding the prevalence of sin.[41]

The eminently dialectical balance of Owen's approach is reflected in his directions for recovery from backsliding through obedience and mortification in *The Glory of Christ Applied unto Unconverted Sinners and Saints under Spiritual Decays* (1691).[42] He simultaneously upheld God's sovereign grace in granting effective calls to repentance and in providing healing.[43] Owen holds these seemingly disparate elements in dynamic equilibrium in two ways: by recognizing that there are two types of promises in the covenant of grace, absolute and conditional, both of which are meant to

[19] *Works*, 1:115–16.
[20] *Works*, 1:390.
[21] *Works*, 4:185.
[22] *Works*, 7:267, 274.
[23] *Works*, 6:10–15 (duty) and 6:18–19 (grace).
[24] *Works*, 1:115–16.
[25] *Works*, 1:280–84.
[26] *Works*, 1:312–22.
[27] *Works*, 1:452–55.
[28] *Works*, 3:230.
[29] *Works*, 2:45, 332.
[30] *Works*, 3:531.
[31] *Works*, 3:703.
[32] *Works*, 4:13.
[33] *Works*, 4:298, 321.
[34] *Works*, 5:553.
[35] *Works*, 6:13–14.
[36] *Works*, 6:110.
[37] *Works*, 6:121.
[38] *Works*, 6:123.
[39] *Works*, 6:750.
[40] *Works*, 6:100.
[41] *Works*, 7:558–59.
[42] *Works*, 1:454.
[43] *Works*, 1:455.

work in complementary lockstep and that God's grace effects His decrees by working in Christian duty in a way of concurrence.[44]

Owen made three predications with regard to gospel promises that are important for a believer to grasp to make progress in sanctification. First, he glories in the reality that God's promises regarding conversion and sanctification of the elect in the covenant of grace are absolute and unconditional: "This is the glory of covenant promises that, as to the communication of grace of conversion and sanctification to the elect, they are absolutely free and unconditional."[45] These absolute promises do not compel Owen, however, to embrace hyper-Calvinism, because he clearly sees gospel promises respecting growth in sanctification as expressly conditional:

> The promises which respect the growth, degrees, and measures of this grace in believers are not [unconditional]. There are many duties required of us, that these promises may be accomplished towards us and in us; yea, watchful diligence in universal gospel obedience is expected from us unto this end (2 Pet 1:4–10). This is the ordinary method of the communication of all supplies of grace to make us spiritually flourish and be fruitful—namely, that we be found in the diligent exercise of what we have received.[46]

Antinomian Error 36 discouraged action by asserting that, "All the activity of the believer is to act to sin."[47]

His third predication regarding gospel promises, and one calculated to sit ill with antinomian writers who denied the reality of divine discipline, is that God usually chastises a Christian's failure, through negligence or sloth, to meet the conditions of the gospel promises with spiritual decay or barrenness.

> Notwithstanding these blessed promises of growth, flourishing and fruitfulness, if we are negligent in the due improvement of the grace which we have received, and the discharge of the duties required of us, we may fall into decays, and be kept in a low, unthrifty state all our days. Fervent

---

[44] *Works*, 3:384–85.

[45] *Works*, 1:441. John Bunyan (1628–1688) makes the same point with a metaphor pregnant in meaning: "The absolute promise is a big-bellied promise, because it has in itself a fullness of all desired things for us; and will, when the time for [the fulfillment of] that promise is come, yield to us mortals that which will verily save us; yea, and make us capable of answering of the demands of the promise that is conditional" (*The Works of John Bunyan*, ed. George Offor [Glasgow: W. G. Blackie, 1854], 1:255). Calvin recognized a similar concept (*Institutes*, II.v.8).

[46] *Works*, 1:441.

[47] Hall, *The Antinomian Controversy*, 228.

prayer, and the exercise of all grace received, with watchfulness unto all holy duties, are required hereunto.[48]

Does Owen hereby fall into the legalistic trap of letting Christian duty dictate to divine grace? Not at all, for he also points out that God may sovereignly heal the believer without awaiting his dutiful performance: "God does sometimes deal otherwise, in a way of sovereignty, and surprises men with healing grace in the midst of their decays and backslidings" (Isaiah 57:17–18).[49] Again, commenting on Canticles 5:4–6, Owen makes a similar point regarding the spouse who found her lover.

> 'She found him'—by what means is not expressed. It often so falls out in our communion with Christ, when private and public means fail, and the soul has nothing left but waiting silently and walking humbly, Christ appears; that his so doing may be evidently of grace. Christ honors his immediate absolute doings sometimes, though ordinarily he crowns his ordinances. Christ manifests himself immediately and out of ordinances to those who wait for him in them.[50]

Like Calvin in the *Institutes*,[51] mainstream Puritans like Owen recognized, then, that God often works above means. Westminster Confession chapter 5, section 3 concurs that, "God in his ordinary providence maketh use of means, yet is free to work without, above, and against them, at his pleasure."

Any perceived contradiction between absolute and conditional promises in the covenant of grace is only apparent and not real. In his treatise *Justification* (1678), Owen reconciles these two types of gospel promises.

> That those who were to be taken into this covenant [of grace] should receive grace enabling them to comply with the terms of it, fulfills its conditions, [and] yield the obedience which God required therein; for, by the ordination of God, [Jesus Christ] did merit and procure for them, the Holy Spirit and all needful supplies of grace, to make them new creatures, and enable them to yield obedience from a new principle of spiritual life faithfully to the end.[52]

[48] *Works*, 1:441.
[49] Ibid.
[50] *Works*, 2:131 (emphasis his).
[51] *Institutes*, I.xvii.1: "God sometimes works through an intermediary, sometimes without an intermediary, sometimes contrary to every intermediary." By "intermediary" Calvin meant "means" or "agency."
[52] *Works*, 5:188. Owen also affirms later in this same treatise that "all the good things… promised in the covenant [of grace] were all procured for us by the obedience and death of Christ" (*Works*, 5:194). See also Bunyan's statement in *Come and Welcome to Jesus Christ*: "There is a blessed harmony between [abso-

Antinomians recoiled from conditional promises and their implications for human activity. Antinomian Errors 27, 28, and 37 expressly rejected faith as a condition of the covenant of grace.[53] Antinomians Errors 38 and 62 spurn conditional promises respecting salvation and Error 48 declares conditional promises to be "legal."[54]

The second way in which Owen held divine grace and human duty in dynamic balance is through his recognition that divine grace communicates grace through Christian duty in a way of concurrence. This constitutes Owen's understanding of the method of grace. Again, in directing the backslider, he insists that although Christian duties may serve as an instrumental cause of healing, they do not constitute the efficient cause:

> Although God will repair our spiritual decays and heal our backslidings freely, yet he will do it so [that] he may communicate grace to us, to the praise of his own glory. These duties are prescribed to us for this purpose: for although they are not the procuring cause of God's healing love and grace, yet they are required, in God's method of the dispensation of grace, to precede their effect.[55]

Furthermore, Owen finds in the concurrence of divine grace and human duty a signal example of the "consistency and harmony" of divine sovereignty and human responsibility:

> Nor have we anywhere a more illustrious instance and testimony of the consistency and harmony between sovereign grace and the diligent discharge of our duty than [in Hosea chapter 14]: for as God promises that he would heal their backslidings out of his free love (verse 4), and would do it by the communication of effectual grace (verse 5), so he enjoins them all these duties [e.g., repentance] thereunto.[56]

A corollary of his position is that grace and duty are not opposite, but complementary and interdependent in the process of sanctification:

lute and conditional promises]. The conditional promise calls for repentance, the absolute promise gives it (Acts 5:31). The conditional promise calls for faith, the absolute promise gives it (Zeph. 3:12; Rom. 15:12). The conditional promise calls for a new heart, the absolute promise gives it (Ezek. 36:25–26). The conditional promise calls for holy obedience, the absolute promise gives it, or causes it (Ezek. 36:27)" (*Works*, 1:255).

[53] Hall, *The Antinomian Controversy*, 226, 229.

[54] Ibid., 229, 235, 232.

[55] *Works*, 1:457.

[56] Ibid.

Our duty and God's grace are nowhere opposed in the matter of sanctification; yea, the one does absolutely suppose the other. Neither can we
perform any duty herein without the grace of God; nor does God give us
this grace for any other end but that we may rightly perform our duty.[57]

Again, he anticipated the worst if duty does not prepare the way for the reception of healing grace. Although Owen clearly believed in "surprisals" of
grace, he does not generally presume their occurrence when the Christian
has demonstrated laziness.

Unless we find these things wrought in us in a way of preparation for the
receiving of the mercy desired, we have no firm ground of expectation
that we shall be made partakers of it; for this is the method of God's
dealing with the church. Then, and then only, we may expect a gracious
reviving from all our decays, when serious repentance, working in the
ways declared, is found in us. This grace will not surprise us in our sloth,
negligence, and security, but will make way for itself by stirring us up
unto sincere endeavors after it in the perseverance of these duties.[58]

What, then, of the common antinomian objection that irresistible
grace rules out the need for Christian duty? For Owen, this objection betrayed serious ignorance of God's method of grace, which operates, after
all, not through the divorce of grace and duty, but through their concurrence.

The only inconvenience wherewith our doctrine is pressed is the pretended difficulty in reconciling the nature and necessity of our duty with
the efficacy of the grace of the Spirit... Not only the necessity of our duty
is consistent with the efficacy of God's grace, but also... we can perform
no duty to God we ought without its aid and assistance, nor have any
encouragement to expect to attempt a work of obedience without a just
expectation thereof so that the work of grace itself is no way effectual but
in our compliance with it in a way of duty: only we give the preeminence
in all to grace, and not to ourselves.[59]

Owen's soteriology, as shown here, consistently upholds the Reformation
principle of *sola gratia*. Elsewhere he undercuts Roman Catholic theology of merit by declaring a Christian, even when obedient to God, has no
qualifications to plead for further grace other than God's promises.[60]

---

[57] Quoted in Gavin J. McGrath, *Grace and Duty in Puritan Spirituality* (Nottingham, England: Grove Books Limited, 1991), 11.

[58] *Works*, 1:457.

[59] *Works*, 3:10.

[60] *Works*, 3:410.

His second counterargument is that God's commands, which spell out the scope of duty, should not encourage sloth. Presumably following Augustine's dictum that God will give what He commands,[61] Owen believed that God's commands should encourage obedience. Antinomian Error 33 went the opposite way: "To act by virtue of, or in obedience to, a command is legal." Owen rebukes the hatred of obedience betrayed by this objection:

> The command of God is the measure and rule of our industry and diligence in a way of duty; and why any one should be discouraged from the exercise of that industry which God requires of him by the consideration of the aid and assistance which He hath promised unto him, I cannot understand. The work of obedience is difficult and of the highest importance; so that if any one [is] negligent therein because God will help and assist him, it is because he hates it, he likes it not.[62]

The "principal" antinomian objection to the working of God's grace in man, as perceived by Owen, is one based on faulty essentialism and the consequent denial of human agency. Owen states the objection fully:

> If not only the working of grace in us, but also the effects and fruits of it, in all its variety and degrees, is to be ascribed unto the Holy Spirit and his operations in us according to his own will, then do we signify nothing ourselves; nor is there any need that we should either use our endeavors or diligence, or at all take any care about the furtherance or growth of holiness in us, or attend unto any duties of obedience. To what end and purpose, then, serve all the commands, threatenings, promises and exhortations of the Scriptures, which are openly designed to excite and draw forth our own endeavors? And this is indeed the principal difficulty wherewith some men seek to entangle and perplex the grace of God.[63]

Error 43, for example, asserts that, "The Spirit acts most in the saints when they endeavor least."[64] Rutherford had earlier cited Error 43 verbatim, condemning it as a "damnable error of libertines."[65]

Owen gave a fivefold reply. First, he points out that God, the source of all goodness, will bless biblical truth to the good of men's souls. Secondly, and more pointedly, he declares:

---

[61] Aurelius Augustine, *Confessions*, trans. R. S. Pine-Coffin (New York: Penguin Books, 1961), 10.29.

[62] *Works*, 3:410.

[63] *Works*, 3:203.

[64] Hall, *The Antinomian Controversy*, 23.

[65] Rutherford, *Trial and Triumph of Faith*, 152.

> It is brutish ignorance to argue from the effectual operations of the Holy
> Spirit for sloth and negligence in duty. He that doth not know that God
> hath promised to 'work in us' in a way of grace what he requires from us
> in a way of duty, hath either never read the Bible or doth not yet believe
> it, either never prayed or never took notice of what he prayed for.[66]

Thirdly, Owen refutes the antinomian denial of human agency by pointing out that "The Holy Spirit works in us by us, and what he does in us is
done by us. Our duty is to apply ourselves to his commands." He observes
in fact that, "Ordinarily the Spirit of grace does not give out His aids and
assistances unless he has prepared the soul with diligence in duty. Because
he acts only in and by our faculties, it is ridiculous for a man to say he will
do nothing because the Spirit of God does all."[67]

Antinomian Errors 1 and 2 illustrate the "brutish ignorance" giving
rise to Owen's complaint. Antinomian Error 1 states that conversion destroyed all human faculties, and Error 2 that the Holy Spirit takes over
their functions. Laying stress on the vital role played by renewed human
faculties in meditation on the glory of Christ, Owen argues:

> If we are spiritually renewed, all the faculties of our souls are enabled to
> exert their respective powers towards [the glory of Christ]. This must be
> done in various duties, by the exercise of various graces, as they are to be
> acted by the distinct powers of the faculties of our minds. This is what is
> intended when we are commanded 'to love the Lord our God with all our
> souls, minds and strength.' All the distinct powers of our souls are to be
> acted by distinct grace and duties in cleaving to God by love.[68]

Finally, he explores the method by which the process of sanctification
ordinarily produces growth. According to Owen, the key is to improve
grace received through diligent use of the means of grace:

> Ordinarily and regularly, the increase and growth of grace, and their
> thriving in holiness and righteousness, depends on the use and improve-
> ment of grace received, in a diligent attendance unto all those duties of
> obedience which are required of us, 2 Peter 1:5–7. And methinks it is the
> most unreasonable and sottish thing in the world, for a man to be sloth-
> ful and negligent in attending unto those duties which God requires of
> him, which all his spiritual growth depends on, which the eternal welfare
> of his soul is concerned in, on pretence of the efficacious aids of the

---

[66] *Works*, 3:204.

[67] Ibid.

[68] *Works*, 1:320. In other words, graces and duties "act" our faculties into loving God.

Spirit, without which he can do nothing, and which he neither has nor can have whilst he does nothing.[69]

Owen's interpretation of 2 Peter 1:5–7 stands poles apart from Cotton's, as discussed in chapter 3. Owen used this passage to encourage human activity, Cotton to discourage it.

In *On the Dominion of Sin and Grace* (1688), Owen seeks to reassure the Christian of the Scriptural promise that sin will not have dominion over him. He emphasizes that God uses the gospel to communicate spiritual strength, or grace, to believers so that sin can be dethroned "in a way of duty." He explains the working relationship between grace and duty in this way:

> The gospel is the means ordained and instrument used by God for the communication of spiritual strength unto them that believe, for the dethroning of sin. It is the "power of God unto salvation," (Rom 1:16), that whereby and wherein He puts forth His power to that end. And sin must be really dethroned by the powerful acting of grace in us, and that in a way of duty in ourselves. We are absolved, acquitted, freed from the rule of sin, as to its pretended right and title, by the promise of the gospel; for thereby are we freed and discharged from the rule of the law [as a covenant of works, but not as a rule of life], wherein all title of sin to dominion is founded, for "the strength of sin is the law:" but we are freed from it, as to its internal power and exercise of its dominion, by internal grace and strength in its due exercise.[70]

It was in this context that Owen makes his clear distinction, already quoted at greater length in chapter 1, between preparation for grace and glory:

> *Remember always the way and method of the operation of divine grace and spiritual aids.* [I]n our first conversion to God, we are as it were surprised by a mighty act of sovereign grace, changing our hearts, renewing our minds, and quickening us with a principle of spiritual life. Ordinarily, many things are required of us in a way of duty in order thereunto: illumination and sense of sin [conviction of sin]; but the work itself is performed by an immediate act of divine power, without any active cooperation on our part. But this is not the law or rule of the communication or operation of actual grace for the subduing of sin. It is given in a way of concurrence with us in the discharge of our duties; and when we are

---

[69] *Works*, 3:204–5. See Antinomian Error 70: "Frequency or length of holy duties or trouble of conscience for neglect thereof, are all signs of one under a covenant of works" (Hall, *The Antinomian Controversy*, 238).

[70] *Works*, 7:546.

sedulous in them, we may be sure we shall not fail of divine assistance, according to the established rule of the administration of gospel grace. If, therefore, we are not diligent in attendance on all the duties whereby sin may be mortified in us, we exceedingly injure the grace of God.[71]

Preparation for grace, then, involves the regeneration of the unregenerate through monergism: regeneration is "surprising" when it occurs and is "performed by an immediate act of divine power without any active [human] cooperation." By contrast, preparation for glory involves the sanctification of the already regenerate through synergism: the "communication or operation of actual grace" is given in a way of concurrence with the Christian in his "sedulous" [thorough] or "diligent" discharge of Christian duties.

After mentioning that legal motives and threats cannot accomplish the overthrow of sin's dominion, Owen lists five gospel motives that can utterly ruin sin "in a way of duty:"

> But the motives and encouragements given by grace to endeavor the utter ruin of sin in a way of duty are such as give life, cheerfulness, courage and perseverance; they continually animate, relieve and revive the soul, in all its work and duty, keeping it from fainting and despondency; for they are all taken from the love of God and of Christ, from the whole work and end of His mediation, from the ready assistance of the Holy Ghost, from all the promises of the gospel, from their own with other believers' experiences; all giving them the highest assurance of final success and victory.[72]

Where does the path of duty lie? To work the ruin of sin, the path of duty, Error 70 and Everarde notwithstanding, runs directly to and through the appointed means of grace:

> The instrumental cause of this freedom [from sin] is the duty of believers themselves in and for the destruction of sin.... This is one of the principal ends of all our religious duties–of prayer, of fasting, of meditation, of watchfulness toward all other duties of obedience; they are all designed to prevent and ruin the interest of sin in us. We are called to fight and contend.... And certainly [what God has appointed and commanded] as the great end of lifelong and constant endeavor is to us of highest importance.[73]

---

[71] *Works*, 7:549 (emphasis his).
[72] *Works*, 7:551.
[73] *Works*, 7:554.

The Bond of Grace and Duty in Preparation for Grace

Owen carefully distinguished between preparation for grace and preparation for glory. It is instructive to examine his analysis of the bond of grace and duty in these two discrete situations. Grace and duty, as one might expect, "bond" differently in these two contexts. In *Pneumatologia*, Owen deals with the objection often made by antinomians and hyper-Calvinists: Why should the unregenerate perform "duties of religious obedience," or preachers press gospel commands and threats, when the religious duties of the unregenerate are at best no more than splendid sins?[74] Owen supplies a detailed reply why preparation for grace should be pursued along these lines. Though the religious duties of the unregenerate are not acceptable to God and thus formally sinful because unsanctified, yet these duties are materially good because they are more likely than inaction to put the sinner in the way of salvation.[75] God has regard to sincere, as opposed to hypocritical, religious duties.[76] Unregenerate man has a remote power, but not an immediate power, to believe and obey God; that is to say, he has faculties capable of being regenerated by God.[77] Preparation for grace insofar as it is founded on natural desires (e.g., the desire to avoid hell) has no disposition to regeneration; yet God in His power may, through the dispensation of the word, work preparatory works upon the regenerate such as illumination (chapter 6), conviction of sin (chapter 7) and legal reformation (chapter 8).

With regard to the preaching of gospel commands and threats, God has not forfeited the power to command simply because man has lost the power to obey. Gospel preachers have a warrant to press on all men the duties of faith, repentance, and obedience because (1) God so commands; (2) such preaching will restrain them from grievous sin that would harden them and render their conversion more difficult, if not desperate; and (3) such warnings will keep them in God's way of appointment whereby real conversion may eventually result.[78]

The Bond of Grace and Duty in Preparation for Glory

Owen also treated the case of preparation for glory in regard to what he called the "grace and duty" of mortification. In this context, he deals

[74] *Works*, 3:292–93.
[75] *Works*, 3:293.
[76] *Works*, 3:293–94.
[77] *Works*, 3:296–97.
[78] *Works*, 3:295.

with two common objections voiced by antinomian writers. The first is, "How can we be exhorted to mortify sin if mortification is the work of the Holy Spirit alone?" Owen offers a threefold reply. First, Philippians 2:13 demonstrates that the Holy Spirit normally works out graces *in* us.[79] Secondly, in contrast to antinomian essentialism and irrationalism, Owen declares that the Holy Spirit communicates grace to the believer to be exercised by him through spiritually renewed faculties; work in mortification of sin uses renewed human faculties, including reason:

> He doth not so work our mortification in us as not to keep it still an act of our obedience. The Holy Ghost works in us and upon us, as we are fit to be wrought in and upon; that is, so as to preserve our liberty and free obedience. He works upon our understandings, wills, consciences, and affections, agreeably to their own natures; he works in us and with us, not against us or without us; so that his assistance is an encouragement as to the facilitating of the work, and no occasion of neglect as to the work itself.[80]

Finally, though mortification is performed in the power of the Holy Spirit, it remains a Christian's duty to mortify sin. Owen infers from Romans 8:13 that, "As it is a work of grace, it is said to be wrought by the Spirit; and as it is our duty, we are said to work it 'through the Spirit'." Furthermore, Owen declares that our consideration of mortification as a work of grace should be the main motive to mortification as a duty. Again citing the Pauline metaphor of the body as the temple of the Holy Spirit, together with severe warnings against defiling that temple (1 Corinthians 3:16–17 and 6:19), he observes, as to every duty, two principal considerations:

> First, the life and spring of [the duty] as wrought in us by grace; secondly, the principal reason of and motive for it to be performed by us in the way of duty. Both of these, in the case of mortification, do centre in this inhabitation of the Spirit. For it is He who mortifies and subdues our corruptions [and] who quickens us to life, holiness and obedience. And the principal reason and motive [care and diligence in performing our duty] is to preserve His dwelling-place [so that we will not be destroyed for defiling it].[81]

A second common antinomian objection, not actually articulated but anticipated by Owen, is to imply that his use of detailed and elaborate

---

[79] *Works*, 6:20.
[80] *Ibid.*
[81] *Works*, 3:550–51.

directions for mortification may lay him open to the charges of semi-Pelagianism or legalism. Owen's reply is incisive. Although mortification is clearly a Christian duty, it is also a grace carried on and accomplished by the Holy Spirit (in a way of concurrence) in all its degrees and particulars. He enumerates no fewer than six ways in which this is true.

1. He alone clearly and fully convinces the heart of the evil and guilt and danger of the corruption, lust or sin to be mortified.

2. The Spirit alone reveals unto us the fullness of Christ for our relief.

3. The Spirit alone establishes the heart in expectation of relief from Christ.

4. The Spirit alone brings the cross of Christ into our hearts with its sin-killing power.

5. The Spirit is the author and finisher of our sanctification; and

6. In all the soul's addresses to God in this condition, it has the support of the Spirit [of supplication].[82]

Finally, faith has a vital role to play in the bond of grace and duty. For Owen, duty is acceptably performed by grace only through faith in Christ.[83] And every grace or duty provides an opportunity for communion with God.[84]

Summary

Unlike Seventeenth-Century antinomians, who thought that Christian morality would flow forth rather effortlessly from regeneration, the early English Reformers were skeptical of such a claim. Owen shared their suspicion and their stress on preparation for grace and the bond of grace and duty. Over against the antinomian disjunction of the two, as stated in Errors 40 and 61, Owen stressed the coordinate bond of word and Spirit. Scripture regulates the scope and parameters of Christian duty, and, through fresh supplies of grace (not immediacy) the Holy Spirit empowers the believer's fulfillment of Christian duty by illuminating the meaning of Scripture through the agency of sanctified human reason, disclosing the believer's spiritual needs and inspiring petitionary prayer for divine assistance, and bestowing spiritual gifts to pastors for the edification of the church. Owen rejected the denial of created graces and spiritual gifts asserted by Errors 15 and 18.

---

[82] *Works*, 6:85–86.
[83] *Works*, 1:136.
[84] *Works*, 2:19.

Owen posited a strong bond of grace and duty. He considered many aspects of Christian conversion and sanctification to be both a grace and a duty and accordingly gave detailed directions for Christian practice. The eminently dialectical balance of his soteriology is reflected, for example, in his approach to recovery from backsliding. While acknowledging God's sovereignty in granting repentance to the backslider, Owen nevertheless emphasized the necessity of obedience and mortification for recovery. Owen held these seemingly disparate elements in dynamic equilibrium by recognizing that absolute and conditional promises work in tandem and that God effects His decrees by working in the Christian (who himself acts as well) in a way of duty.

With regard to gospel promises, Owen declared that promises of conversion and definitive sanctification are absolute, whereas those respecting growth in sanctification are conditional and that God usually visits the lackadaisical Christian who ignores the conditions with spiritual barrenness. Even here, however, though he did not generally expect it where sloth has prevailed, Owen made room for a "surprisal" of grace to magnify the preeminence of God's grace and sovereignty.

That divine grace communicates spiritual strength and power through the believer's acting of Christian duty in a way of concurrence represents Owen's understanding of the "method" of grace. Grace and duty are complementary and interdependent in establishing the "consistency and harmony" of divine sovereignty and Christian responsibility. Although God's promises regarding the conversion and definitive sanctification of his elect are absolute and unconditional, Owen regarded those respecting growth in sanctification as expressly and properly conditional. In opposition to a cluster of Antinomian Errors, Owen affirmed the propriety of conditional promises and unlike Cotton, interpreted 2 Peter 1:5–8 to require activity, not passivity.

The seventeenth-century antinomian interposed two objections to this theological analysis. The first objection disparaged the importance of Christian duty because of the irresistible efficacy of grace. Owen responded that God's method of grace operates through the conjunction of grace and duty, not their divorce and that God's commands, presumably on the Augustinian principle that God gives what He commands, ought to encourage diligence rather than sloth. The second antinomian objection was based on faulty essentialism and a consequent denial of human agency. Owen's counter-arguments are that the "commands, threatenings, promises and exhortations of Scripture"[85] make no sense except as an encouragement to activity and that the Holy Spirit renews human faculties

---

[85] *Works*, 3:203.

in regeneration, so that He is able to act through them in sanctification, without overriding human agency: "The Holy Spirit works in us by us, and what He does in us is done by us."[86] Furthermore, progress in sanctification ordinarily depends on the diligent and obedient improvement of grace: over against Cotton, Owen stresses that actual grace for the subduing of sin is "given in a way of concurrence with us in the sedulous [thorough] discharge of our duties."

Owen clearly distinguished, as other Puritans did, between preparation for grace, which is monergistic, and preparation for glory, which is synergistic. God's method of grace accordingly differs between the two. With respect to preparation for grace, Owen had to deal with an antinomian objection that religious duties of the unregenerate were nothing but "splendid sins." Antinomian Error 36 considers all activity of a believer to be sinful. Owen replies that the unregenerate should keep seeking God because such duties are a material factor (though not an efficient one) in conversion because God may use gospel preaching to restrain them from heart-hardening sins that would put them out of the way of salvation.

With respect to preparation for glory, matters stand on a different footing. Though mortification is a Christian duty for whose performance Owen gave very detailed directions (see chapter 11), it is nonetheless a grace carried forward and accomplished by the Holy Spirit through conviction of sin, revelation to the believer of Christ's remedies, and upholding the believer's practice of petitionary prayer.

[86] *Works*, 3:83.

5

The Means of Grace

A characteristic feature of Puritan theology is the prominence accorded to the means of grace. This emphasis played a central role in the theology of Richard Greenham (ca.1535–ca.1599), considered the pioneer of Puritan practical divinity. Greenham, widely regarded as "a pastoral counselor of great skill"[1] by his peers, took strategic advantage of his church's proximity to Cambridge University and gave ministry training to several university students including Henry Smith, the "Chrysostom" of early Puritanism, and Arthur Hildersam, whom Baxter considered a "must-read."[2] John Primus, his modern biographer, correctly lays stress on the central role played by the doctrine of means in Greenham's practical theology:

> *The means to faith*—this is a doctrine that *does* occupy a central position in Greenham's practical divinity. That God does not work by remote control but uses human, historical means is a pervasive, virtually omnipresent theme in Greenham's *Workes*. Younger contemporaries like William Perkins and Richard Rogers also emphasized the doctrine of means, but Greenham was one of the first to give it preeminence. Moreover, for Greenham it was not a doctrine artificially contrived in order to carve out a place for human responsibility in a system otherwise dominated by the sovereignty of God. Rather, it issued quite naturally from his doctrine of God as one who normally works through creaturely agency. God's eternal promises are realized and secured in temporal ways. Hence, these

[1] Packer, *A Quest for Godliness*, 43.
[2] Ibid., 340.

promises 'do not make such as fear [God] to be careless, but careful to use the means.' In the doctrine of means, the realms of grace and nature intersect.[3]

As this quotation implies, the Puritan doctrine of the means, by connecting the realms of grace and nature, stands in direct opposition to the hyper-supernaturalism promoted by seventeenth-century antinomian writers. A primary characteristic of seventeenth-century English antinomians (as witnessed in Chapter 2) was "a propensity to argue that the Mosaic Law, including the Decalogue, was in some sense abolished, abrogated or superseded for Christians."[4] As will be seen in chapter 14, this distinctive emphasis generally entailed the disparagement of Christian sanctification and consequently of the means of grace, since sanctification depends on their constant use and improvement.

The Westminster standards, representative as they are of mainstream Puritan divinity, provide a convenient starting point for discussion of Owen's doctrine of means. Against the hyper-supernaturalism of contemporary antinomians, chapter 5, sections 2 and 3 of the Westminster Confession affirm God's providential use of secondary causes. Section 2 declares that:

Although in relation to the foreknowledge and decree of God, the first cause, all things come to pass immutably and infallibly; yet by the same providence he orders them to fall out according to the nature of second causes, either necessarily, freely or contingently.

Chapter 5, section 3 balances the previous statement in section 2 by adding a caveat that God is not in any way limited to using second causes: "God in his ordinary providence makes use of means, yet is free to work without, above and against them at his pleasure." Though section 3 stresses God's untrammeled freedom not to use any means, it still yields no support whatever to antinomian hyper-supernaturalism for two reasons. First, section 3 is meant to safeguard God's sovereignty over the efficacy of means, not to discourage Christian use of the means of grace. Second, because the word "ordinary," means "ordered, regular, and always expected" in Puritan usage, section 3 instead signals the mainstream Puritan expectation, especially in conversion, that God will normally choose not to operate outside His appointed means since "faith comes by hearing, and hearing by the word of God" (Romans 10:17).

---

[3] Primus, *Richard Greenham*, 127 citing "Of Prayer and Meditation" in *Workes*, 777.

[4] Como, *Blown by the Spirit*, 34.

Other statements in the Westminster Confession also reinforce God's "ordinary" use of gospel ordinances and sacraments for conversion and sanctification. Chapter 7, section 6 provides that the ordinances by which the gospel is dispensed are "the preaching of the word, and the administration of the sacraments of baptism and the Lord's Supper" through which the gospel is "held forth in more fullness, evidence and spiritual efficacy."[5] Chapter 25, section 3 points out that such ordinances are made effectual by the Holy Spirit according to God's promise.[6]

As Hambrick-Stowe points out, the Puritans typically distinguished between sacraments and ordinances. The two sacraments, both of which served as "seals of the covenant" of grace, were baptism and the Lord's Supper; these were considered more special means of grace.[7] The term "ordinances" was used to describe ordinary means of grace such as prayer, meditation, conference, and preaching.[8] Owen nowhere gives an exhaustive list of means of grace, but varies his list slightly in different contexts. In *The Glory of Christ*, he enumerated "prayer, meditation, mourning [over sin], reading and hearing of the Word, all ordinances of private and public worship, and diligent obedience."[9] In *An Exposition of Psalm 130*, he mentioned mortification, prayer, meditation, gospel ordinances, and godly counsel.[10] The reading of Scripture is mentioned as a means of grace in *The Divine Original of Scripture* (1659).[11] His view of Christian obedience as a means of grace is discussed in chapter 13.

Question and answer 153 of the Larger Catechism takes the position that the diligent use of the means of grace is not only important for conversion but crucial for perseverance as well:

Q. 153   What does God require of us, that we may escape the wrath and curse due us by reason of the transgression of the law?

A. 153   That we may escape the wrath and the curse of God due to us by the transgression of the law, he requires of us repentance toward God, and faith toward our Lord Jesus Christ, *and the diligent use of the outward means whereby Christ communicates to us the benefits of His mediation.*

[5] See also question 35 of the Larger Catechism. The answer to question 154 also adds prayer as an ordinance.
[6] A similar sentiment is echoed in the answers to questions 155 and 161 of the Larger Catechism.
[7] Owen concurred with this judgment. See *Works*, 1:490–91.
[8] Hambrick-Stowe, *The Practice of Piety*, 123.
[9] *Works*, 1:319.
[10] *Works*, 6:618.
[11] *Works*, 4:12.

Question and Answer 153 is remarkable because the answer about the path to salvation goes beyond the expected references to faith and repentance by adding a statement about the ongoing importance of the continued utilization of the means of grace, even after conversion. It was this insistence on perseverance in improving the means of grace ("the diligent use of the outward means") in sanctification that strongly set the Puritans apart from their antinomian opponents.

In Puritan theology, a person's zeal for the means of grace was thought to demonstrate sincerity and promote sanctification. God condescended to work through the means of grace, even though the seeker's diligence could not force God's gracious hand. Como explains:

> While use of these means did not guarantee salvation (God's grace was still assumed to be free and unmerited), the diligence and pleasure with which a person approached God's ordinances was taken to be a good, rough indicator of his or her spiritual estate; moreover, the means, zealously applied, were the only way that a believer could possibly continue to grow upward and outward in divine grace. In Puritan spirituality God did not come *because* someone engaged in a certain exercise; but if God was [were] going to come, He would do it through means of that exercise.[12]

Eaton's attack made against the continued use of the means of grace beyond conversion is typical antinomian fare. He held the primary means of the believer's sanctification was simply to pray and meditate on "the power of free justification." As Como points out,

> This violated the traditional Puritan understanding of the means of grace. For the godly, all the ordinances of God could serve as means. This included preaching, public worship and the sacraments, as well as more informal, private devotions such as reading, fasting, conference, and mutual communion with other saints. It was precisely a reliance upon such 'duties' that Eaton and his followers sought to undermine. Such an illuminism [focused on meditation on 'free justification'] in their [the Puritan] view violated the commandment of God to work out their salvation in fear and trembling.[13]

Though Owen recommended prayer and meditating on the glory of Christ, as discussed further in Chapter 13, he unlike Eaton does not recommend prayer and meditation to the exclusion of the sacraments and gospel ordinances. Eaton's elevation of meditation on the "power of free justification" as the preeminent means of grace means downgrading, if not eliminating

---

[12] Como, *Blown by the Spirit*, 124 (emphasis his).
[13] Ibid., 208.

altogether, daily repentance and the use of the sacraments and gospel ordinances.

Use of Means by the Unregenerate in Preparation for Grace

Question and answer 153 of the Larger Catechism demonstrates the mainstream Puritan view that the means of grace are indispensable to both preparation for grace and preparation for glory. Hambrick-Stowe demonstrates the Puritan view that preparation for glory was conceived of as a lifelong process designed to bring out progressively deeper conviction of sin, faith, and repentance, with sanctification reflecting the basic pattern of conversion.[14] Owen distinguished different duties for the unregenerate in preparation for grace and for the regenerate in preparation for glory.[15]

Owen stressed that in regeneration the Holy Spirit usually works by the ordinary means appointed in Scripture and especially by preaching.[16] In consequence, he refuses to embrace "thunderbolt" theology by merely emphasizing, as Marrow theologians have often done, that religious duties performed by the unregenerate are nothing better than "splendid sins."[17] On the contrary, the Holy Spirit's employment of ordinary means in regeneration makes putting oneself "in the way of" salvation all the more important. Owen pointed out two duties of the unregenerate in preparation for grace:

There are some things required of us in a way of duty in order to our regeneration, which are so in the power of our natural abilities as that nothing but corrupt prejudices and stubbornness in sinning do keep or hinder men from the performance of them. And these we may reduce to two heads: (1) Outward attendance on the dispensation of the word of God, with those other external means of grace which accompany it or are appointed therein. 'Faith cometh by hearing, and hearing by the word of God.' (Rom. 10:17) That is, it is hearing the word of God, which is the ordinary means of ingenerating faith in the souls of men. (2) Diligent intension of mind, in attendance on the means of grace, to understand and receive the things revealed and declared as the mind and will of God. For this end has God given men reason and understanding to use and exercise about their duty to him.[18]

---

[14] Hambrick-Stowe, *The Practice of Piety*, 199.

[15] *Works*, 3:10.

[16] *Works*, 3:213, 225.

[17] *Works*, 3:292–95.

[18] *Works*, 3:229–30. Owen insists that such preparatory activities, though well worth pursuing, are not meritorious. See a fuller discussion in chapter 9.

Owen again issues the reminder that God normally rewards the diligent use of the ordinary means of grace with special grace:

> Ordinarily, God in the effectual dispensation of his grace meets with those who attend with diligence on the outward administration of the means of [grace]. He does so, ordinarily, in comparison [to his treatment of] those who despise and neglect [the means of grace]. Although sometimes he will go out of his way to save a persecutor like Saul, nevertheless he ordinarily dispenses his peculiar, special grace among those who attend to the common means [of grace]; for he will both glorify his word thereby and give out pledges of his approbation of our obedience to his commands and institutions [appointed ordinances].[19]

God may have gone "out of His way" to save Saul of Tarsus, but this exception only proves the general rule.

Owen also elevates the importance of seeking and prayer by the unregenerate. He rebuts two relevant objections to this kind of preparation for grace. Owen considers the antinomian objection— that prayer for the Holy Spirit by the unregenerate renders the covenant of grace improperly conditional— to be ill founded:

> It will be said that we are bound to pray for him [for our first conversion to God] and therefore the bestowal of him depends on a condition to be by us fulfilled; for the promise is, that 'our heavenly Father will give the Holy Spirit to them that ask him.' Luke 11:13. But this does not prove that the bestowal and reception of [the Holy Spirit] is not absolutely free. Nay, it proves the contrary. It is 'undeserved grace' that is the proper object of prayer. And God, by these encouraging promises, does not abridge the liberty of his own will, nor derogate from the freedom of His gifts and grace, but only directs us into the way whereby we may be made partakers of them, to His glory and our own advantage. And this very praying for the Spirit is a duty that we cannot perform without his assistance. 1 Cor. 12:3.[20]

Owen also disputes the hyper-Calvinistic objection that it is improper for an unregenerate person to pray for the Holy Spirit because he does not know whether or not he is one of the elect. Surprisingly, because of his belief in illuminism, the antinomian thought he could tell which people including himself were elect. Antinomian Error 24 insists that, "He that has the seal of the Spirit may certainly judge of any person whether he be elected or no."[21] Antinomian Error 32 asserts that, "After the revelation

---

[19] *Works*, 3:231.
[20] *Works*, 3:109.
[21] Ibid., 226.

of the Spirit, neither devil nor sin can make the soul to doubt [its salvation]."[22]

Owen's makes short work of this objection. He replies that people under conviction of sin ought to pray for salvation because they cannot plead any special promise made under the secret decree of election, but that they "may plead for the grace and mercy declared in the [indefinite gospel] promises."[23] Again, Owen contends that duties should be pressed on the unregenerate: even if the duties are "splendid sins", they are still materially good because their performance may put the sinner in the way of salvation.[24]

Owen expresses a profoundly optimistic soteriology regarding diligent use of the means of grace, founded both on God's faithfulness to divine promises of mercy and grace and His propensity to reward those who seek him diligently (Hebrews 11:6). Owen remarks:

> The rule in this case is, Hosea 6:3: 'Then shall we know, if we follow on to know.' Are you in the way of knowing Christ in the use of means, hearing the word, and sincere endeavors in holy duties? Though you cannot yet attain to any evidence that you have received him, have closed with him, nothing can ruin you but giving over the way wherein you are; for then shall you know, if you follow on to know the Lord.[25]

Owen's optimism encourages perseverance in preparation for grace and discourages giving up.

Use of Means by the Regenerate in Preparation for Glory

The antinomian (given his essentialism and irrationalism) thought the importance of the means of grace dwindled to or near the vanishing point as soon as a sinner experienced the new birth. Yet on the heels of discussing regeneration in *Pneumatologia*, Owen takes great pains to mark the vital importance of persevering with the means of grace: "The whole that God requires of us in a way of duty is, that we should be holy, and abide in the use of those means whereby holiness may be attained and improved in us."[26] Owen leaves no reasonable doubt that the means of grace are inextricably bound to the ongoing administration of the covenant of grace. In

---

[22] Ibid., 32.
[23] *Works*, 3:412. Thus Owen embraces the "free offer of the gospel."
[24] *Works*, 3:293.
[25] *Works*, 1:429.
[26] *Works*, 3:377.

A Brief Instruction in the Worship of God and Discipline of the Churches of the New Testament (1667), he blasts the antinomian chimera that the necessity of the means of grace for believers has for the most part ceased:

> Q. 6.   May not such an estate of faith and perfection in obedience be attained in this life, as wherein believers may be freed from all obligation for the observation of gospel institutions?

> A. 6.   No; for the ordinances and institutions of the gospel being inseparably annexed to the evangelical administration of the gospel of grace, they may not be left unobserved, disused, or omitted, whilst we are to walk before God in the covenant, without contempt of the covenant itself, as also of the wisdom and authority of Jesus Christ.[27]

In fact, constant and diligent use of the means of grace in undertaking sanctification is both an objective and a subjective necessity. Owen considers the greatest Christian duty in sanctification to be that of sanctifying God's name and insisted that it is accomplished *objectively* through obedient observance of gospel ordinances:

> Q. 8.   How may we sanctify the name of God in the use of gospel institutions?

> A. 8.   By a holy reverence of his sovereign authority in appointing them; a holy regard to his special presence in them; faith in his promises annexed to them; delight in his will, wisdom, love and grace manifested in them; constancy and perseverance in obedience to God by their due observation.[28]

The *subjective* sanctification of God's name is accomplished through appropriating God's presence in the ordinances when the Holy Spirit gives efficacy to the word of God, thereby communicating grace and mercy to the church and granting special blessings on Christian growth and holiness.[29]

What difference does it make if the means of grace are neglected? Does the doctrine of divine preservation guarantee the same outcome, as the antinomians suggested, regardless of whether the means of grace are improved?[30] What about using the mortification of sin as a test case?

---

[27] *Works* 15:454.

[28] *Works*, 15:456.

[29] *Works*, 15:458.

[30] See Owen's warning against presumptuous reliance on the doctrine of perseverance at *Works*, 6:147–48.

Owen warned of specific danger from the neglect of mortification: "[T]his is the reason why we have so many withering professors among us, decayed in their graces, fruitless in their lives, and every way conformed to the world."[31] Antinomian Error 70, by contrast, takes to task those legalists whose consciences were smitten by their neglect: "Frequency of length of holy duties or trouble of conscience for neglect thereof, are all signs of one under a covenant of works."[32]

Without continued diligence in the use of means of grace, Owen holds out little hope of perseverance, regarding such neglect as a repeat performance of Adam's original folly:

> We may not think to find acceptance with God, or to inherit the promises, if we neglect that which is external and of his free appointment: for besides that we renounce thereby our inward dependence on him also, in not observing his commands, as Adam did in transgressing an institution, we become wholly useless for all the ends of his glory in the world; this is not the way to come to an enjoyment of God.[33]

Further, he points out grievous consequences from the neglect of the word of God. The preaching of the word produces illumination, obedience, holy and heavenly affections, spiritual strength, and fruitfulness in good works.[34] Owen describes the power of the preached word in strong terms:

> [U]nbelievers were sensible of a divine authority, which they could not stand before, or withstand in life and power of conviction of sin. As men found an authority in the dispensation of the word, so they felt and experienced an efficacy in the truths dispensed. By it were their minds enlightened, their consciences awakened, their minds convinced, their lives judged, the secrets of their hearts made manifest until they cried out in multitudes, 'Men and brethren, what shall we do?'[35]

Finally, he observes that those who sit under the preaching of the word without any experience of these powerful spiritual effects run the grave danger of becoming gospel-hardened.[36] As quoted in chapter 2, Owen insists that constant and diligent attendance on the means of grace, part of

---

[31] *Works*, 3:45.
[32] Hall, *The Antinomian Controversy*, 238.
[33] *Works*, 15:448.
[34] *Works*, 7:540.
[35] *Works*, 4:484.
[36] Ibid.

the created order that God has appointed to use supernaturally, is imperative for Christian growth and obedience:

> There is not any thing in the whole course of our obedience wherein the continual exercise of faith and spiritual wisdom is more indispensably required than the due improvement of gospel privileges and ordinances: for there is no other part of our duty whereon our giving glory to God and the eternal concern of our own souls does more eminently depend. Gospel institutions of worship are the only ordinary outward means whereby the Lord Christ communicates his grace to us, and whereby we immediately return love, praise, thanks and obedience to him, on which spiritual intercourse, our spiritual growth does depend. It is therefore certain that our growth or decay in holiness [and] our steadfastness in, or apostasy from, profession, are greatly influenced by the use or abuse of those privileges.[37]

Again working consistently with his theology regarding the bond of grace and duty, Owen gives five directions to keep the heart "tender" under the word of God. He counsels (1) casting out all vicious habits of mind; (2) recalling the power and efficacy the word has previously had on one's soul;[38] (3) laying aside all prejudices against the preacher; (4) keeping the heart humble and teachable; and, above all, (5) praying for God's blessing on the word preached.[39]

Owen points out that sin has dominion over the Christian when his spiritual deadness and decay is not recoverable by ordinary means of grace, especially preaching. He cites David as a Christian under dominion of sin who had to be awakened by extraordinary means, a visit from Nathan.[40] As quoted in chapter 4, Owen leaves no doubt where the path of Christian duty lies for accomplishing the ruin of sin. The path of duty runs directly to and through the appointed means of grace:

> The instrumental cause of this freedom [from sin] is the duty of believers themselves in and for the destruction of sin.... This is one of the principal ends of all our religious duties–of prayer, of fasting, of meditation, of watchfulness toward all other duties of obedience; they are all designed to prevent and ruin the interest of sin in us. We are called to fight and contend... And certainly [what God has appointed and commanded]

---

[37] *Works*, 7:250.

[38] Compare Antinomian Error 58: "To help my faith and comfort my conscience in evil hours from former experience of God's grace in me, is not a way of grace" (Hall, The *Antinomian Controversy*, 234).

[39] *Works*, 7:559.

[40] *Works*, 7:540.

as the great end of lifelong and constant endeavor is to us of highest importance.[41]

Owen never tires of pointing out the dire necessity of constant and diligent use of the means of grace for Christian growth and obedience. Nothing but the "due improvement of gospel privileges and ordinances" will promote thriving Christian growth and holiness.

> There is not anything in the whole course of our obedience more indispensably required to become a spiritually thriving Christian than the due improvement of gospel privileges and ordinances, especially since worship is the only ordinary outward means of spiritual intercourse between Christ and us whereby He communicates His grace to us and we return love, praise, thanks and obedience to Him. This is what our growth depends on.[42]

For Owen, not using the means of grace consistently throughout the Christian life precludes growth in grace and perseverance.

Summary

Mainstream Puritan pastors followed the lead of Richard Greenham in repudiating the disparagement of the means of grace current among Seventeenth-Century antinomian authors. Mainstream Puritanism rejected the presuppositions of hyper-supernaturalism, essentialism, illuminism, and irrationalism that informed their position on the dispensability of the means of grace especially regarding sanctification. Instead, Owen and mainstream Puritans affirmed that in salvation, God normally works through means that are part of the created order, that the means of grace also play a pivotal role in lifelong sanctification, and that God works His good pleasure in Christians through "acting" their renewed faculties which they themselves "act" as well.

Question and answer 153 of the Larger Catechism shows the mainstream Puritan view of perseverance, namely that constant and diligent use of the means of grace is indispensable both in preparation for grace and preparation for glory. It declares that "escape [from] the [legal] wrath and curse of God... requires repentance, faith and the diligent use of the outward means whereby Christ communicates the benefits of His mediation." Owen, who concurred that salvation is to be worked out with fear and trembling, discussed both aspects of Christian duty towards the means

[41] *Works*, 7:554.
[42] *Works*, 7:250.

of grace: the duty of the unregenerate in preparation for grace and that of the regenerate in preparation for glory.

Owen emphasized three major duties incumbent on the unregenerate to prepare for grace: outward attendance on the means of grace, diligent intention of mind to grasp God's mind and will as revealed in Scripture, and prayer for the gift of the Holy Spirit in regeneration. Because of his profound soteriological optimism that God rewards those who seek him diligently, Owen did not hesitate to press these duties on the unregenerate. Even though these may be regarded as "splendid sins," no one should lose sight of the fact that they are formally good because of their designed tendency to put the sinner "in the way of" salvation.

Owen repeatedly stressed the need for the regenerate to prepare for glory, not by resting on their laurels but by pressing on, through steady improvement of the means of grace, to Christian maturity. In contrast to those antinomian authors who depreciated the continued need for their full use following conversion, Owen insisted that the means of grace are indispensable to the ongoing administration of the covenant of grace and for the Christian to receive the benefits of Christ's mediation. He held that the means of grace are necessary not only for sanctifying God's name but also for enjoying fellowship with God and experiencing growth in holiness and usefulness. Owen considers the greatest Christian duty to be that of sanctifying God's name, which duty is accomplished *objectively* through obedient observance of gospel ordinances in faith and delight and *subjectively* through apprehending God's presence in gospel ordinances and His special blessing on Christian growth and holiness.[43] The neglect of means of grace leads to backsliding, not often recoverable by ordinary means, and even total apostasy, which is irrecoverable. Owen warns that Christians will never accomplish their duty of destroying indwelling sin unless they are willing "to walk over the bellies of their lusts" (in Owen's vivid image from *On the Mortification of Sin*) through utilizing means of grace such as mortification, prayer and fasting, meditation, watchfulness, and obedience.

[43] *Works*, 15:458.

6

Preparation for Grace: Illumination

Illuminism versus Illumination

Though both words share the same root, the Latin word *lumen* meaning "light, what Owen means by *illumination* is diametrically opposed to the *illuminism* advocated by seventeenth-century antinomian writers. Owen defines illumination as "that supernatural knowledge that any man has or may have of the mind and will of God, as revealed to him by supernatural means, for the law of his faith, life and obedience."[1] Illuminism, by contrast, is belief in continuing direct or immediate inspiration from the Holy Spirit, based on an primitivist assumption that the Holy Spirit operates the same now in every respect as in apostolic times. Illuminism is also marked by a strong tendency to dispense with the means of grace and to ground assurance solely in the direct revelation of the Holy Spirit. Illumination is an operation of *the Holy Spirit working in, by, and through the word of God* to create spiritual understanding of God's will and man's duty, whereas the direct revelation embraced by illuminism is new revelation independent of Scripture that lays claim to infallibility.[2]

As seen in chapters 1 and 2, Owen's response to antinomian illuminism, up to this point, has been fourfold. First, he blames illuminism for

---

[1] *Works*, 4:6.
[2] Nuttall, *The Holy Spirit*, 49.

false guidance that leads to pursuit of duties nowhere described in Scripture. Secondly, consistent with "the characteristic Puritan understanding of the Reformed conjunction of Word and Spirit,"[3] Owen insists that the Holy Spirit does not work apart from the word of God. Thirdly, he fleshes out the doctrine of cessationism sketched by Calvin, holding that prophecy in the sense of foretelling, which even in apostolic times paled in importance compared to preaching, is a spiritual gift that ceased with the close of the canon of Scripture. Finally, he rejects the notions of immediate revelation and direct assurance from the Holy Spirit, insisting on confirmation of assurance by the practical syllogism.

The Reformed Background

Not only did the Protestant Reformation recover the doctrine of justification by faith, but it also placed a fresh and powerful new emphasis on the person and work of the Holy Spirit. Luther stressed the importance of praying and meditating on Scripture for correct understanding. Concerning Luther's approach, David Steinmetz writes:

> Scripture is not in our power. It is not at the disposal of our intellect and is not obliged to render up its secrets to those who have theological training, merely because they are learned. Scripture imposes its own meaning; it binds the soul to God through faith. Because the initiative of Scripture remains in the hands of God, we must humble ourselves in his presence and pray that he will give understanding and wisdom to us as we meditate on the sacred text. While we may take courage from the thought that God gives understanding of the Scripture to the humble, we should also heed the warning that the truth of God can never coexist with human pride.[4]

It remained for Calvin, however, whom B. B. Warfield called "the theologian of the Holy Spirit," to put special emphasis on the work of the Holy Spirit in inner witness, union with Christ and sanctification, which marked a much needed departure from His neglect by medieval Roman Catholic theologians.[5] Calvin's groundwork prepared the way for Puritans

---

[3] J. I. Packer, "Foreword".

[4] David C. Steinmetz, "Hermeneutic and Old Testament Interpretation in Staupitz and the Young Martin Luther," *Archiv Für Reformationgeschichte* 70 (1979): 71.

[5] B. B. Warfield, "Introductory Note" to Kuyper's, *The Work of the Holy Spirit*, xxxiii and also see his remarks in *Calvin and Augustine* (Philadelphia: Presbyterian and Reformed, 1956 reprint), 487.

like Owen and Thomas Goodwin (1600 –1680) to write more extensive works on the Holy Spirit.

As to the indwelling of the Holy Spirit, Calvin states that "by the inspiration of his power he so breathes divine life into us that we are no longer actuated by ourselves but are ruled by his action and prompting. Accordingly... without him [we have nothing but] darkness of mind and perversity of heart."[6] The sealing of the Spirit, according to Calvin, has two principal effects. The first is to give us the witness of the Holy Spirit regarding the divine inspiration of Scripture: "[I]llumined by his power, we believe neither by our own nor by anyone else's judgment that Scripture is from God."[7] The second related effect of the sealing of the Spirit is to grant assurance of salvation, which is directly linked to belief in the veracity of Scripture and God's promises.

Calvin insists on the necessity of illumination by the Holy Spirit for personal salvation: "The way to the Kingdom of God is open only to him whose mind has been made new by the illumination of the Holy Spirit."[8] By illumination, our corrupted human nature is restored, in all its faculties, to the image of God.[9] "Without the illumination of the Holy Spirit, the Word can do nothing."[10] The Holy Spirit and Scripture do not contradict each other. "The Holy Spirit so inheres in [Scripture] that only when proper reverence and dignity are given to the Word does the Holy Spirit show forth his power."[11] Calvin declares that, "Scripture exhibits fully as clear [an] evidence of its own truth as white and black things do of their color, or sweet and bitter things do of their taste." In other words, he regards Scripture as self-authenticating through the illumination of the Holy Spirit.

> Scripture indeed is self-authenticating; hence, it is not right to subject it to proof and reasoning. And the certainty that it deserves with us, it attains by the testimony of the Spirit. For even if it wins reverence for itself by its own majesty, it seriously affects us only when it is sealed upon our hearts through the Spirit. Therefore, illumined by his power, we believe neither by our own nor by anyone else's judgment that Scripture is from the very mouth of God.[12]

---

[6] *Institutes*, III.i.3.

[7] *Institutes*, I.vii.5 and III.i.1.

[8] *Institutes*, II.ii.20.

[9] *Institutes*, I.xv.4.

[10] *Institutes*, III.ii.33.

[11] *Institutes*, I.ix.3.

[12] *Institutes*, I.vii.5.

Calvin mentions that Scripture "wins reverence for itself by its own majesty" through the sealing of the Holy Spirit, so that belief in Scripture as coming "from the very mouth of God" is neither merely rational nor secondhand.

Since Scripture is indeed self-authenticating, Calvin notes that the apostles did not dwell on rational proofs. Instead, "the highest proof of Scripture derives in general from the fact that God in person speaks in it."[13] The self-authenticating nature of Scripture leads to the corollary that reason, although useful, is insufficient to lead a person to a saving knowledge of God. Calvin insists:

> Unless this certainty, higher and stronger than any human judgment, be present, it will be vain to fortify the authority of Scripture by arguments, to establish it with common agreement of the church, or to confirm it with other helps. For unless this foundation is laid, its authority will always remain in doubt. Conversely, once we have embraced it devoutly as its dignity deserves, and have recognized it to be above the common sort of things, those arguments – not strong enough before to engraft and fix the certainty of Scripture in our minds – become very useful aids. What confirmation ensues when we ponder the economy of divine wisdom, so well ordered and disposed; the completely heavenly character of its doctrine, savoring of nothing earthly; the beautiful agreements of the parts with one another.[14]

Again, Calvin repeats the point that certainty in Scripture as God's very words cannot be established by rational arguments, though these may serve as useful confirmation.

Calvin mentioned other rational proofs including the great antiquity of Scripture, miracles and fulfilled prophecy, the providential preservation of the Bible, and the consent of the church to the canon of Scripture.[15] The limitations of human reason, nevertheless, remain very real:

> Yet of themselves these [rational proofs] are not strong enough to provide a firm faith. Scripture will ultimately suffice for a saving knowledge of God only when its certainty is founded upon the inward persuasion of the Holy Spirit. Indeed, these human testimonies will not be vain as secondary aids if they follow that chief and highest testimony.[16]

---

[13] *Institutes*, I.vii.4.
[14] *Institutes*, I.viii.1.
[15] *Institutes*, I.viii.1–13.
[16] *Institutes*, II.ii.18.

The most penetrating and exhaustive coverage of the Holy Spirit's role in illumination in Christian literature takes place in Owen's *Pneumatologia*. His defense of the sufficiency and perspicuity of Scripture over against Roman Catholic, Socinian, antinomian, and Quaker theologies hinges on the pivotal dual role played by the Holy Spirit in enabling the Christian to believe Scripture to be the word of God and interpret it correctly for a life of faith and obedience *coram Deo*. Owen, like other Protestant scholastic theologians, employed the term "illumination" in two discrete senses:[17] illumination connotes either a preparatory work of grace by the Holy Spirit (hereafter referred to as "pedagogical illumination") or regeneration itself (hereafter "salvific illumination"). Owen acknowledged as much himself.

> [Because of natural depravity], hence both is illumination sometimes taken for the whole work of conversion to God [i.e. salvific illumination], and the spiritual actings of the mind, by renovation of the Holy Ghost, [that] precede any gracious actings in the will, heart and life [i.e. pedagogical illumination].[18]

Owen used illumination in the pedagogical sense when he treated the subject of preparatory works toward regeneration.

> There are certain internal spiritual effects wrought in and upon the souls of men, whereof the word preached is the immediate instrumental cause, which ordinarily do precede the work of regeneration, or real conversion unto God. And they are reducible to three heads: 1. Illumination; 2. Conviction; 3. Reformation. The first of these respects the mind only; the second, the mind, the conscience and affections; and the third, the life and conversation [behavior].[19]

So pedagogical illumination, which influences the mind, is clearly involved in preparation for grace as it is one of the three "internal spiritual effects … which ordinarily do precede the work of regeneration, or real conversion unto God."

Owen again uses the term in the former sense of preparatory illumination when he states:

> In order of nature [illumination] is previous to a full and real conversion to God, and is materially preparatory and dispositive thereunto; for sav-

[17] Muller, "Illuminatio," *Dictionary of Latin and Greek Theological Terms*, 142–143. Salvific illumination can be both *legalis* (by means of the law) and *evangelica* (by the gospel).
[18] *Works*, 3:281.
[19] *Works*, 3:231.

ing grace enters into the soul by light. As it is therefore the gift of God, so it is the duty of all men to labor after a participation [in] it, however by many it be abused.[20]

Owen goes on to explain what he means by the phrase "materially preparatory and dispositive:"

> A material disposition is that which disposes and somehow makes a subject fit for the reception of that which shall be communicated, added or infused into it as its form. So wood by drying and a due composure is made fit and ready to admit of firing, or continual fire.[21]

The next-to-the-last statement reveals a great deal about Owen's understanding of the bond of grace and duty. Although illumination is a gracious gift of God, the recipient of illumination has a duty to use and improve the gift toward conversion. Failure to improve the gift duly is called "abuse" by Owen. As seen in Chapter 5, Owen's optimistic soteriology once more comes to the fore:

> Every one who takes care of his own present and eternal welfare may and shall, in the due use of the means appointed, and discharge of duties prescribed to that end, with a due dependence on the aid and assistance which [God] will not withhold from any who diligently seek him, infallibly attain such measure of the knowledge of his will and mind, with full assurance [of salvation] therein, as will be sufficient to guide him to eternal blessedness.[22]

Owen ordinarily expects eschatological salvation, then, for every person who, depending on the Holy Spirit's gracious assistance, duly discharges his duties in preparation for regeneration.

Owen' use of the word "illumination" in two different senses to express either "pedagogical" or "salvific" illumination is relevant to Owen's demarcation of three degrees of illumination. The first two degrees are pedagogical; only the third degree is salvific. The first degree is merely natural knowledge of spiritual truth attained by reason alone, while the second is supernatural knowledge given by the Holy Spirit that makes the gospel clearer, compels mental assent to it, and grants joy and even spiritual gifts.[23] The third degree of illumination, to which the first two degrees

---

[20] *Works*, 3:233.
[21] *Works*, 3:229.
[22] *Works*, 4:119.
[23] *Works*, 3:231–32.

of illumination normally (but not invariably) lead, is regeneration itself. He writes: "There is an effectual, powerful, creating act of the Holy Spirit put forth in the minds of men in their conversion to God, enabling them spiritually to discern spiritual things; wherein the seed and substance of divine faith is contained."[24] Here Owen clearly connects salvific illumination with regeneration.

His treatises *The Reason of Faith (or The Grounds Whereon the Scripture is Believed to be the Word of God with Faith Divine and Supernatural)* (1677) and *Causes, Ways and Means of Understanding the Mind of God* (1678) answer two related lines of inquiry, both of which implicate the necessity of illumination: How do we believe the Scripture to be the word of God, and how do we understand God's mind and will as expressed in Scripture?[25] Owen asserts that *salvific* illumination, the third degree of illumination, is not only involved in regeneration but also necessary for true belief in the divine inspiration of Scripture:

> The work of the Holy Ghost for this purpose consists in the saving illumination of the mind; and the effect of it is a supernatural light, whereby the mind is renewed. Hereby we are enabled to discern the evidences of the divine original and authority of Scripture that are in itself, as well as assent to the truth contained in it; and without it we cannot do so, for 'the natural man receives not the things of the Spirit of God, for they are foolishness to him, neither can he know them, because they are spiritually discerned.' 1 Cor. 2:14.[26]

Owen specifies, with respect to salvific illumination, that "this revelation of the Spirit [also works by] … freeing our minds from darkness, ignorance and prejudice, enabling them to discern spiritual things duly."[27]

The Internal and External Witness of the Holy Spirit

The Puritans closely followed Calvin's lead in affirming the role of the inner witness of the Holy Spirit in demonstrating the Bible to be the very Word of God. Chapter 1, section 5 of the Westminster Confession can be taken as a fair summary of Calvin's teaching:

> We may be moved and induced by the testimony of the Church to an high and reverend esteem of the Holy Scripture, and the heavenliness of

---

[24] *Works*, 3:332.
[25] *Works*, 4:6.
[26] *Works*, 4:57.
[27] *Works*, 4:60.

the matter, the efficacy of the doctrine, the majesty of the style, the consent of all the parts, the scope of the whole (which is to give all glory to God), the full discovery it makes of the only way of God's salvation, the many other incomparable excellencies, and the entire perfection thereof, are arguments where it doth abundantly evidence itself to be the word of God: yet, notwithstanding our full persuasion and assurance of the infallible truth and divine authority thereof is from the inward work of the Holy Spirit bearing witness by and with the word in our hearts.

The Westminster Confession hews closely to Calvin's line of approach: while rational arguments and the testimony of the church may increase one's belief that Scriptures are probably the word of God, it is only the inward witness of the Holy Spirit "by and with the word in our hearts" that gives "full persuasion and assurance of [Scripture's] infallible truth and divine authority."

According to Owen, the inner witness of the Holy Spirit testifies in three ways. He bears witness through "the impressions or characters which are subjectively left in Scripture and upon it by the Holy Spirit, its author, of all the divine excellencies or properties of the divine nature."[28] Moreover, He gives an experience of the power of Scripture.

He gives unto believers a spiritual sense of the power and reality of the things believed, whereby their faith is greatly established.... It is the greatest corroborating testimony. This is that which brings us to the "riches of the full assurance of understanding." And on account of this spiritual experience is our perception of spiritual things so often expressed by acts of sense, as tasting, seeing, feeling and the like.[29]

He too dispels temptations to doubt.[30]

Most importantly, Owen goes beyond Calvin by making explicit what the latter has left implicit: the external witness of the Holy Spirit. Owen defines the external witness as "the external work of the same Holy Spirit giving evidence in and by the Scripture unto its divine original."[31] Packer comments:

The [external witness of the Holy Spirit] presupposes, and is correlative to, the [internal witness of the Holy Spirit], and both belong to the

[28] *Works*, 4:91.
[29] *Works*, 4:64.
[30] *Works*, 4:65.
[31] *Works*, 4:102.

statement of the classic Reformed doctrine, first given prominence by
Calvin in the *Institutes*, of the witness of the Spirit as the ground of faith
in the Scriptures. In stating this against the Church of Rome, Calvin had
stressed the internal witness of the Spirit and had given no separate attention to the point that there is also an external testimony of the Spirit
to which his inward witness in the believer's heart corresponds. What is
distinctive about Owen's presentation of this doctrine, as compared with
Calvin's, is the stress that he lays on the Spirit's external witness. His
doctrine is thus of a double testimony of the Holy Spirit to Scripture; its
effect is to draw out and make explicit what is implicit in Calvin's statements at points where these statements are not fully developed.[32]

The Holy Spirit gives external testimony to the divine inspiration and
authority of Scripture by producing five effects (one principal effect and
four related effects).[33] The main effect consists "in the conversion of the
souls of sinners to God"[34] when the Holy Spirit, acting by and through
the word, exerts "power and authority over the minds and consciences of
men" by manifesting "the secrets of the heart."[35] Owen described this work
metaphorically in *The Divine Original of Scripture* (1659) as "its diving into
the hearts, consciences and secret recesses of the minds of men; its judging
and sentencing of them in themselves; its convictions, terrors, conquests,
and killing of men."[36]

Owen also mentioned four related effects that result from the same
bond of word and Spirit. The Holy Spirit causes involuntary conviction of
sin and makes conscience submit to God's judgment of conduct.[37] Again,
He gives "spiritual illuminating efficacy" to the word of God.[38]

> Those who believe find by it a glorious, supernatural light introduced into
> their minds, whereby they who before saw nothing in a distinct, affecting
> manner in spiritual [matters], do now clearly discern the truth, the glory
> and the beauty of heavenly mysteries, and have their minds transformed
> into their image and likeness.[39]

[32] Packer, *A Quest for Godliness*, 90.
[33] Owen defined the authority of Scripture as "its power to command and
require obedience, in the name of God" (*Works*, 16:308).
[34] *Works*, 4:94.
[35] *Works*, 4:93.
[36] *Works*, 16:322.
[37] *Works*, 4:96.
[38] *Works*, 4:97.
[39] *Works*, 4:98. Elsewhere Owen described this quality of light imparted to
Scripture as "nothing but the beaming of the majesty, truth, holiness and authority of God" (*Works*, 16:322).

Indeed, He evokes awe of God and the Bible even among the unsaved.[40] Finally, He administers strong comfort and consolation to believers in the deepest distress."[41]

Having delineated the great sweep of the Holy Spirit's internal and external witness to the divine inspiration and authority of Scripture, Owen still saw reason as having a significant complementary role to play in illumination, though limited in power, because God works in illumination through man's rational faculties. To demonstrate this proposition, however, Owen had to straddle a tightrope between antinomian and Quaker illuminism and irrationalism on the one side and Socianian rationalism and reductionism on the other. Against illuminism and irrationalism, Owen made four counterarguments. The first is that the Holy Spirit works in, by, and through Scripture, which is the sole external means of grace that gives revelation. It is irrational to believe, as the antinomians and Quakers did, that the Holy Spirit and Scripture can contradict each other. The second counterargument is that there is no new revelation because the antinomians and Quakers misunderstood the Holy Spirit's ministry as a "Spirit of revelation" (Ephesians 1:17). Owen linked cessationism with *sola Scriptura*:

> It is a revelation that the apostle prays for, or a Spirit of revelation to be given to them. This greatly offends some at first hearing, but wholly without cause; for he understands not a new *immediate external revelation* from God. Believers are not directed to look after such revelations for their guide. Ever since the Scripture was written, the generality of the church was obliged to attend [to Scripture] alone, as their only rule of faith and obedience.[42]

The "Spirit of revelation" that Paul sought for the Ephesian church is not, then, one granting new revelation but one giving insight into and understanding of the meaning and application of the Scriptures.

His third counterargument involves the necessity of the continued use of reason. Against Socianians and Anglican moralists, Owen denied the sufficiency of reason alone to confirm the inspiration and authority of Scripture. He also found that reason cannot grant stable assurance of the truthfulness of Scripture in the same way the Holy Spirit can.[43] Against antinomians and Quakers, Owen complained of their erroneous belief that the necessity of illumination eliminates the need for the exercise of reason

---

[40] *Works*, 4:98.

[41] *Works*, 4:99.

[42] *Works*, 4:134 (emphasis his).

[43] *Works*, 4:150, 152. The "highest assurance" of the truth of Scripture is the experience of its power in the believer's heart.

in the use of external means.[44] After pointing out that the illumination of the Holy Spirit is expressed in Scripture by "teaching, leading and guiding into the truth," Owen levels a powerful blast against their irrationalism:

> And two things are supposed in this expression of teaching: first, a mind capable of instruction, leading and conduct. The nature must be rational and comprehensive of the means of instruction, which can be so taught. Wherefore, we do not only grant herein the use of the rational faculties of the soul, but require their exercise and utmost improvement. If God teach[es], we are to learn, and we cannot be learn but in the exercise of our minds. And it is vainly pretended that God's communication of a supernatural ability to our minds and our exercise of them in a way of duty, are inconsistent, whereas indeed they are inseparable in all that we are taught of God; for at the same time he infuses a gracious ability into our minds, he proposes the truth to us concerning which that ability is to be exercised. And if these things are inconsistent, the whole real efficacy of God in the souls of men must be denied; which is to despoil him of his sovereignty.[45]

Once again, as stated above, Owen does not relax his firm theological grip, which holds together the bond of grace and duty: "God's communication of a supernatural ability to our minds and our exercise of them in a way of duty are [not] inconsistent ... [but] inseparable... for at the same time he infuses a gracious ability into our minds, he proposes the truth to us concerning which that ability is to be exercised."

His fourth counterargument against illuminism and irrationalism concerns the ongoing necessity of the means of grace. Because Scripture is the believer's sole guide and there is no new revelation, he must resort to the means of grace that are designed to make Scripture, the "only external means of divine revelation,"[46] effective to the soul. These include Bible reading and meditation, "without [which] it would be vain to expect illumination from the word,"[47] conference among Christians, and attendance to the preaching of the word.[48]

Owen also had to address the rationalism and reductionism of the Socinian approach that limited revelation by the rule of reason. This approach eliminated all gospel mysteries including the incarnation, the deity of Christ, and the Trinity. To begin with, Owen points out the irony that

[44] *Works*, 4:162.
[45] *Works*, 4:167.
[46] *Works*, 4:12.
[47] Ibid.
[48] *Works*, 4:13.

the insufficiency of reason makes the rationalism of Socinianism not only reductionistic but also irrational as well:

> The work of the Spirit is to bring into captivity to the obedience of faith every thought that might arise from our ignorance, or the impotency of our minds to comprehend the things to be believed. And that new religion of Socianianism, which pretends to reduce all to reason, is wholly built upon the most irrational principle that ever befell the minds of men. It is this alone: *"What we cannot comprehend in things divine and infinite, as to their own nature, that we are not to believe as to their revelation [in Scripture]."* On this ground alone do the men of that persuasion reject the doctrine of the Trinity, of the incarnation of the Son of God, of the resurrection of the dead, and like mysteries of the faith.[49]

In other words, Owen criticizes Socianianism for teaching a version of Christianity that claims to be rational but irrationally strips the Christian faith of all mysteries "beyond reason" such as the Trinity and the incarnation.

Moreover, he maintains that faith and reason are supposed to function in a complementary and consistent way. Owen mentions an ascending hierarchy consisting of three means of mental assent: natural light, reason, and faith.[50] Though faith is superior to natural light and reason, it does not dispense with them but draws them out in proper use.[51] Further, he insists that reason must remain dependent on the guidance of the Holy Spirit.

> [W]hatever perfection there seems to be in our art of reasoning, it is to be subject to the wisdom of the Holy Ghost in the Scripture. His way of reasoning is always his own, sometimes sublime and heavenly, [soaring above] the common rules of our arts and sciences, [with] instructive, convictive and persuasive efficacy.[52]

Fourthly, using an argument borrowed from Calvin against the Socinians, Owen stresses the primacy of gospel preaching in the mission of the church over against the rational arguments of apologetics. Apologetics serves a useful function, Owen conceded, but should remain subordinate to gospel preaching.[53]

---

[49] *Works*, 4:195–96 (emphasis his). Owen mentioned that these doctrines are "above reason" (*Works*, 4:54). He is not using "mystery" in a Pauline sense.

[50] *Works*, 4:82–91.

[51] *Works*, 4:85.

[52] *Works*, 4:224.

[53] *Works*, 4:103.

The Holy Spirit as Interpreter

How then can the believer understand Scripture to live out a life of faith and obedience to God? Owen argues that divine illumination is as necessary to live out the Christian life as to believe in the divine authority and infallibility of Scripture. In explaining how Christians come to know the mind of God as revealed in Scripture, Owen describes the "principal efficient cause" as none other than the Holy Spirit.[54]

> There is an especial work of the Holy Spirit on the minds of men, communicating spiritual wisdom, light and understanding to them, necessary for their discerning and apprehending aright the mind of God in his word, and the understanding of the mysteries of heavenly truth contained therein. And among all the false and foolish imaginations that ever Christian religion was attacked or disturbed withal, there never was any, there is none more pernicious than this, that the mysteries of the gospel are so exposed to the common reason and understanding of men that they may know and comprehend them usefully and dutifully without the effectual aid and assistance of the Holy Spirit.[55]

Thus, the Holy Spirit has an indispensable role in causing believers to comprehend the mysteries of the Christian faith that would otherwise be impossible for them to understand.

Owen did not deny that a nominal Christian can understand the propositional truths set forth in Scripture. This is a far cry from asserting, however, that such a person believes these propositions, grasps the mind and will of God in the Bible, and comes away from the encounter transformed into the *imago Dei*. Owen would probably regard much modern academic theology as currently practiced in the secular university as a travesty:

> This knowledge [attained without the supernatural aid of the Holy Spirit] does only inform the mind in the way of an artificial science, but does not really illuminate it; and to this end men have turned divinity into an [academic] art to be learned instead of a spiritual wisdom and understanding of divine mysteries.[56]

[54] *Works*, 4:124.

[55] Owen's view harmonizes with that of other mainstream Puritan writers. Packer quotes Baxter and Goodwin; both declare the necessity of praying for the Holy Spirit's supernatural assistance in interpreting Scripture. The underlying rationale is that the Holy Spirit, as the inspirer and inditer of Scripture, is its matchless interpreter (Packer, *A Quest for Godliness*, 100). Bunyan characterized the Holy Spirit as Interpreter in *Pilgrim's Progress*.

[56] *Works*, 4:224.

Owen was well aware that owing to human depravity, spiritual illumination is anything but automatic. Hindrances include spiritual ignorance, spiritual pride, love of honor, corrupt traditionalism, sloth, love of sin, and Satanic blinding.[57] Owen specified a threefold mode of operation by which the Holy Spirit removes these hindrances. He first communicates spiritual light into the mind. Then He frees the mind from corrupt affections and prejudices. Last, according to Owen:

> He implants in our mind spiritual habits and principles, contrary and opposite to those corrupt affections, whereby they are subdued and expelled. By him are our minds made humble, meek, teachable through submission to the authority of the word, and a conscientious endeavor to conform ourselves thereto.[58]

Anticipating Jonathan Edwards and Thomas Chalmers, Owen is impressed by the expulsive power of newly implanted spiritual affections.

There are three types of divinely appointed means for the interpretation of God's word. The first type is internal, whereas the second and third are external. As an internal means of interpreting Scripture, prayer is considered critical. Owen recommends prayer for spiritual enlightenment with regard to difficult passages of Scripture. He even declares: "There is not a duty in this world we perform to God that is more acceptable to him than fervent prayers for a right understanding of his mind and will in his word; for hereon all the glory we give him, and all the due performance of our obedience do depend.[59] Owen insists that a believer must be teachable. To be ready to obey God a believer must first understand Scripture: "God himself has plainly declared the qualifications of those souls meet to be partakers of divine teachings. These are meekness, humility, godly fear, reverence, submission to the authority of God, with resolution and readiness for all obedience."[60]

The second and third specified means are external. The second type of means for interpreting Scripture, which Owen calls "disciplinarian," encompasses knowledge of original biblical languages, history, geography, chronology, hermeneutics, logic, and other arts and sciences. The third type is ecclesiastical. While rejecting Roman Catholic and patristic authors as safe guides,[61] he expresses a decided preference for Reformed theolo-

---

[57] *Works*, 4:174–84.
[58] *Works*, 4:185.
[59] *Works*, 4:205–8.
[60] *Works*, 4:185–86.
[61] *Works*, 4:78.

gians,[62] though critical of most biblical commentators for blazing no new trails mainly because they neglect to pray to the Holy Spirit for illumination of the text.[63]

Summary

The illuminism espoused by Seventeenth-Century antinomians, the belief in new revelation and direct assurance from the Holy Spirit, differs greatly from what Owen called "illumination." The latter is the operation by which the Holy Spirit creates spiritual understanding of God's will and man's duty by working in, by, and through the Scriptures. In rebutting illuminism, Owen stressed its falsity, insisted that word and Spirit always go together, staked out a cessationist position regarding prophecy, and maintained that full assurance is attained only through progress in sanctification.

Both Luther and Calvin helped recover the biblical emphasis on the person and work of the Holy Spirit. Calvin regarded the Scriptures as self-authenticating through the inner witness of the Holy Spirit testifying to its divine infallibility and authority. This supernatural certainty transcends the probability suggested by rational proofs alone. Owen developed Calvin's teaching on the inner witness farther by dwelling on the external witness of the Holy Spirit's power in conviction, conversion, and re-creation.

For Owen, illumination has degrees and may be preparatory or salvific. The unregenerate have a duty to "improve" preparatory illumination so that by the grace of God it may become salvific. Owen's soteriology is optimistic: he expected the outcome to be salvation for every sincere and diligent seeker of God, though it must be noted that those adjectives 'sincere' and 'diligent' are loaded with content in his theology. Salvific illumination creates belief in Scripture's divine inspiration and transforms one into the image of God.

Yet for all this emphasis on the Holy Spirit, reason still has an important role to play. Striking a balance between the extremes of antinomian and Quaker illuminism and irrationalism on the one hand and Socinian rationalism and reductionism on the other, Owen insisted that the Holy Spirit empowered "exercise and utmost improvement of the rational faculties." Though faith is superior to reason, faith does not dispense with reason but instead draws it out to its proper use. Salvific illumination goes beyond the mere understanding of the propositional truth set forth in Scripture to empower regeneration and sincere Christian obedience.

[62] *Works*, 4:226–29.
[63] *Works*, 4:205.

7

Preparation for Grace: Conviction of Sin

This miry slough is such a place as cannot be mended. It is the descent whither the scum and filth that attends conviction of sin doth continually run, and therefore it is called the Slough of Despond: for still, as the sinner is awakened about his lost condition, there ariseth in his soul many fears, and doubts, and discouraging apprehensions, which all get together and settle in this place. And this is the reason of the badness of the ground. It is not the pleasure of the King that this place should remain so bad; his laborers have been employed about this patch of ground for above 1600 years, [yet] here have been swallowed up at least 20,000 cartloads and millions of wholesome instructions. True, there are, by the direction of the Lawgiver, certain good and substantial steps, placed even through the very midst of this slough, but when this place doth much spew out its filth, these steps are hardly seen...

Help's speech to Christian in John Bunyan's *Pilgrim's Progress*

The Antinomian Attitude toward Conviction

Seventeenth-Century English antinomians seldom if ever extolled the virtues of conviction of sin. On the other hand, some antinomians, particularly those of the imputative category, continued to believe in the necessity of preparation for grace, albeit a very passive one, accomplished by way of the preparatory work of the law. The semi-antinomian New England pastor Cotton is representative of this view when he asserts, "God prepares these [His people under the covenant of grace] by a spirit of poverty.... For if a soul was never yet bruised with sin, and with the sense of sin, he never yet laid hold upon Christ with true justifying faith."[1]

A difference of opinion emerges between the antinomian and the Puritan attitude toward the continuing role of conviction of sin in the Christian life. Given the disparagement of Christian duties and self-examination of the antinomian authors, it should come as no surprise that they would have looked askance at Owen's injunction, quoted below, to "improve" conviction of sin. They would have especially failed to see how conviction of sin remains important in preparation for glory, as this excerpt from Thomas Shepard's diary implies.

> July 9 [1641]. Being suddenly surprised by a sin before the sacrament, my conscience was awakened, and my heart checked me for it. Yet the Lord turned the meditation of the evil of this great sin to great good to me.... I saw I was to fly to Christ's blood and righteousness for satisfaction and peace.[2]

It would be hard to imagine such a testimony for the ongoing benefits of conviction of sin coming from a seventeenth-century English antinomian author. Eaton, as quoted in chapter 2, recommended meditation on free justification rather than confession of sin or repentance to those smitten by troubled consciences.[3] The most charitable construction that can be placed on the antinomian attitude toward conviction of sin is that it is useful before conversion but useless thereafter; in fact, it may be worse than useless thereafter, even positively dangerous in that supposedly morbid introspection could imperil the joys of full and free assurance. Unsavoury Speech number 3, also compiled by the Newtown Synod in 1637 to evidence dangerously spreading antinomian sentiment, declared, "If I be holy, I am never the better accepted of God; if I be unholy I am never the worse. He that elected me must save me."[4] Hooker had earlier observed this antinomian laxity toward conviction of sin; he complained that the antinomians "think it is unprofitable for a believer to trouble himself for his sins, and to go up and down with heart full of grief."[5] Yet Owen viewed conviction of sin as a boon both before and after conversion and stressed,

---

[1] Murray, "*Antinomianism*," 41. See also the textbook-perfect statement of preparation for grace from Cotton quoted in Murray, 44–45.

[2] Cited in Ibid., 61.

[3] Eaton, *Honeycombe*, 18.

[4] Hall, *The Antinomian Controversy*, 245.

[5] Bush, *The Writings of Thomas Hooker*, 83 citing Hooker, *The Soules Exaltation* (London, 1638), 226–27.

as quoted in chapter 4, that both conversion and recovery from backsliding are normally dependent on prior conviction of sin.

The Reformed Heritage and Owen's View of Conviction

Owen taught, like most Reformed divines including David Dickson in *The Sum of Saving Knowledge*, that there are two types of conviction of sin: legal, based on the law which must generally be experienced by adult converts, and evangelical, based on the gospel. This becomes quite clear in his treatise *The Doctrine of Justification by Faith* (1677) in chapter 1 entitled, "The Causes and Object of Faith." He framed the question to be answered as, "What is required on our part, in a way of duty, prior to [justifying] faith?"[6] Like Luther and Calvin, Owen declared that legal conviction of sin, the *preparatory* work of the law, is required for conversion.[7] Owen defined the work of conviction by writing that,

> The work of conviction [is] in general whereby the soul of man has a practical understanding of the nature of sin, its guilt, and the punishment due to it; and is made sensible of his own interest both in original and in actual sin and in his utter disability to deliver himself [out of a state of bondage].[8]

He declared the important general rule that "the work of the law in the conviction of sin is a necessary antecedent to justifying faith in the adult.[9] Owen believed that powerful convictions exposed the otherwise hidden motives of the heart and took away the self-righteousness of the nominal Christian.

---

[6] *Works*, 5:74.

[7] Luther, for example, wrote that, "The Scripture sets before us a man who is not only bound, wretched, captive, sick and dead but who through the operation of Satan his lord, adds to his other miseries blindness, so that he believes himself to be free and possessed of liberty. The function preformed by the law is most emphatically serious and necessary. It is to lay open to man his own wretchedness so as to make him ready for grace" (*Bondage of the Will*, 162).

[8] *Works*, 5:74.

[9] Ibid. See also William Guthrie, *The Christian's Great Interest* (Edinburgh: Banner of Truth, 1969), 37–52, for the view that the preparatory work of the law as prerequisite to conversion is the normal rule subject to exception, especially with children. Owen likewise recognized that there were exceptions, so-called "surprisals of grace," to the general rule when Christ found those who were not seeking him (*Works*, 9:361).

Effectual convictions draw out the soul's inward principles which are not otherwise to be discovered. Many have notionally received the doctrine of free justification only to discover the iniquity of their self-righteousness when any great conviction or pressing danger befalls them.[10]

Owen's use of the adjective "free" seems to be an oblique reference to contemporary antinomians who touted themselves, after all, as the champions of "free" justification, Eaton's favorite term. This does not mean, however, that conviction of sin invariably, or even generally, leads to conversion. Owen reiterates his opposition to Roman Catholic doctrine of condign merit, as he did not consider preparation for grace as a way of acquiring merit:

Not every one who is convinced must necessarily be justified. There is not any disposition or preparation of the subject by this conviction and its effects such that justification must necessarily ensue, as the Papists [believe]. Nor is there any such preparation that can claim a divine promise of pardon and justification.[11]

In several treatises, Owen explained how convictions can become lost or unimproved. In *Pneumatologia* (1674) he furnishes three examples of abuse.

Some are no way careful or wise to improve this light and conviction to take them off their self-confidence and to direct them to Christ. In some they are overborne by the power and violence of their lusts. Some rest in these things, as though they comprised the whole work of God towards them.[12]

He seemed to be pondering the plight of the negligent, the tempted and the complacent.

In *The Grace and Duty of Being Spiritually Minded* (1681), though acknowledging that great and effectual convictions of sin stir up strong affections, he still insisted that people under conviction often cannot grasp that Christ and His righteousness is the sole means of relief. Because such people lack faith in Christ, their convictions either decay utterly or produce formalism or legalism.[13] In his treatise on *Mortification*, he similarly

---

[10] *Works*, 9:85.
[11] *Works*, 5:75.
[12] *Works*, 3:234.
[13] *Works*, 7:446. Owen seems to have separately considered the plight of Socinians, Anglican moralists, and antinomians when conviction miscarries. The first become legalists and the second formalists, while the third remain nominal Christians.

declares, "There is a peculiar convincing power in the word, which God is oftentimes pleased to put forth, to the wounding, amazing and [legal] humbling of sinners, though they are never converted."[14] In *An Exposition Upon Psalm 130* (1688) Owen devoted an entire chapter to the danger of resting in conviction of sin. He states that this danger takes two forms: "Some rest in it and press no farther; some rest in it and suppose that [conviction of sin] is all that is required of them."[15] With regard to the first manifestation, Owen used "rest" as a term of art; he defined "resting" as despondency resulting from disbelief in the prospect of deliverance.[16] Owen gave two reasons why nothing is more dangerous than this state of mind:

1. It insensibly weakens the soul, and disables it for present duties and future endeavors.

2. This frame will insensibly give countenance to hard thoughts of God, and to repining and weariness in waiting on him. Secret thoughts arise that God is austere, inexorable and not to deal withal. Here, in humiliation [prior to] conversion many a convinced person perishes. They cannot await God's season and perish under their impatience.[17]

For those guilty of the second error, that of equating conviction with conversion, this state of mind is equally dangerous because they rest in their self-righteousness and do not seek after true forgiveness of sin.[18]

Temporary convictions or habits, Owen declared in *The Grace and Duty of Being Spiritually Minded* (1681), differ from truly spiritual affections in three major ways. The first difference is that the former merely restrain sin and idolatry by altering the course of the affections, whereas the latter restore every faculty of the person so that these cleave to God's presence in spiritual things.[19] The second difference between the two is the ground and motive given for delight in worship; the former make use of carnal motives for delight in worship such as outward show or admiration of the pastor's gifts, whereas the latter take true delight in worship because of communion with God in Christ and the spiritual efficacy of ordinances.[20] The third difference is that temporary convictions wither and die for lack of faith in a proper object, whereas faith in Christ causes spiritual affec-

---

[14] *Works*, 6:38.
[15] *Works*, 6:376.
[16] Ibid.
[17] *Works*, 6:377.
[18] *Works*, 6:378–79.
[19] *Works*, 7:410–21.
[20] *Works*, 7:423–45.

tions to be assimilated to spiritual and heavenly things.[21] Nevertheless, even temporary convictions are to be improved toward conversion.[22]

Owen gave four reasons why, in the order of nature, conviction precedes conversion. The first is that conviction alone "puts the soul on flight to the mercy of God in Christ, to be saved from the wrath to come."[23] The second reason is that the sentence and curse of the law must become a felt reality for a sinner to long for the deliverance promised by the gospel.[24] The third ground is Christ's insistence that he "came not to call the righteous, but sinners to repentance." The fourth is that after the Fall, God confronted Adam with the curse of the law before announcing the promise of the coming Messiah.[25]

Owen specified two effects of such conviction that motivate all preconversion religious duties—temporary faith and legal conviction.[26] Owen mentioned three internal and three external duties, or works, prompted by real conviction of sin. The first internal duty is sorrow and shame for sin. The second internal duty is fear of punishment because of the sentence and curse of the law. Owen, in his commentary on Hebrews, vividly described this frame of mind:

> A full conviction of sin is a great and shaking surprisal to a guilty soul. Hence in such a one here [in Heb 6:17–20] tacitly compared to [a man-slayer]. Though immediately before in a condition of peace and safety, fear within and danger without beset him on every hand. The commandment comes and discovers their guilt and danger and unveils the curse, which until now was hidden from them, as the avenger of blood ready to execute the sentence of the law. Hence those cries, 'What shall we do to be saved?' argue great distress and amazement.[27]

The third internal duty, as one might now expect, is a consuming desire for deliverance.[28]

Owen described the three external duties prompted by conviction. The first is abstinence from known sin to the utmost of one's limited power. This usually takes the form of promises and vows not to sin, followed by repeated surprisals into sin.[29] The second is pursuit of "the duties of reli-

---

21 *Works*, 7:445–55.
22 *Works*, 7:417.
23 *Works*, 4:75.
24 *Works*, 4:75.
25 *Works*, 4:76.
26 *Works*, 4:77.
27 *Works*, 21:278 or 5:278.
28 *Works*, 4:77–78.
29 *Works*, 4:78.

gious worship, in prayer and hearing of the word, with diligence in the use of the ordinances of the church."[30] A third and related external duty is reformation of life.[31] In the case of abstinence and reformation, God uses conviction as a means of restraining grace; such conviction regards a particular sin, however, not sin universally.[32] Owen warned that conviction miscarries where, as here, "[Y]ou set yourself against a particular sin, and do not consider that you are nothing but sin."[33]

Against Roman Catholic opponents, Owen elaborated on his earlier assertion that such preparation for grace is not meritorious. Neither do preparations for grace have any "certain infallible connection" with conversion, a perspective he supported with four reasons.[34] First, these are not conditions of justification, because although they are generally a necessary condition of justification, they are not a sufficient one since God nowhere promises to reward them with justification.[35] Secondly, instantaneous conversions, such as that of the Philippian jailer, do sometimes occur.[36] Thirdly, they do not formally dispose anyone to justification because no new principle of grace is added to the soul. Fourthly, they do not morally dispose anyone to justification since they involve merely the exercise of legal repentance, not saving faith.[37]

Once more relying on God's dealing with Adam as a model, Owen posits three degrees of legal conviction:

1. The opening of the eyes of the sinner, to see the filth and guilt of sin in the sentence and curse of the law applied to his conscience. Romans 7:9–10.

2. Ordinarily, God by his providence or in the dispensation of the word, gives peculiar power to the work of the law, so that the sinner is consciously [left without excuse and any means of self-deliverance]; and

3. It is a mere [pure] act of sovereign grace, regardless of the foregoing, that calls the sinner to faith.[38]

In *An Exposition Upon Psalm 130* (1688), Owen delved into the workings of the Holy Spirit in the conviction of sin. Although Owen had to

---

[30] Ibid.
[31] Ibid.
[32] *Works*, 6:270–71.
[33] *Works*, 6:38.
[34] *Works*, 4:78.
[35] *Works*, 4:78–79.
[36] *Works*, 4:79.
[37] Ibid.
[38] *Works*, 4:81.

deal primarily with evangelical conviction of sin in Psalm 130, legal conviction still figures large because it precedes the former in order of nature. In applying his exposition of this psalm to preparation for grace, it is important to recognize that he regards conversion and recoveries from backsliding, though significantly different, to be analogous in terms of the means employed and the effects produced.[39]

Again, the first step in conviction is legal conviction, or the preparatory work of the law: the law visits condemnation on his sins and the curse of the law fills him with dread and terror.[40] Because the convicted sinner receives no relief from Christ, hope is nowhere to be found. Owen discussed four possible routes of deliverance, all of which are discovered to be unavailing: the insensibility of the judge, the prospect of an intercessor, the relaxed application of the law, or the interposition of a legal defense.[41]

The second step is evangelical conviction consisting of three elements: "sincere sense of sin; acknowledgment of sin; and self-condemnation [together with] the justification of God."[42] A sincere sense of sin consists in "deep apprehension of sin and its evils" which produces "humiliation, sorrow, and self-abhorrency."[43]

> It is [the Holy Spirit] who [reveals] to us and spiritually convinces us of the pollution of sin and our defilement thereby. Something, indeed, of this kind will be wrought by the power of natural conscience, awakened and excited by ordinary outward means of conviction; for wherever there is a sense of guilt, there will be some kind of sense of filth, as fear and shame are inseparable. But this sense alone will never guide us to the blood of Christ for cleansing. Such a sight and conviction of it as may fill us with self-abhorrence and abasement, as may cause us to loathe ourselves for the abomination that is in it, is required of us; and this is the work of the Holy Spirit belonging to that peculiar conviction of sin, which is from the Holy Spirit alone (John 16:8). I mean that self-abhorrency, shame, and confusion of face with respect to the filth of sin, which is so often mentioned in the Scripture as a gracious duty; as nothing is a

---

[39] Works, 6:361. "In a sin-perplexed soul's addresses to God, the first thing that presents itself to him is God's marking sin according to the tenor of the law. The case is the same in this matter with all sorts of sinners, *whether before conversion or in relapses and entanglements after conversion*. There is a proportion between conversion and recoveries. They are both wrought by the same means and ways, and have both the same effects upon the souls of sinners, although in sundry ways they differ" (emphasis mine).

[40] Works, 6:360–62.

[41] Works, 6:365–68.

[42] Works, 6:362.

[43] Works, 6:369–70.

higher aggravation of sin than for men to carry themselves with a carnal boldness with God and in his worship, whilst they are unpurged from their defilements. Without this preparation whereby we come to know the plague of our own hearts, the infection of our leprosy, the defilement of our souls, we shall never make application to the blood of Christ for cleansing in a due manner.[44]

It also involves judging sin according to the strict tenor of the law: There can be no due consideration of sin where the law has no place. By the law the sinners see sins to be 'exceedingly sinful.' Romans 7:13. The more a man sees of the excellency of the law, the more he sees the vileness of his sin [and its inexorable condemnation by the law]. As ever you would have your souls justified by grace, take care to have your sins judged by the law.[45]

Owen's statement that there can be no due consideration of sin without the second use of the law has profound implications for antinomian practice. Antinomians like Eaton considered the law useful for creating conviction of sin prior to justification. Eaton spilled much ink in *Honeycombe of Free Justification* expounding breaches of the Decalogue in traditional Reformed fashion[46] but insisted that after conversion the believer automatically knew how to keep the "spiritual" meaning of the Decalogue.[47]

Owen insisted that the second element of evangelical conviction involves the free and full acknowledgment of sin.[48] (Eaton, by comparison, downplayed confession of sin in favor of meditation on free justification.) By "free" Owen means "voluntary" despite the shame of sin. A voluntary confession of sin, suggested Owen, argues for the presence of the Holy Spirit.

The confession of a person under the convincing terrors of the law or dread of imminent judgments is that of malefactors on the rack [i.e. in-

---

[44] *Works*, 3:442–43.

[45] *Works*, 6:370. The evangelical, as opposed to merely legal, conviction worked by the Holy Spirit in a backslidden Christian who is returning goes farther: "Though a believer be less under the power of the law than others, yet he knows more of its authority, spirituality and holiness" (ibid.). Moreover, He brings to the returning backslider's remembrance the love of God and the blood and cross of Christ: "Such a soul now looks on Christ, bleeding, dying, wrestling with wrath and curse for him, and sees his sin in the streams of blood that issued from his side" (*Works*, 6:372).

[46] Eaton, *Honeycombe*, 11–17.

[47] Ibid., 7.

[48] *Works*, 6:373.

voluntary and coerced]. The returning soul has never more freedom and liberty of spirit than when he acknowledges what he is most ashamed of. This is no small evidence that it proceeds from the Holy Spirit. 2 Cor. 3:17.[49]

Acknowledgment of sin must also be full. By "full" Owen denotes a universal acknowledgment of all known sin, with nothing being withheld. Noting the strong connection in Scripture between confession of sin and pardon, he warns, "If there be remaining a bitter root of favoring any one lust or sin, of any occasion of or temptation to sin, let a man be as open, free and earnest as can be imagined in the acknowledgment of all other sins and evils, the whole duty is rendered abominable."[50] Owen's emphasis on "full" confession harmonizes with his insistence on "universal obedience", which does not mean perfect obedience but sincere obedience that has respect to all of God's commands.

The third indispensable element of evangelical conviction is self-condemnation coupled with the sinner's vindication of God. Godly sorrow and self-judging cause the soul to acquiesce in God's judgment on sin. How do these three elements of evangelical conviction prepare for grace, or as Owen put it, "make way for the exaltation of grace"? He explains:

> Grace will not seem high until the soul be laid very low. And this also suits or prepares the soul for the receiving of mercy in a way of pardon, the great [goal of] the sinner; and it prepares it for every duty incumbent on him in his condition. This brings the soul to waiting with diligence and patience. The soul in this frame is contented to await the pleasure of God. And it puts the soul on prayer always. And there is nothing more evident than that want [lack] of a thorough engagement to the performance of these duties is the great cause why so few come clear off from their entanglements all their days. Men heal their wounds slightly.[51]

Owen's observations of human response to conviction of sin tally with Jesus' promise that the humble will be exalted, and the exalted humbled (Matthew 23:12; Luke 14:11).

In his treatise *The Holy Spirit as a Comforter* (1693), Owen noted that the Holy Spirit reproves or convinces sinners by His "internal efficacy in the dispensation of the word."[52] Owen interpreted the Greek verb expansively to mean "by undeniable argument and evidence, to convince the world, or the adversaries of Christ and the gospel, so that they have noth-

---

[49] Ibid.
[50] *Works*, 6:374.
[51] *Works*, 6:375–76.
[52] *Works*, 4:364.

ing to reply."[53] Having stressed in *The Grace and Duty of Being Spiritually Minded* (1681) that conviction of sin is involuntary,[54] Owen observes what probably follows as a corollary, that convinced sinners react in either of two diametrically opposite ways: "They yield to the truth and embrace it, as finding no ground to stand upon in refusing it; or they fly into desperate rage and madness."[55] He contrasted those who repented upon hearing Peter' sermon at Pentecost with those who upon hearing Stephen's defense stoned him to death.[56]

Owen interpreted John 16:8–11 to mean that the Holy Spirit convicts or persuades the sinner through the gospel regarding sin, righteousness, and judgment.[57] Owen followed the clear import of John 16:9 in declaring the sin of unbelief is primarily in view, a refusal to acknowledge Jesus as the Son of God.[58] Of the righteousness that John 16:10 associates with Jesus' exaltation, Owen stated that, objectively, "both the personal righteousness of Christ and the righteousness of his office are intended."[59] This means that, subjectively, "The Holy Spirit so convinces men of an impossibility for them to attain a righteousness of their own, that they must either submit to the righteousness of God in Christ or die in their sins."[60] Finally, the Holy Spirit convinces the world of judgment because Satan as prince of the world is judged and is "by the gospel laid open [as] an accursed apostate, a murderer and the great enemy of mankind."[61]

In Chapter 6 of *Pneumatologia* (1674), Owen treated Augustine's conversion account as normative.[62] Based on his study of Augustine's *Confessions*, Owen formulated morphologies of both sin and conversion. Sin develops according to five discernible steps. First, in infancy natural depravity generally prevents all the actings of grace in us.[63] Next, the actings of sin increase with the growth and maturation of faculties, which serve as "instruments of unrighteousness."[64] Thirdly, actual sins such as lying and stealing break out into the open; and lying may well occasion a child's

---

[53] Ibid.
[54] *Works*, 7:390.
[55] *Works*, 4:365.
[56] Ibid. In both cases the Greek text says that the audience was "cut to the heart."
[57] *Works*, 4:365.
[58] *Works*, 4:366.
[59] *Works*, 4:367.
[60] *Works*, 4:367.
[61] *Works*, 4:367–68.
[62] *Works*, 3:349.
[63] *Works*, 3:338–39.
[64] *Works*, 3:339–40.

first conviction of sin.[65] Fourthly, as people mature, sin gains ground both subjectively and objectively. Sin even abuses the commandment so as to increase sinning, and worldly temptations and youthful lusts multiply. When they succumb to temptation and fall into great actual sins, once again sinners respond in either of two diametrically opposed ways:

> God sometimes takes occasion from [great sins] to awaken their consciences to a deep sense not only of that sin in particular but of their other sins also. With others it proves a violent entrance into a farther pursuit of sin. Because they are emboldened to greater wickedness, their conversion is rendered more difficult and they wander away to the greatest distance recoverable by grace.[66]

Finally, habits of sinning develop. Habituation to sinning removes the sinner's sense of sin and the world dulls the shame of it. Love of sin makes for greedy pursuit except as God's restraining grace is pleased to prevent total degradation. Yet this still does not amount to the unpardonable sin.[67] But it does make conversion more difficult, at least from the human standpoint.[68]

In his morphology of conversion, Owen identified at least seven discrete steps. The first is that a few are regenerated in youth.[69] Second, God works upon men by his Spirit and outward means to cause them to consider His holiness and their estrangement from Him on account of sin. These outward means take the form of sudden astonishing judgments, remarkable deliverances and mercies, godly Christian example, and personal afflictions. Of this Owen pointed out:

> Affliction naturally bespeaks anger [over] sin [serving as] God's messenger to call sin to remembrance. Hence great thoughts of the holiness of God and his hatred of sin with some sense of men's own guilt and crimes will arise; and these effects many times prove preparatory and *materially dispositive* unto conversion.[70]

Convictions of sin also arise from the word and keep men devoted to religious duties such as prayer and reformation.[71] With some, their sustained devotion makes a nearer approach to conversion. Yet with many, pursuit of

[65] *Works*, 3:341.
[66] *Works*, 3:342–43.
[67] *Works*, 3:343–45.
[68] *Works*, 5:298.
[69] *Works*, 3:345–46.
[70] *Works*, 3:347 (emphasis his).
[71] *Works*, 3:347–48.

salvation fades away for any of six reasons: mental darkness, presumption, bad company, decay, Satanic agency, and love of lusts.[72]

Third, the Holy Spirit convicts men of sin mainly through the preaching of the law (the preparatory work of the law). Conviction impresses on the "vain" mind of an unregenerate sinner "a due sense of sin's nature, tendency and end... manifesting itself in suitable affections such as trouble, sorrow, disquiet and fear of ruin."[73] This legal work of conviction entangles and perplexes the sinner, who is unable to extricate himself speedily.[74] Just as before, some improve legal convictions in a way of duty toward conversion but many fall away for the same reasons mentioned above, especially if they receive no gifts of the Holy Spirit (presumably because gifts help stir up graces) and if they lose their awe of God's judgment simply because nothing bad has yet befallen them.[75]

Fourth, two things ordinarily happen to adults who improve these convictions toward conversion. The first is that their convictions battle their corruptions, especially a darling sin, such that they discover the power of sin (Romans 7:7–9) and their own disability to resist. They make attempts and promises of reformation but typically hold out only until the next occasion of sinning presents itself. This conflict produces great conflict and even despair. In some instances, God secretly regenerates them during this time.

> Under this work God often "uses a word in season"[76] secretly to communicate a principle of grace or spiritual life to the will. This begins its conflict effectually to eject sin from its throne and dominion. The Spirit begins to lust against the flesh. There was upon bare conviction a contest merely between the mind and conscience and the will. Now the conflict begins to be in the will itself. This fills the mind with amazement and brings some to the very door of despair for deliverance.[77]

The second thing that often results is a spirit of bondage. It manifests itself in sorrow and shame for sin, fear of eternal wrath, perplexity over deliverance and a quest for reformation.[78]

Fifth, yet a spirit of bondage does not necessary have to usher in conversion. Because of God's sovereign and "unspeakable variety" displayed

---

[72] *Works*, 3:348.
[73] *Works*, 3:350–51.
[74] *Works*, 3:350.
[75] *Works*, 3:353–54.
[76] *Works*, 3:357.
[77] *Works*, 3:356.
[78] *Works*, 3:357–59. Owen refuted the charge of novelty.

in conversion, some experience the spirit of bondage, while others are surprised by grace in the first visitation.[79] Owen was unwilling to limit the Holy One of Israel: "No certain rule or measure of [the spirit of bondage] can be prescribed as necessary ... [prior] to conversion. Conviction of sin is a duty, but not legal sorrow or a spirit of bondage."[80] Sixth, Owen discussed here only two requirements of conviction: a sinner's conviction of original sin, sinfulness and actual sins, evoking the curse of the law and his settled conviction of no deliverance existing outside Christ. A convinced sinner should not apply himself to every remedy that promises fair. For example, reformation of life, or legal righteousness, is deceptively attractive because conversion clearly requires it (although in its proper place and order following regeneration) and the law seems to call for it. Yet because it will not deliver the sinner, he must seek the imputed righteousness of Christ. Seventh, conversion is completed when God implants faith in Christ.[81] Owen rebutted the charge that justification by faith leads to loose morals by pointing out that faith in Christ is always accompanied by universal repentance, which produces in turn reformation of life and fruitful obedience.[82]

Summary

Unlike imputative antinomians, Owen thought that conviction of sin was beneficial and essential before and after conversion, especially since it was normally a necessary condition of both conversion and recovery from backsliding. By conviction of sin Owen meant the second use of the law. Legal conviction caused men to grasp their predicament of hopeless bondage to both original and actual sin and long for outside deliverance. Rejecting the Roman Catholic idea of condign merit, Owen pointed out how readily conviction of sin could fall short of the mark of conversion by lack of due improvement, overpowering lusts, or premature equation of conviction with conversion. Conviction of sin could turn out to be merely temporary. Genuine legal conviction of sin causes, in Owen's view, sorrow and shame for sin, fear of punishment and a consuming desire for deliverance leading to a serious attempt to avoid sinning and worship God. Though legal conviction works gradually, it becomes evangelical conviction only through the regenerating power of God's sovereign grace. Evangelical conviction has three essential elements: self-hatred over one's sinfulness,

---

[79] *Works*, 3:360–61.
[80] *Works*, 3:360.
[81] *Works*, 3:362.
[82] *Works*, 3:364.

free and voluntary confession of sin to God, and self-condemnation combined with a vindication of Gods' justice. Owen observes that, "Grace will not seem high until the soul be laid very low. And this prepares the soul for receiving pardoning mercy, and for every duty incumbent on him, and for prayer."[83] The Holy Spirit convinces such that "they must either submit to the righteousness of God in Christ or die in their sins."[84]

Treating Augustine's conversion account as normative, as was fairly typical of Reformed and Puritan divines, Owen outlined morphologies of both sin and conversion. Sin increases with age, development of natural faculties, and continued exposure to the ways of the world. Great sins may sear the conscience and plunge one into even great depths of depravity. Owen pointed out several key instrumental factors in conversion: remarkable mercies or afflictions, the power of godly Christian example, and attentiveness to preaching and prayer. Conviction of sin wages a pitched battle with indwelling sin, especially any darling sin, and makes the sinner long for deliverance. God is often moved to intervene decisively in the conflict by granting regeneration. The sinner's fruitless attempts at self-reformation must ultimately yield to his trust in the imputed righteousness of Christ.

---

[83] *Works*, 6:375.
[84] *Works*, 4:367.

8

Preparation for Grace: Legal Reformation

The Antinomian Hostility to Reformation

The hostility of Seventeenth-Century antinomians to the concept of reformation stemmed largely from their failure to distinguish between legal reformation, which occurs prior to conversion and is natural, partial, and temporary, and evangelical reformation, which occurs after and in consequence of conversion and is supernatural, universal, and permanent. If only evangelical reformation is permanent, then why did Owen make a place for legal reformation in his morphology of conversion? Seventeenth-Century antinomians could see no rationale for this approach, so they accused Puritan divines of reinstituting a covenant of works. Even a noted Puritan scholar like Bozeman levels a similar accusation:

> Of course, in Puritan circles, there could be no ascription of saving efficacy to the penitent's preparatory activity. Yet [Puritan pastors insisted that even before conversion] inner warfare against sin must begin and produce substantial modification of the penitent's attitude and behavior. With its call for behavioral change a condition of access to the Atonement, this strain of preparationist doctrine... requires revision of the widely held notion that in Puritan theology 'first came the traumatic conviction of sin, then the awakening hope of mercy, and finally the transformation of behavior'.[1]

[1] Bozeman, *The Precisianist Strain*, 109–10.

As will be seen, it is the conspicuous failure to differentiate between legal reformation and evangelical reformation common to both Bozeman and Seventeenth-Century antinomians that leads them astray on this matter. No revisionism whatever regarding Puritan theology is called for. Eaton himself seemed to be blind to this distinction, and his blindness permitted him to rail against the Puritans, accusing them for good measure of being "in a damnable estate," having "dead faith" and being stuck in the gear of "earnest *legal* repentance."[2]

Owen divulged the answer to this riddle in his discussion of the third benefit of legal reformation, which is to drive the sinner under conviction of sin to salutary self-despair, so that he gives up all hope of self-help and looks solely to Christ for salvation. As Packer observed,

> The old [Puritan Reformed] gospel stresses something that the new [modern] gospel ignores–that sinners cannot obey the gospel, any more than the law, without renewal of heart.... Thus it labours to overthrow self-confidence, to convince sinners that their salvation is completely out of their hands, and to shut them up to a self-despairing dependence on the glorious grace of a sovereign Saviour, not only for their righteousness but for their [gift] of faith too.[3]

Owen's Distinction Between Legal Reformation And Evangelical Reformation

Owen used the word "reformation" in two distinct senses. "Reformation" could refer to both the Protestant Reformation of the sixteenth century[4] and to the efforts of the post-Reformation church to continue the reformation of the church, as for example the Puritan program to "purify" the Church of England. The second sense in which he thought of "reformation" was to describe a change in personal life. Whenever Owen used the word "reformation" in this second sense, it is important to determine the timing of reformation in the *ordo salutis*. More specifically, is Owen describing activity that takes place before or after conversion? Legal reformation,[5] though often a preparation for grace, is a very different thing

---

[2] Eaton, *Honeycombe*, 6-7.

[3] Packer, *A Quest for Godliness*, 143.

[4] *Works*, 7:72. Here Owen enumerated the considerable blessings brought about through the Protestant Reformation and stressed the necessity of continued diligence.

[5] I have coined this term to describe Owen's concept. Though he never used it himself, he did in other contexts of preparation for grace distinguish between

from evangelical reformation. The former is inspired by moralism, partial in scope (and thus subject to repeated failure), and not acceptable to God as a work or duty, whereas the latter is effected by regeneration, universal in scope, and acceptable to God through Christ. Of evangelical reformation Owen declared,

> Regeneration always certainly and infallibly produces reformation of life. In some it does so more completely; in others more imperfectly; but in all sincerely. For the same grace in nature and kind is communicated unto several persons in various degrees, and is by them used and improved with more or less care and diligence.[6]

Similarly and more fully, he rejoins,

> This acting of faith in Christ, through the promise of the gospel, for pardon, righteousness and salvation, is inseparably accompanied with, and [saving] faith is the root and infallible cause of, a universal engagement of the heart to all holy obedience to God in Christ, with a relinquishment of all known sin, necessarily producing a thorough change and reformation of life and fruitfulness in obedience. [The new creature] can no more refrain from the love of holiness and the watchful pursuit of universal obedience than a newborn can from [breathing or eating]. Vain and foolish are the reproaches of [the worldly and profane] who charge justification by faith with a neglect of holiness, righteousness and obedience to God. The faith that does not purify the heart and reform the life is dead.[7]

Chapter 8 will explore the reality suggested by the second sense of this word as a change in life and primarily the phenomenon of legal reformation as a preparation for grace. In Owens's *ordo salutis*, illumination (chapter 6), conviction of sin (chapter 7), and legal reformation of life precede regeneration, though the latter does not invariably result from these preparatory works.[8] Despite that, Owen insists that, "In their own nature [preparatory works] are good, useful and material preparations for regeneration, disposing the mind to the reception of the grace of God."[9]

legal and evangelical illumination and between legal and evangelical conviction of sin. Thus this coinage seems consistent with his other usage and accurate, because reformation of life that occurs before conversion takes place through the preparatory work of the law on the sinner's conscience.

   [6] *Works*, 3:219.

   [7] *Works* 2:425-426

   [8] *Works*, 3:231. These are normally wrought by the Holy Spirit acting in, by and through the preached word (*Works*, 3:235).

   [9] *Works*, 3:234.

Indeed, conviction of sin, unless suppressed, normally leads to legal reformation. Owen described three external duties prompted by conviction, the first and third of which are intimately associated with legal reformation. The first is abstinence from known sin to the utmost of one's limited power. This duty follows from conviction of sin naturally for "they who begin to find that it is an evil and bitter thing to sin against God, cannot [help] but endeavor future abstinence."[10] It usually takes the form of promises and vows not to sin, followed by what Owen called "surprisals" into sin. The second is pursuit of "the duties of religious worship, in prayer and hearing of the word, with diligence in the use of the ordinances of the church."[11] A third, and closely related external duty, is [legal or moral] reformation of life. In the case of abstinence and reformation, God uses conviction as a means of restraining grace; such conviction is ineffective, however, in that it restrains a particular sin, not sin universally.[12] Owen warned that conviction miscarries where, as here, "You set yourself against a particular sin, and do not consider that you are nothing but sin."[13] Owen also gave a pertinent word of advice for gospel preaching.

> A skilful [preacher] lays his axe at the root, drives still at the heart. To inveigh against particular sins is a good work; but yet at best it may produce merely formality or hypocrisy. It is like beating an enemy in an open field, only to drive him into an impregnable castle where he cannot be prevailed against. To break men off particular sins, and not to break their hearts, is to [work contrary to their conversion].[14]

Benefits and Dangers of Legal Reformation

Legal reformation has at least three beneficial effects. First, it restrains the outbreak of further sin in a person's life. Secondly, by restraining sin, it may make conversion easier. Owen observed that developed habits of sinning take away a sinner's sense of sin and that the continued love and practice of sin makes for total degradation except as God restrains it. This habituation to sin makes conversion more difficult, at least from the human standpoint.[15] Thirdly, because legal reformation is not produced by regeneration and empowered by the Holy Spirit, it will result in repeated

[10] *Works*, 5:78.
[11] Ibid.
[12] *Works*, 6:270–71.
[13] *Works*, 6:38.
[14] *Works*, 6:39.
[15] *Works*, 3:298.

failure to stop sinning; this repeated frustration will prove beneficial, however, only if it pushes the convinced sinner to salutary self-despair and the only remedy, regeneration, that will meet his need for salvation.

Ironically, however, legal reformation, though generally a necessary preparation for grace, has four serious dangers. The first, as already mentioned, is that repeated failures to stop sinning lead to so-called "surprisals" into sin. A sinner's convictions battle his corruptions, especially any darling sin, such that he discovers the power of sin (Romans 7:7–9) and his own inability to resist. He makes attempts and promises to reform but typically holds out only until the next occasion of sinning promises fair. This conflict produces great distress of soul, even despair, unless and until God sees fit to regenerate the convinced sinner.

> Under this work God often 'uses a word in season' secretly to communicate a principle of grace or spiritual life to the will. This begins its conflict effectually to eject sin from its throne and dominion. The Spirit begins to lust against the flesh. There was upon bare conviction a contest merely between the mind and conscience and the will. Now the conflict begins to be in the will itself. This fills the mind with amazement and brings some to the very door of despair for deliverance.[16]

The second pitfall stems from the convinced sinner's response to the necessarily partial character of legal reformation. He may focus on the reformation of one particular sin to the exclusion of all other sins and fail to grasp that his overriding problem is the plague of his heart, which expresses itself in manifold sins. Or he may simply exchange one sin for another and doom his efforts at reform because they are not universal in scope. Owen discussed what we might call pseudo-reformation under the name of "diversion" in his treatise on *Mortification*.

> A sin is not mortified when it is only diverted. Simon Magus for a season left his sorceries; but his covetousness and ambition remained still. Therefore, Peter tells him, 'I perceive that thou art in the gall of bitterness.' The same lust now exerts and puts itself forth another way. And this diversion often befalls men [for reasons] wholly foreign to grace.[17]

The third serious danger is that reformation will succeed to the degree that it becomes self-righteousness, which the convinced sinner clings to, in the vain hope of self-justification under the covenant of works. Owen, like other mainstream Puritan divines, distinguished between the covenant of

[16] *Works*, 3:356–57.
[17] *Works*, 6:26.

works applicable to Adam and Eve and the covenant of grace applicable to all human beings since the Fall. The main difference between the two is that the former depends on perfect obedience such as could have been performed by Adam; the latter on the imputation of the righteousness of Christ to Adam's fallen offspring.[18] (The obedience rendered by the Christian under the covenant of grace should be sincere and universal, as discussed in chapter 12.) Legal reformation cannot, however, supply the spiritual strength or grace necessary to satisfy the requirements of either covenant. Owing to natural depravity, there is an absence of any principle of spiritual life in the unregenerate that would avail to meet the conditions of either the covenant of works or the covenant of grace.[19] Likening a sinner under serious conviction of sin to a manslayer fleeing to the city of refuge Owen warns how either may resort to a foolish stratagem: "[Both] might have many contrivances suggested in his mind how he might escape the danger to which he was exposed. A righteousness of the works of the law [will be suggested to his mind as a means of relief] and with many is effectual to his ruin."[20] Self-righteousness is such a plausible and pleasing remedy to the convinced sinner because, as Owen writes:

> That which is pressed with most vehemence and plausibility, being suggested by the law itself, in a way of escape from the danger of its sentence, is legal righteousness, to be sought after in amendment of life. This proposes itself to the soul with great importunity and advantages to further its acceptance: for first, [reformation of life] is so unquestionably necessary, that without it in its proper place and end, there is no sincere conversion to God; and secondly, [reformation] is looked on as the sense of what will satisfy the law. But this proposal is deceitful, and if amendment of life is leaned on for satisfaction of the law's sentence, it will prove a broken reed.[21]

Owen stresses, in opposition to the emphasis on mere moralism by certain Anglicans, that reformation of life can proceed so far in the unregenerate that it becomes the form of godliness lacking the power thereof: "A common work of grace upon unregenerate men may be carried on so far that it is very difficult to discern between its effects and those of saving grace."[22] He recasts several of the same points given above in elaborating on the threefold defect of legal (or moral) reformation of life:

---

[18] *Works*, 5:275–76.
[19] *Works*, 3:287.
[20] *Works*, 21:341.
[21] *Works*, 3:362.
[22] *Works*, 3:309.

1. It will consist [coexist] with and allow raging and reigning sins of igno-
    rance. The conducting light in this work not leading to an abhorrence of
    all sin as sin, nor to a pursuit of universal holiness fully conformable to
    Christ, often leaves great sins unregarded [unreformed].

2. Its reformation is seldom universal as to all known sins, unless for a sea-
    son produced by affliction, judgment or the like.

3. Such behavior fades and decays over time as convictions of sin wear off.
    Sin gains ground, and they become walking and talking skeletons in re-
    ligion—dry, sapless, useless worldlings.[23]

The fourth and final danger is that reformation will be pursued only
temporarily, so that the convinced sinner (owing to the great power of
indwelling sin) becomes entangled again in sin and lapses ultimately into
total apostasy. Owen declares that indwelling sin shows off its formidable
power by stifling the power of conviction of sin, reformation, and gospel
light wrought no less than by the word of God:

> It [indwelling sin] stops or controls the exceedingly great power that
> is put forth in the word in their conviction and reformation. We see by
> experience that men are not easily wrought upon by the word. Mighty
> difficulties and prejudices must be conquered, and great strokes given to
> the conscience before this can be brought about. It is as the stopping of
> a river in his course, and turning his streams another way. To turn men
> from their corrupt ways, sins and pleasures; to make them pray, fast, hear,
> to cause them to profess Christ and the gospel are the effects of mighty
> power and strength. Indeed, the power that the Holy Ghost puts forth by
> the word, in the staggering and conviction of sinners, in the wakening of
> their consciences, the enlightening of their minds, the changing of their
> affections, the aweing of their hearts, the reforming of their lives and
> compelling them to duties, is inexpressible.
>
> But when sin is once enraged, conscience is stifled, reputation in the
> church of God despised, light supplanted, the impressions of the word
> cast off, convictions digested, heaven and hell despised; sin makes it way
> through all, and utterly turns the soul from the good and right ways of
> God.[24]

Only regeneration through the power of the Holy Spirit can put matters
right.

---

[23] *Works*, 3:240–41.
[24] *Works*, 6:309–10.

Placing Regeneration in the Ordo Salutis between Legal and Evangelical Reformation

As chapter 9 will discuss in greater depth, Owen devoted Book 3 of *Pneumatologia* to the topic of regeneration. He wrote against a number of theological opponents—including moralists who mocked regeneration as enthusiasm—and identified various counterfeits of regeneration including legal (or moral) reformation.[25] Given the reality of natural human depravity, Owen specifically denies any equivalence between moral reformation and regeneration:

> Whatever preparations they may be for it and dispositions to it, the bringing forth of a [new creature occurs] in an instant. This, therefore, cannot consist in a mere reformation of life. So are we said herein to be the 'workmanship of God, created in Christ Jesus for good works.' There is a work of God in us preceding all our good works towards him; for before we can work any of them, in order of nature, we must be the workmanship of God, created for them, or enabled spiritually to perform them.[26]

Contrary to what Bozeman and Owen's antinomian opponents thought, mainstream Puritans like Owen maintain that regeneration, by infusing a new, real spiritual principle into the soul and its faculties, infallibly produces moral reformation (or what Scripture calls fruits of repentance or that holiness without which no man will see the Lord).[27] His definition of regeneration makes it clear that regeneration must, in the order of nature and salvation, precede legal (or moral) reformation: "Regeneration is the begetting, infusing, creating, of a new principle of life, light and power in the soul, antecedent to true evangelical reformation of life, in the order of nature, and enabling men thereunto, according to the mind of God."[28] Reformation is a universal duty that must take place in the context of true gospel obedience.[29] Changing the order of nature and putting moral reformation first as though it amounted to regeneration is raising a roof before a foundation is laid. Owen declares, "The doctrine of regeneration does not exclude morality but puts it on its proper founda-

---

[25] *Works*, 3:2–3.

[26] *Works*, 3:222.

[27] *Works*, 3:219. The degree of moral reformation is not uniform for all the regenerate, but varies based on the Holy Spirit's communication of grace and the Christian's exercise or improvement of the grace given.

[28] *Works*, 3:222.

[29] *Works*, 3:219.

tion."[30] He rejected as sheer folly the notion that putting regeneration first in order of nature produces antinomianism.[31]

Owen related three ways in which the grace of regeneration improves nature. First, it transforms the performance of moral duties into evangelical obedience acceptable to God. Secondly, the communication of grace to the regenerate gives the strength necessary to perform spiritual duties.[32] Lastly and most importantly, the method of the gospel is to proclaim gospel mysteries first as the foundation of faith and obedience, and only then to enforce moral duties. Owen notes the way in which the natural mind perverts this gospel method by inverting the order: "Natural men invert that order and set up moral duties as the foundation of a covenant of works. Then they despise or reduce the gospel, thereby destroying the foundation of all true morality."[33]

Summary

The fatal flaw in the antinomian scheme of hostility to legal (or moral) reformation on the ground that it was setting up a covenant of works was their failure to distinguish carefully between legal and evangelical reformation. Indeed, legal reformation is designed to lead to regeneration and consequent evangelical reformation by inducing salutary self-despair. Thus it is vitally necessary in Owen's usage to ascertain in context which type of reformation he is referencing. Legal reformation, which precedes regeneration, is natural, partial, and temporary, whereas evangelical reformation, which temporally and causally follows regeneration, is supernatural, universal, and lasting. Conviction of sin usually leads to legal reformation. The latter takes the shape of abstaining from known sins and pursuing changed behavior. Legal reformation not only restrains sin but it provokes indwelling sin to raise a pitched battle whereby the sinner may be pushed to despair of self and seek Christ.

Despite the benefits of legal reformation, four serious dangers accompany it. The first is that repeated "surprisals" into sin result when the sinner's resistance backfires and provokes worse bouts of sinning. The second snare is that a sinner may settle for partial reformation rather than universal. The third pitfall is that the sinner may resort to the highly plausible yet ultimately foolish stratagem of self-righteousness. A fourth serious danger

---

[30] *Works*, 3:218
[31] Ibid.
[32] *Works*, 3:278–79.
[33] *Works*, 3:279.

is that, tired of constant defeat, the convinced sinner may give in to sin by succumbing to hypocrisy or apostasy.

Though identifying moral reformation as a counterfeit of regeneration, Owen still insisted that in the order of nature, regeneration must precede, just as it infallibly produces, moral transformation. The antinomians mistook the matter in Owen's opinion by jumping to the conclusion that Puritan preachers were seeking to raise the roof of moral reformation before laying the foundation of union with Christ. Exactly the opposite turns out to be true.

9

Regeneration

Antinomian Denial of Three Key Aspects of Regeneration

The seventeenth-century antinomian concept of regeneration involved three key denials. The first denial stemmed from essentialism, the view that regeneration implanted the divine essence itself. The negative corollary of this view was the antinomian denial that regeneration implanted created graces in the convert. The second denial, based on irrationalism, took the form of antinomian insistence that regeneration bypassed human rational faculties. The third key denial was the antinomian claim that regeneration had nothing to do with the renewal of the faculties of understanding, will, and heart. The New England Antinomian Controversy also put the antinomian understanding of regeneration on display. The list of 82 antinomian errors compiled by the Newtown (Cambridge, Massachusetts) Synod dealt largely with regeneration. Antinomian Error 1 claimed that conversion, far from restoring them, actually destroyed the human faculties, while Antinomian Errors 14 and 15 averred that because Christ works in the regenerate as if the latter were dead; therefore graces reside only in Christ and not in Christians themselves.[1] Antinomian Error 35 asserted, "The efficacy of Christ's death is to kill all activity of graces in his members, that he might act all in all."[2] Similarly, in accordance with the immediatist presupposition of antinomians, Antinomian Error 18 asserted

[1] Hall, *The Antinomian Controversy*, 219, 223.
[2] Ibid., 228.

that the Holy Spirit works in hypocrites by gifts and graces but in the regenerate "immediately."[3] Antinomian Error 23 declared that one should pray only for Christ, not for gifts and graces.[4] Wheelwright's Fast Day sermon took the line that Christ's entry into the soul "maketh the creature nothing."[5] John Cotton supported Wheelwright's stand, probably because his own definition of "gifts of spiritual grace," as discussed in chapter 3, amounted to very much the same thing. As Stoever observed,

> Cotton's theological posture was governed was a conception of the order of regeneration in which union with Christ was the primary, overruling moment. Creaturely agency and the mediation of second causes, in accomplishing and evidencing regeneration, are wholly subordinate if not irrelevant.[6]

By contrast, the mainstream Puritan understanding of God's 'efficiency' in the accomplishment of redemption means that "regeneration is properly defined not as the impinging of omnipotence directly upon human nature, but rather as the operation of God's efficient power through means appropriate to human capacity, including mental faculties."[7]

Owen's Response to Three Key Antinomian Denials

Before discussing Owen's soteriology of regeneration more generally, I will briefly summarize Owen's response to these three key denials of Seventeenth-Century antinomian theology. As discussed in chapter 4, he rejected the essentialist view of regeneration that the divine essence was implanted in believers whose role thus remained completely passive, such that Christ believed and repented in the stead of the believer. Owen instead insisted on the reality of human agency: "The Holy Spirit works in us by us, and what he does in us is done by us."[8] Owen's major stress on the importance of illumination (see chapter 6) on the path of conversion reflected his opposition to the antinomian view, founded on irrationalism, that regeneration bypasses rational faculties. Owen blasted antinomian irrationalism regarding divine illumination as involved in regeneration and conversion:

[3] Ibid., 223.
[4] Ibid., 225.
[5] Cited by Bozeman, *The Precisianist Strain*, 302.
[6] Stoever, '*A Faire and Easye Way to Heaven*', 79.
[7] Ibid., 89.
[8] *Works*, 3:204.

We do not only grant herein the use of the rational faculties of the soul, but require their exercise and utmost improvement. If God teach, we are to learn, and we cannot be learn but in the exercise of our minds. And it is vainly pretended that God's communication of a supernatural ability to our minds and our exercise of them in a way of duty, are inconsistent, whereas indeed they are inseparable in all that we are taught of God; for at the same time he infuses a gracious ability into our minds, he proposes the truth to us concerning which that ability is to be exercised.[9]

He also took issue with the third key antinomian denial that regeneration involves the renewal of human faculties, affirming the contrary:

If we are spiritually renewed, all the faculties of our souls are enabled to exert their respective powers.... This must be done in various duties, by the exercise of various graces, as they are to be acted by the distinct powers of the faculties of our minds.... All the distinct powers of our souls are to be acted by distinct grace and duties in cleaving to God by love.[10]

Further, Owen insisted that regeneration, by infusing a new, real spiritual principle into the soul and its faculties, infallibly produces moral reformation.[11]

Owen's Soteriology of Regeneration

In Owen's *ordo salutis*, regeneration follows enlightenment, conviction, and reformation of life, though it does not invariably result from these preparatory works.[12] It is important to recognize that Owen, like many Seventeenth-Century theologians, used the terms 'regeneration' and 'conversion' interchangeably.[13] As Packer points out,

Many Seventeenth-Century Reformed theologians equated regeneration with effectual calling and conversion with regeneration (hence the systematic translation of epistrepho [be converted] in the AV); later Reformed theologians have defined regeneration more narrowly, as the

---

[9] *Works*, 4:167.

[10] *Works*, 1:320. In other words, graces and duties "act" our faculties into loving God.

[11] *Works*, 3:219. The degree of moral reformation is not uniform for all the regenerate, but varies based on the Holy Spirit's communication of grace and the Christian's exercise or improvement of the grace given.

[12] *Works*, 3:231. These are normally wrought by the Holy Spirit acting in, by and through the preached word (*Works*, 3:235).

[13] *Works*, 3:9.

implanting of the 'seed' from which faith and repentance spring in the course of effectual calling.[14]

It would be a serious mistake to infer from Owen's usage, however, that he would not acknowledge the distinction made by later Reformed divines. In *Pneumatologia* (1674) Owen grasped fully that the will is passive in regeneration:

> The will, in the first act of conversion (as even sundry of the schoolmen acknowledge), acts not but as it is acted, moves not but as it is moved; and therefore is passive therein.... In order of nature, the acting of grace in the will in our conversion is antecedent unto its own acting; though in the same instant wherein the will is moved it moves, and when it is acted it acts itself, and preserves its own liberty in its exercise. There is, therefore, herein [in regeneration] an inward almighty power of the Holy Ghost, producing or effecting in us the will of conversion unto God, so acting our wills as that they also act themselves, and that freely.[15]

He clearly understood the distinction between the order of nature and the order of time in salvation: the will acts in conversion at the very moment in time as God acts upon it in regeneration, though the latter precedes the former in the order of nature.

Writing specifically against Socinians, Anglican moralists, and antinomian "enthusiasm," Owen devoted Book 3 of *Pneumatologia* to the topic of regeneration. Socinians denied original sin and thus the necessity of regeneration, Anglican moralists mocked regeneration as "enthusiasm," and antinomians denied the involvement of any human faculties or created graces in regeneration.[16] He also had to deal in passing with Roman Catholics who equated regeneration with baptism and Arminians who considered regeneration a product of synergism between God and man. Owen was convinced that the necessity of regeneration cannot be understood apart from natural depravity[17] for the latter necessitates an "internal, especial, immediate, supernatural, effectual, enlightening act of the Holy Ghost."[18] It is natural depravity that causes violent opposition to arise against the doctrine of regeneration, ironically, such as Owen himself encountered from his theological opponents while insisting on the necessity of regeneration.[19]

---

[14] J. I. Packer, "Regeneration," in *Evangelical Dictionary of Theology*, ed. Walter A. Elwell (Grand Rapids: Baker, 1984), 925.

[15] *Works*, 3:319–20.

[16] *Works*, 3:2–3.

[17] *Works*, 3:9.

[18] *Works*, 3:282.

[19] *Works*, 3:212.

Owen laid down certain general principles concerning regeneration. The Holy Spirit is the author or principal efficient cause of regeneration and it is by regeneration that He applies the benefits of redemption. Regeneration is called in Scripture a "vivification" or "quickening" because it communicates a new spiritual life.[20] Though great variety may result from a host of variables including the external means of grace, the order of regeneration (i.e., the morphology of conversion), the degrees of preparation for grace, and even the human perception of the process, regeneration works essentially the same state in all who are born again.[21] Despite any preparation for grace that may have taken place, regeneration is an instantaneous event.[22]

Though regeneration is instantaneous, Owen, in contrast to Seventeenth-Century antinomians who denied the role of human agency in regeneration altogether, posited two duties that lie within the free agency of the unregenerate: outward attendance on the appointed means of grace and a diligent intensity both to understand and to receive the impact of divine revelation.[23] Furthermore, Owen believed that regeneration more frequently results when the unregenerate have been seeking God or preparing for grace. "Surprisals of grace," such as Paul's experience on the road to Damascus and subsequent conversion, are the exception rather than the rule because God normally "meets with" those attending to the appointed means of grace and thus rewards those who diligently seek Him.[24] But this does not mean fulfillment of these preparatory duties somehow merits further grace. Owen specifically rejected the Roman Catholic concept of congruent merit.[25] Elsewhere he affirmatively stated, "All that we receive from him [the Holy Spirit] and by him, we have by the way of free gift or donation."[26]

Even more importantly, utilizing Aristotle's categorization of causes, Owen stated that duties preparatory to regeneration cannot serve as formal or efficient causes thereof. Aristotle had posited four types of causes:

1. An efficient cause is that by which some change is wrought.

2. A final cause is the end or purpose for which the change is produced.

3. A material cause is that out of which a change is wrought.

---

[20] *Works*, 3:209.
[21] *Works*, 3:213, 215.
[22] *Works*, 3:222.
[23] *Works*, 3:230.
[24] *Works*, 3:231.
[25] *Works*, 3:241.
[26] *Works*, 4:139.

4. A formal cause is that into which something is changed.[27]

Owen made a critical distinction between material and formal causes of (or dispositions toward) regeneration. He rightly insisted that duties preparatory to regeneration are a material, but not a formal, cause of regeneration:

> A material disposition is that which disposes and somehow makes a subject fit for the reception of that which shall be communicated, added or infused into it as its form. So wood by drying and a due composure is made fit and ready to admit of firing, or continual fire. A formal disposition is where one degree of the same kind disposes the subject to further degrees of it; as the morning light... disposes the air to the [noonday sun]. The former we allow here, but not the latter.[28]

Nor can duties preparatory to regeneration serve as an efficient cause thereof. Because duties preparatory are natural, nothing supernatural can derive from them. Duties preparatory to regeneration still merit vigorous pursuit because they put one in the way of salvation.

> No doubt unregenerate men may perform many external duties which are good in themselves, and lie in the order of the outward disposal of the means of conversion; nor is it questioned but they may have real designs, desires and endeavors after [salvation]–but so far as these desires are merely natural, there is no disposition in them to spiritual life or spiritual good. So far as they are supernatural, they are not of themselves, for although there are no preparatory inclinations in men, there are preparatory works upon them... wrought by the power of God, exerted in the dispensation of the word. They are not educed out of the natural faculties of men.[29]

Owen discussed three counterfeits of regeneration. The first is seemingly direct inspiration, often accompanied by seemingly miraculous gifts.[30] Owen took direct aim here at the illuminism of both antinomians and Quakers. The second impostor is baptism, even when accompanied by an adult profession of faith.[31] This stricture applies to Roman Catholics and Anglo-Catholic Anglicans who believe in baptismal regeneration, even of infants, and also to Protestant churches who mistake the outward symbols of baptism and profession of faith for the inward reality. The third pretender, championed by Socinians, is moralism. Owen claimed that it was a repudiation of original sin that forced them into this unten-

---

[27] Taylor, "Causation," 2:56.
[28] *Works*, 3:229.
[29] *Works*, 3:296.
[30] *Works*, 3:214, 224.
[31] *Works*, 3:216.

able position.[32] Owen insisted that regeneration, by infusing a new, real spiritual principle into the soul and its faculties, infallibly produces moral reformation.[33] Regeneration must, in the order of nature, precede moral reformation.[34] Reformation is a universal duty that must take place in the context of true gospel obedience.[35] Changing the order of nature and putting moral reformation first as though it amounted to regeneration is raising a roof before a foundation is laid. Owen declared, "The doctrine of regeneration does not exclude morality but puts it on its proper foundation."[36] He rejected as sheer folly the notion, often advanced by Roman Catholics, Socinians, and Anglican moralists, that putting regeneration first in order of nature produces antinomianism.

Owen then turned his attention to natural depravity on the assumption that regeneration cannot be otherwise understood. In fact, natural depravity and regeneration are discussed in *Pneumatologia* in roughly equal length. Owen observed that each person is either regenerate or unregenerate and that there is no middle state.[37] He cited three aspects of natural depravity: (1) corruption of mind, also called spiritual darkness or blindness; (2) corruption of the will and affections, also called impotency; and (3) spiritual death of the entire soul. Spiritual blindness prevents the spiritual discernment of saving truth; not even human reason, which Socinians and Anglican moralists exalt, can discern the gospel savingly.[38]

Corruption of the Mind: Spiritual Blindness

Original sin, or natural depravity, has caused spiritual blindness by corrupting all human faculties.[39] The mind, the ruling faculty, follows vain pursuits in confusion and disorder. Understanding, the judging faculty, is even more corrupt than the mind. The heart, the practical principle of operation that includes the will and affections, stubbornly resists gospel light and conviction of sin.[40] A vicious circle comes in being because the mind is

[32] *Works*, 3:223.
[33] *Works*, 3:219. The degree of moral reformation is not uniform for all the regenerate, but varies based on the Holy Spirit's communication of grace and the Christian's exercise or improvement of the grace given.
[34] *Works*, 3:222.
[35] *Works*, 3:219.
[36] *Works*, 3:218.
[37] *Works*, 3:243, 258.
[38] *Works*, 3:244–49.
[39] *Works*, 3:250.
[40] *Works*, 3:250–52.

the ruling faculty whose lead the understanding and heart must follow. In saving illumination or regeneration, "light is used by the mind, applied by the understanding, and used by the heart."[41] But in an unregenerate state, the mind, unable to perceive the worth of spiritual truth, blocks the reception of light and grace and leads the other faculties astray:

> Nothing in the soul, nor the will and affections, can will, desire or cleave unto any good but what is presented to them by the mind, and as it is presented. The good, whatever it be, which the mind cannot discover, the will cannot choose nor the affections cleave to. So where the mind is practically deceived, or in any way captivated by the power of prejudices, the will and the affections can [in] no way free themselves from entertaining that evil which the mind has perversely assented to.[42]

Because of this vanity of the mind, Calvin considered the mind an idol factory; Owen called it the mother of monstrous births.[43] It gives rise to an unteachable spirit that prefers any other life to a life of faith and obedience to God.[44] Even under affliction or conviction, the carnal mind will find moralism, as urged by Socianians or certain Anglicans, more appealing than the gospel summons to regeneration.[45] As implied by the use of gospel warnings, exhortations, promises, and precepts, the mind possesses a natural power to discern the propositional truths set out in Scripture but that natural power is insufficient for two reasons. First, Owen insisted, against the semi-Pelagianism of Socinians and Arminians, that the revelation of biblical duties does not imply the existence of human power to perform them acceptably to God.[46] Secondly, Owen pointed out that to receive spiritual knowledge "really" as opposed to "notionally," one must discern its revelation of God's wisdom, goodness, and holiness and its suitability to God's glory and the believer's good.[47]

Corruption of the Will and Affections: Moral Impotency

The second aspect of natural depravity revealed in Scripture is moral impotency, as opposed to what Owen called natural impotency. Because of

---

[41] *Works*, 3:252.
[42] *Works*, 3:281.
[43] *Works*, 3:254.
[44] *Works*, 3:255.
[45] *Works*, 3:256.
[46] *Works*, 3:262.
[47] *Works*, 3:260–61.

natural impotency, man cannot receive spiritual truth savingly; because of moral impotency, he *will* not.[48] Moral impotency is no good excuse before God because it remains both the punishment and cause of sin.[49] This moral impotency manifests itself in pernicious ways. First, moral impotency keeps the natural man from fully using the means of grace.[50] Secondly, it fills the natural man with such enmity against God that he, even under gospel preaching, will dread God as unapproachable or contrariwise assume that an all-too-approachable God is more than willing to wink at his sins.[51] Thirdly, such enmity produces hatred of all God's ways and fills the mind with vain and lustful imaginations toward sensual and worldly objects.[52] Fourthly, it fills the mind with countless prejudices against the gospel.[53]

Owen related three ways in which the grace of regeneration improves nature. It transforms the performance of moral duties into evangelical obedience acceptable to God. The communication of grace to the regenerate gives the strength necessary to perform spiritual duties. The method of the gospel, contrary to what Socinians and Anglican moralists conceived, is to proclaim gospel mysteries first as the foundation of faith and obedience, and only then moral duties.[54] With regard to this last improvement, Owen noted the perversion of it by the natural mind: "Natural men invert that order and set up moral duties as the foundation of a covenant of works. Then they despise or reduce the gospel, thereby destroying the foundation of all true morality."[55]

Corruption of the Soul: Spiritual Death

The third aspect of natural depravity is spiritual death. The natural man, dead as he is in sins and trespasses, cannot receive spiritual things. Owen saw three implications emanating from spiritual death. First, the principle of spiritual life capable of meeting the conditions of either the covenant of works or the covenant of grace is completely lacking.[56] Secondly, as discussed, the natural man is morally impotent. Thirdly, moral

[48] *Works*, 3:266 (emphasis his).
[49] *Works*, 3:267.
[50] *Works*, 3:268.
[51] *Works*, 3:271, 273.
[52] *Works*, 3:274.
[53] *Works*, 3:275.
[54] *Works*, 3:278–79. Owen is discussing evangelical, not legal, reformation as the two are distinguished in chapter 8.
[55] *Works*, 3:279.
[56] *Works*, 3:287.

persuasion, though a necessary condition of regeneration, is not a sufficient one; regeneration requires a "physical, immediate operation of the Holy Spirit" and involves the real renovation of all human faculties into the *imago Dei*.[57] This final implication constitutes a major area of disagreement between Reformed theology on the one hand and both Arminian (or semi-Pelagian) theology and antinomian theology on the other. The Arminian, based on belief in a largely unimpaired human freewill, would claim moral suasion sufficient to effect regeneration. Owen pointed out that moral suasion "confers no new supernatural strength."[58] The antinomian, because of his essentialist presupposition, denied that human faculties are ever physically regenerated. Owen bolstered his case that regeneration is not only a moral but also a physical operation of the Holy Spirit through adducing compelling linguistic usage from Scripture.

> And hence the work of grace in conversion is constantly expressed by words denoting a real internal efficiency; such as creating, quickening, forming, giving a new heart. Whenever this word is spoken of with regard to an active efficiency, it is ascribed to God; he *creates* us anew, he *quickens* us, he *begets* us of his own will. But where it is spoken with respect to us, there it is passively expressed; we *are created* in Christ Jesus, we are *new creatures*, we are *born again*, and the like: which one observation is sufficient to evert [overthrow] the whole hypothesis of Arminian grace.[59]

He also cited 1 Peter 1:23 and John 1:13 as excluding the human will as a cause of regeneration.[60]

Owen's Reply to Antinomian Objections

Owen immediately felt compelled to address three frequently posed antinomian objections. The first objection centered on the claim that if what Owen said is true, then gospel commands, promises, and warnings are useless. Owen begged to differ on four grounds. To begin with, these "moral instruments" work suitably to the faculties of the unregenerate person, who has a "remote, passive,"[61] not a "next"[62] or "immediate,"[63] power

[57] *Works*, 3:316. The context is adult conversion. Owen took virtually the same position as did William Guthrie in *A Christian's Great Interest*: the usual rules for adult conversion often do not apply to infants and youth.

[58] *Works*, 3:309.

[59] *Works*, 3:317 (emphasis his).

[60] *Works*, 3:336.

[61] *Works*, 3:289.

[62] *Works*, 3:321.

[63] *Works*, 3:295.

to obey. He defined a "remote power" as faculties lacking immediate power but capable of being graciously wrought upon by the Holy Spirit.[64] Next, he pointed out again that these "moral instruments" define human duty, not human power,[65] contrary to the semi-Pelagian claim later embraced by Charles Finney (1792–1875). In addition, God has appointed these "moral instruments" as means of grace.[66] Finally, Owen declared that moral persuasion has a "powerful persuasive efficacy"[67] to regeneration if utilized by the Holy Spirit because it instructs the hearer in both God's will and man's corresponding duty toward God.[68] Despite grasping the significance and importance of moral suasion, Owen contended that moral suasion alone would leave the depraved human will indifferent to conversion. He wrote, "The most effectual persuasions cannot prevail with such [unregenerate men] to convert themselves, any more than arguments can prevail with a blind man to see, or with a dead man to rise from the grace, or with a lame man to walk steadily."[69] He likewise found the Arminian hypothesis of synergism and the antinomian hypothesis of total passivity both contradicted by prayers for conversion commonly made by the Christian church.

The second objection of the hyper-Calvinist or perfectionistic antinomian follows next. If religious duties performed by the unregenerate are at best "splendid sins," then why preach biblical commands, promises and threats?[70] Owen's five-part reply is given below:

1. Though their duties are formally sin, yet these performances are materially good [because they may put them in the way of salvation].[71]

2. God has regard to sincere, as opposed to, hypocritical performances.

---

[64] *Works*, 3:295.

[65] *Works*, 3:289.

[66] *Works*, 3:290.

[67] *Works*, 3:304. Owen gave five reasons for the efficacy of preaching: evidence of the truth, proposal of God as the chief good and sin as the worst temporal evil, artful presentation of motives to conversion, God's appointment, and the spiritual gifts accorded preachers.

[68] *Works*, 3:303–4.

[69] *Works*, 3:313.

[70] *Works*, 3:292–93.

[71] Earlier Owen stressed that "surprisals" of grace are the exception. God ordinarily meets with those attending to the means of grace to glorify His word and to reward obedience even though performed in an unregenerate state. Thomas Cobbett (1608–1685), a famous New England prayer warrior, expressly endorsed prayer for conversion by the unregenerate in his treatise *Gospel Incense* (1657), but the practice was condemned by the Presbyterian Board of Publications when it reprinted his work in the nineteenth century.

3. The same outward duty may be accepted in some, rejected in others.

4. God has not forfeited his power to command simply because man has lost the power to obey.

5. Gospel preachers have a warrant to press on all men the duties of faith, repentance, and obedience because God so commands and such preaching will restrain them from grievous sin and further gospel-hardening and keep them in God's way of salvation.[72]

A third antinomian objection is implicit in Owen's discussion. Why does the Holy Spirit not finish the work through regeneration that He began in moral suasion? The antinomians thought all the Holy Spirit's operations were immediately efficacious. Although the internal efficiency of the Holy Spirit is always infallible (or irresistible),[73] Owen countered that He in His sovereignty determines the measure of His efficacy.[74] As Owen had pointed out earlier in *Pneumatologia* with regard to other types of preparation for grace, the operations of the Holy Spirit need be only (1) good and holy and (2) effectual in accordance with the extent of His sovereign design: "That he should always design them to the utmost length of what they have a moral tendency towards, though no real efficiency for, is not required."[75]

Self-examination, the importance of which antinomians were loathe to admit, is vital to Owen because this incomplete work of moral suasion may too closely resemble regeneration and conversion. Owen gave five guidelines to avoid self-deception (what he called "speaking peace" to oneself) and ultimate destruction.

1. Though conviction of sin may restrain the will in its pursuit of sin, the will is not changed or renewed.

2. Only saving illumination gives the mind a transforming delight and complacency in spiritual things.

3. The preparatory work does not produce a conscience that hates sin enough to apply the blood of Christ for cleansing.

---

[72] *Works*, 3:293–95.

[73] Owen took pains to point out that the Holy Spirit does not work by compulsion; no one is dragged kicking and screaming into the kingdom of God (*Works*, 3:318–19, 225).

[74] *Works*, 3:317–18. Owen points out that the regenerate sometimes reject His motions to the detriment of their greater sanctification.

[75] *Works*, 3:237.

4. The preparatory work does not fix the affections on spiritual things or fill the affections with them.

5. Reformation of life under this preparatory work suffers from a threefold defect:

    a.   Great sins often continue to reign;

    b.   Behavior is seldom reformed universally as to all known sin; and

    c.   Moral behavior will decay over time, as holiness does not thrive.[76]

How then does regeneration redress natural depravity? First, God makes a new creature by His resurrection power.[77] Secondly, contrary to the antinomian claim, regeneration renovates all human faculties.[78] From Scripture the mind receives saving light and spiritual understanding.[79] The will becomes willing in the day of God's power and freely obedient.[80] Love of God and all His ways, causing the soul to cleave with rest and delight, is implanted in the heart.[81] In fact, the new creature is even said by Owen to possess a new faculty.[82] Further, in conversion God works faith and repentance in the convert[83] which ultimately lead to fruitful obedience.[84]

Pastoral Advice

Owen's advice to ministers on the subject of regeneration, though scattered about, is also well worth pondering. He painstakingly insisted that a theological and evangelistic grasp of preparation for grace is "of great benefit" to the church.[85] Without defending the accuracy of every single assertion made by Puritan authors marking out this topic,[86] Owen also asserted that Puritan sermons and theological treatises sounding this theme,

---

[76] *Works*, 3:238–41.
[77] *Works*, 3:323–24.
[78] *Works*, 3:219.
[79] *Works*, 3:331.
[80] *Works*, 3:324, 335.
[81] *Works*, 3:335.
[82] *Works*, 3:252.
[83] *Works*, 3:323–24.
[84] *Works*, 3:364. This line of argument is pursued most successfully by Robert Traill in his masterful treatise *Justification Vindicated from the Unjust Charge of Antinomianism* (1692).
[85] Works, 3:241.
[86] *Works*, 3:359.

though increasingly mocked in his day,[87] had redounded "to the great profit and edification of the church of God"[88] and caused many learned divines
and ministers to enjoy fruitful evangelistic ministry.[89]

According to Owen, it is pointless for ministers to expect to preach effectively for conversion without a firm understanding of regeneration and
the normal morphology of conversion. Reformed churches were already
declining from their glory through the ministrations of pastors ignorant
of these matters and lacking their own personal experience of God's re-
generative power. His warning should cause all ministers of any period in
church history to sit up and take notice if they want to fulfill their solemn
responsibility before God.

> It is a duty indispensably incumbent on all ministers of the gospel to
> acquaint themselves thoroughly with the nature of this work, that they
> may be able to comply with the will of God and grace of the Spirit in
> the effecting and accomplishment of it [regeneration] upon the souls of
> them to whom they dispense the word. Neither, without some compe-
> tent knowledge hereof, can they discharge any one part of their duty and
> office in a right manner. If all that hear them are born in trespasses and
> sins, if they are appointed of God to be the instruments of their regenera-
> tion, it is a madness, which must one day be accounted for, to neglect a
> sedulous inquiry into the nature of this work, and the means whereby it
> is wrought. And the ignorance hereof or negligence herein, with the want
> of an experience of the power of this work in their own souls, is one great
> cause of that lifeless and unprofitable ministry among us.[90]

Summary

The seventeenth-century antinomian concept of regeneration involved
three key denials. The antinomian writers of this era denied that: (1) regeneration implanted created graces in the convert; (2) regeneration involved
employment of human rational faculties; and (3) regeneration in fact
caused the renewal of human faculties of understanding, will, and heart.
Owen made short shrift of these denials, all of which served to undermine
the efficacy of regeneration. Rejecting the antinomian view of regeneration, informed as it was by essentialist, irrational, and hyper-supernatural
presuppositions, Owen stressed that God communicates a "supernatural
and gracious ability" to the human mind to comprehend divine revelation

[87] *Works*, 3:235.
[88] *Works*, 3:366.
[89] *Works*, 3:234.
[90] *Works*, 3:227–28.

preparatory to regeneration and insisted that regeneration, by God's putting forth of irresistible resurrection power, causes the powerful renewal of human faculties through the implantation of a new principle of spiritual life, and that this new principle enables the renewed human faculties to act and implanted created graces to exercise and grow.

Although Owen, like many Seventeenth-Century theologians, used the terms 'regeneration' and 'conversion' interchangeably, he fully recognized that the human will is passive in regeneration yet active in conversion and that there is both an order of nature and one of time involved. Though non-meritorious preparatory works like illumination, conviction, and reformation of life may and often do precede regeneration, the latter being instantaneous when it occurs, Owen nonetheless challenged the facile antinomian assumption that human agency has no role to play. He posited two duties incumbent on the unregenerate: to make full use of the means of grace and an intense effort to grasp and internalize, as it were, divine revelation. He was also convinced, despite exceptional "surprisals" of grace, that regeneration occurs far more frequently when an unregenerate person has been earnestly seeking God for some time. These preparatory duties, however, are a material cause of regeneration, neither a formal nor efficient one.

Regeneration is made indispensable by and cannot be fully understood apart from natural depravity. Regeneration redresses the havoc wrought upon human faculties by natural depravity: that of spiritual blindness, by giving the mind understanding of spiritual truths; that of moral impotency, by producing a sin-hating conscience and an obedient will; and that of spiritual death, by giving a new heart of flesh that takes delight in spiritual matters. Regeneration works by renovating these human faculties physically, not merely by persuading them morally.

Owen also rebutted three common antinomian objections by demonstrating that gospel exhortations and promises work to stir up human activity, that unregenerate activity though formally sinful is still materially useful to put a person in the way of salvation, and that the Holy Spirit does not, and need not, always bless conviction with regeneration in the way antinomians fond of immediatism imagined He should.

Owen attributed the newly burgeoning evangelistic deadness of the Reformed churches largely to ministerial ignorance concerning God's method of grace and the normal morphology of conversion for regeneration. The typical pastor thus found himself in the unenviable position of being unable to design sermons calculated to further the divine work of regeneration among his flock.

10

The Importance of Being Spiritually Minded

Putting Regeneration to the Test

Owen did not content himself merely with developing a thoroughly wrought-out soteriology of regeneration. He thought it absolutely vital that the reality of regeneration manifest itself in spiritual-mindedness and conflict against sin (see chapter 11). Owen's mainstream Puritan theology retained the strong distinctive emphasis placed by Calvin on the indissoluble link between justification and sanctification. He thereby erected another bulwark against Seventeenth-Century antinomians, who considered sanctification a *fait accompli* not affected by the ravages of indwelling sin. This concern appears in Owen's treatise *The Grace and Duty of Being Spiritually Minded* (1681), an extended treatment of Romans 8:6, "To be carnally minded is death, but to be spiritually minded is life and peace," which Thomas Chalmers (1780–1847) lauded for its deep searching of the heart and "forcible application of truth to the conscience."[1]

Owen sought to highlight pressing Christian duties, pointing out that many professing Christians through worldliness found themselves indisposed to perform spiritual duties or stir up graces.[2] According to Owen, these self-deceived nominal Christians, possessing the notional faith boasted by antinomians and spurning the rigors of self-examination, "ad-

[1] *Works*, 7:262.
[2] *Works*, 7:263.

mit of sacred truths in their understanding and assent to them, but take not in the power of them on their consciences, nor strictly judge of their state and condition by them."[3] Owen complained that even the majority of true Christians weakened the link between justification and sanctification and incurred great guilt by foolishly contenting themselves with low measures of grace.[4] Their presumed objection that sanctification is too difficult did not impress Owen in the least. He gave two basic replies. The first is that the general reason for this lack of growth is negligence and sloth, especially by those holding on to a darling sin. The second is that new Christians tend to get frustrated by their repeated failures to resist sin and do not thoroughly mortify sin: they deal with sin merely to stave off convictions of sin, not to glorify God in overcoming it.[5] He believed that Christians would lack assurance of salvation unless they strove after the "highest degree of being spiritually minded."[6] Owen's more rigorous approach to assurance stands in bold relief to that of Seventeenth-Century English antinomians, who believed that the Holy Spirit directly granted full assurance of salvation independently of any exercise or growth of graces.

According to Owen, Romans 8:6 implies that every person is either carnally minded or spiritually minded, spiritually dead or alive. While the "flesh" is fallen human nature, the "spirit" stands for "the holy, vital principle of new obedience wrought in the souls of believers by the Holy Ghost, enabling them to live unto God."[7] Owen pointed to three aspects of this "great" duty of being spiritual-minded: (1) fixing one's thought life on spiritual things; (2) setting one's heart on them; and (3) cleaving to them with relish and delight. He commented that, "There is a salt in spiritual things, making them savory to a renewed mind, though to others they are like the tasteless white of an egg."[8]

A Spiritually-Minded Thought Life

Owen considered the "predominancy of voluntary thoughts" the surest index of the presence or absence of genuine regeneration.[9] Opening

[3] *Works*, 7:272.

[4] Owen mentions five aggravating circumstances: the expected growth of grace is thwarted, God's promises slighted, God dishonored, Christianity's reputation blackened, and assurance undermined (*Works*, 7:541–42).

[5] *Works*, 7:454.

[6] *Works*, 7:274.

[7] *Works*, 7:269.

[8] *Works*, 7:270.

[9] *Works*, 7:277.

Matthew 12:35, Owen points out that grace and sin do not decrease by expenditure but rather increase by exercise.

> There is a good and bad treasure of the heart. This treasure is opening, emptying, and spending itself continually, though it can never be exhausted; for it has a fountain, in nature or grace, which no expense can diminish, yea, it increases and gets strength by it. The more you spend of the treasure of your heart in any kind, the more will you abound in treasure of the same kind.[10]

As if to anticipate how Edwards in *The Distinguishing Marks of the Spirit* (1738) would subsequently distinguish between negative (insufficient) and positive evidence of true revival, Owen set out negative and positive evidences of spiritual-mindedness. Three negative evidences are coming under conviction of sin, sitting under gospel preaching, and praying. His overarching point was that use of the outward means of grace, though important, does not guarantee spiritual-mindedness. Because Owen views convictions of sin as *involuntary* thoughts, they do not necessarily prove spiritual-mindedness:

> Convictions put a kind of force upon the mind, or an impression that causes it to act contrary to its own habitual disposition and inclination. [In the same way, water naturally descends unless artificially forced upwards]. When any efficacious conviction presses on the mind, it forces the egress of its thoughts upwards towards heavenly things. But as soon as the power of conviction decays or wears off, [so] that the mind is no more sensible of its force and impression, its thoughts return again to their descent.[11]

Likewise, merely sitting under gospel preaching does not lead to spiritual transformation unless the truth is received in love.[12] Finally, praying does not necessarily establish spiritual-mindedness because in prayer "spiritual thoughts may be raised in a person in his own duty *by the exercise of his gifts*, when there is no acting of grace at all."[13] Owen defended this proposition, that a person may possess gifts yet not graces, at greater length in *A Discourse of Spiritual Gifts* (1693).

---

[10] *Works*, 7:275–76.

[11] *Works*, 7:280. He has in view the "foxhole religion" of Psalm 78. He also compared convictions of sin to thundershowers rather than living springs.

[12] *Works*, 7:283.

[13] *Works*, 7:284 (emphasis his).

Owen concedes the truth of the ancient complaint that "spiritual things are filled with great obscurity and difficulty."[14] He gave two reasons why, the first being that fear, self-love, and indwelling sin may cause self-deception. The second reason is the "great similitude between *temporary* faith and that which is *saving and durable*, and between graces and gifts in their operation."[15] Given these seemingly insuperable difficulties, how can a Christian undertake satisfactory self-examination? Owen trusted that impartial self-examination by Scripture accompanied by fervent prayer for the Holy Spirit to search the heart will suffice.[16] He also gave characteristics of sincere spiritual affections[17] and criteria for distinguishing temporary faith from saving faith.[18]

The first positive evidence of spiritual-mindedness is that of genuine, as opposed to merely formal, prayer. Distinguishing between the two types of prayer is not easy. Neither sharpness of convictions nor fervency in prayer necessarily proves it to be gracious.[19] Instead, Owen looks to several marks of genuine prayer. First, genuine prayer "make[s] the soul humble, holy, watchful and diligent in universal obedience."[20] Secondly, in genuine prayer, the Christian's duty of prayer is founded in holy delight:

> This holy complacency, this rest and sweet repose of mind, is the foundation of the delight of believers in this duty. They do not pray only because

[14] *Works*, 7:285.

[15] *Works*, 7:286 (emphasis his).

[16] *Works*, 7:286–87.

[17] Sincere spiritual affections are stable, relish spiritual things, give rise to spiritual thoughts, prevail against various temptations, and promote the mortification of indwelling sin (*Works*, 7:483–87).

[18] Temporary convictions or habits differ from truly spiritual affections in three major ways. The first difference is that the former merely restrain sin and idolatry by altering the course of affections, whereas the latter restores every faculty of the person so that these cleave to God's presence in spiritual things (*Works*, 7:410–21). The second difference between the two is the ground and motive given for delight in worship; the former makes use of carnal motives for delight in worship such as outward show or admiration of the pastor's spiritual gifts, whereas the latter takes true delight in worship because of communion with God in Christ and the spiritual efficacy of ordinances (*Works*, 7:423–45). The third difference is that temporary convictions wither and die for lack of faith in a proper object, whereas faith in Christ causes spiritual affections to be assimilated to spiritual and heavenly things (*Works*, 7:445–55). Nevertheless, even temporary convictions are to be improved toward conversion (*Works*, 7:417).

[19] *Works*, 7:290–91.

[20] *Works*, 7:288.

it is their duty to do so, nor yet because they stand in need of it, so as that they cannot live without it, but they have delight in it; and to keep them from it is all one as to keep them from their daily food and refreshments.[21]

Thirdly, genuine prayer is animated by spiritual affections and a duly prepared heart. Owen stresses that grace is supposed to lead gifts, not vice versa:

This is the natural order of these things: grace habitually inclines and disposes the heart to this duty; providence and rule give the occasions for its exercise; sense of duty calls for preparation. Grace coming into actual exercise, gifts come in with their assistance. If gifts lead, all is out of order.[22]

The second positive evidence of spiritual-mindedness is that of abundantly occurring gracious thoughts about spiritual matters: "We can have no greater evidence of a change in us than a change wrought in the course of our thoughts."[23] Again, conviction of sin, though a necessary condition of genuine conversion, is not a sufficient one:[24]

The design of conviction is to put a stop unto [the multiplicity of] these [carnal] thoughts, to take off from their number, and thereby to lessen their guilt. It deserves not the name of conviction of sin which respects outward actions, and regards not the inward actings of the mind; and this alone will for a season make a great change in the thoughts, especially it will do so when assisted by superstition such as Roman Catholic devotional religion. Conviction labors to put some stop and bounds unto thoughts absolutely evil and corrupt, and superstition suggests other objects for them, which they readily embrace.[25]

To find relief from conviction of sin, Owen pointed to the necessity of opening new channels for thought-life through regeneration.[26] Contrary to the view of God's law held out by Seventeenth-Century English antinomians, Owen has great expectations that Christians would continually contemplate God's law: "The holy men of old, who obtained this testi-

---

[21] *Works*, 7:292–93. This delight springs from three sources: (1) the approach made to the lovingkindness of God; (2) the due exercise of faith, love and delight; and (3) the testimony of conscience.

[22] *Works*, 7:296.

[23] *Works*, 7:299.

[24] *Works*, 7:291.

[25] *Works*, 7:299–300.

[26] *Works*, 7:300.

mony that they pleased God, meditated continually on the law; thought of God in the night seasons; spoke of his ways, his works, his praise; their whole delight was in him, and in all things they 'followed hard after him.'"[27] Owen gave two specific directions toward achieving a spiritually-minded thought life. First, a Christian should have a greater proportion of spiritual thoughts than temporal ones; the former should be more constant and intense than the latter.[28] Second, one should observe whether spiritual thoughts occur during prayer, bedtime, and leisure.[29] A gracious soul bewails his sins of omission, whereas a carnal person remains careless and unconcerned.[30] The neglect of appointed devotional times fosters evil thoughts and sinful miscarriages.[31]

Spiritual thoughts have three objects: (1) chastening providences; (2) temptations; and (3) any other matters of Christian faith and practice.[32] As to "frowning" providences, the Christian has a twofold duty: to discover the true cause of God's displeasure and to resign himself to God's will by mortifying his desire for the recovery of his losses.[33] The Seventeenth-Century English antinomian would have found both of Owen's emphases puzzling because the former regarded the sins of the elect as invisible to God (see chapter 2) and mortification of sin redundant (see chapter 12).

Owen recognizes that it is unwise for a Christian to direct his thought life toward temptations (see chapter 11) because temptations grow stronger when his thoughts about the object of temptation multiply and start becoming delicious:

> Men may begin their thoughts of any object [of temptation] with abhorrence and detestation, and end them with complacency and approbation. The deceitfulness of sin lays hold on something that lust in the mind finds delectable and so corrupts the gracious whole frame of spirit which began the duty.[34]

Owen gave two directions for the remedy. First, "[t]hink of the guilt of sin, that you may be humbled. Think of the power of sin, that you may seek strength against it. Think not of the matter of sin, lest you be more and

---

[27] *Works*, 7:301.

[28] *Works*, 7:301–5.

[29] *Works*, 7:305–6.

[30] *Works*, 7:307.

[31] *Works*, 7:306. He quotes Micah 2:1, "They devise iniquity upon their beds, and when the morning is light they practice it."

[32] *Works*, 7:308–31.

[33] *Works*, 7:309–11.

[34] *Works*, 7:313.

more entangled."[35] Most importantly, "act faith" on Jesus Christ, our merciful and faithful High Priest, for sufficient grace for deliverance.[36]

The third object of spiritual thoughts centers on other matters of Christian faith and practice. Owen emphasized the importance of heavenly-mindedness for growth in knowledge and grace. Heavenly-mindedness is necessary both for the exercise of faith and hope and for the endurance of suffering. Owen's side comment sheds much light on his theology of grace and duty and his rejection of easygoing antinomian immediatism:

> I know God can come in by the mighty power of His Spirit and grace to support and comfort the souls of them called and even surprised into the worst of sufferings; yet do I know also that it is our duty not to tempt Him in the neglect of the ways and means which He hath appointed for the communication of His grace unto us.[37]

He clearly rejects as feckless a "let go, and let God" approach.

Owen gave specific directions for the cultivation of heavenly-mindedness to stifle worldliness and promote Christlikeness.[38] The first direction is to meditate on heaven:

> Spiritual thoughts of this heaven, consisting principally in freedom from all sin, in the perfection of all grace, in the vision of the glory of God in Christ, and all the excellencies of the divine nature as manifested in him, are an effectual means for the improvement of all graces in us: for they cannot but effect an assimilation [in us].[39]

His second direction is to compare heaven to hell, which makes for hating sin, walking humbly, and admiring God's saving grace.[40] His final directions are to meditate on the glory of Christ[41] and to meditate on the person and attributes of God with delight and godly fear.[42] This delight in communion with God gives a "threefold" evidence of spiritual-mindedness. It evinces participation in the covenant of grace and personal experience of transformation into the image of God, yielding a foretaste of heaven.[43]

[35] *Works*, 7:314.
[36] *Works*, 7:314–15.
[37] *Works*, 7:325.
[38] *Works*, 7:326–27, 338.
[39] *Works*, 7:341.
[40] *Works*, 7:342–43.
[41] *Works*, 7:344–48.
[42] *Works*, 7:362–67.
[43] *Works*, 7:362–63.

Owen defines spiritual-mindedness in such a way that it serves as a foil to the kind of notional faith espoused by Seventeenth-Century antinomians:

> Let us not mistake ourselves. To be spiritually minded is not to have the notion and knowledge of spiritual things in our minds; it is not to be constant, no, nor to abound in the performance of our duties: both which may be where there is no grace in the heart at all. It is to have our minds really exercised with delight about heavenly things, especially Christ himself as at the right hand of God.[44]

In contrast to the easy familiarity presumed by seventeenth-century English antinomians in their approaches to God, Owen laid heavy stress on the infinite distance between God and man, which makes communion with God an astonishing act of condescension on God's part and godly fear the appropriate response. In a way that would have surprised "bold, careless" antinomians, Owen makes the profound point that only spiritual-mindedness can reconcile Scripture's admonition to fear God with its encouragement to approach God with confidence and boldness:

> These things carnal reason can comprehend no consistency in: what it is afraid of, it cannot delight in; and what it delights in, it cannot long fear. But the consideration of faith, concerning what God is in Himself and what He will be to us, gives these different graces their distinct operations, and a blessed reconciliation in our souls.[45]

Owen gave seven general directions for meditation. First, a sense of the vanity of one's mind should humble us.[46] Secondly, our insufficiency and God's sufficiency should be borne in mind.[47] Thirdly, spiritual-mindedness does not have to mean attaining a higher level of solemn meditation.[48] Fourthly, growth in spiritual-mindedness, like that in all other graces, requires "diligence, watchfulness, and spiritual striving in all holy duties."[49] Fifthly, it is important to dedicate time to meditation every day.[50] Sixthly, subjects of meditation should be planned in advance.[51] Lastly, persevere in meditation because practice makes perfect.[52]

[44] *Works*, 7:348.
[45] *Works*, 7:365.
[46] *Works*, 7:380.
[47] *Works*, 7:383.
[48] *Works*, 7:384–85.
[49] *Works*, 7:385
[50] *Works*, 7:391–93.
[51] *Works*, 7:393.
[52] *Works*, 7:394.

The Bent of Spiritual Affections

Dealing with the second aspect of the "great" duty of spiritual-mindedness, Owen emphasized that the bent of the spiritual affections is absolutely crucial because God and the world compete for our hearts which are all we have to give. Owen recited six devices by which God seeks to wean the heart from the world: (1) the contempt shown worldly things by the example and cross of Christ; (2) the shortness and uncertainty of life; (3) the ruinous effect of worldly temptations; (4) the necessity of spiritual wisdom to distinguish between the use and abuse of worldly things; (5) the embarrassment caused men by their bondage to carnal lusts; and (6) the reality of hell waiting for those who love the world and hate God.[53]

Though Christian conversion is normally accompanied by vigorous spiritual affections, Owen took note of the inevitability and danger of spiritual decays. Spiritual decays pose grave danger to the Christian because they displease Christ, grieve the Holy Spirit, provoke God to wrath, undermine assurance, and cause gospel-hardening, backsliding and even apostasy.[54] To anyone seeking recovery, Owen recommended that he recall his first love to Christ and see how far he has fallen away, bear in mind Scripture's warnings against backsliding as well as its promises of healing, and make thorough work of repentance through fully using the means of grace.[55]

Spiritual affections and graces are supposed to energize the fulfillment of Scriptural duties. "The graces required [in Scripture] are to act themselves by [spiritual affections]; the duties it prescribes are those which they stir up and enliven; the religious worship it appoints is that wherein they have exercise."[56] Owen gave three characteristics of an attainable measure of spiritual-mindedness. The first is that spiritual affections, improved by exercise, readily entertain spiritual thoughts. The second is that they find a relish in spiritual matters, even crosses and losses. The third is that they prove to be fertile soil for the growth of Christian graces.[57]

Spiritual Delight

Although Owen gave four reasons why spiritual affections delight in spiritual things, his discussion of the first reason–that the infinite beauty,

---

[53] *Works*, 7:397–410.
[54] *Works*, 7:456–63.
[55] *Works*, 7:467.
[56] Works, 7:469.
[57] Works, 7:470–42.

goodness, and love of God in Christ draw our love—merits attention because he responded directly to the Christian convert who complains of no experience of any preparation for grace. Owen's response demonstrates his wisdom, like that shown by Edwards in *A Surprising Narrative*, by recognizing the great variety of the Holy Spirit's dealings in conversion and not making a one-size-fits-all morphology of conversion.

> Some cannot say that a distinct apprehension of these things was the first foundation and cause of their love to God; yet are they satisfied that they do love him in sincerity, with all their souls. And I say it may be so. God sometimes casts the skirt of his own love over the heart of a poor sinner, and efficaciously draws [him] to Himself, without a distinct apprehension of these things, by a mere sense of the love [he] has received.[58]

Owen closed his treatise by discussing how spiritual-mindedness promotes life and peace. Spiritual-mindedness infuses a principle of faith and obedience enabling us to live for God. Owen took "peace" in Romans 8:6 to refer primarily to assurance, not reconciliation. The latter is immediate and instantaneous, whereas the former depends on ongoing diligence in duty and the exercise of all grace. Again rejecting the immediatism espoused by Seventeenth-Century English antinomian writers, he declared,

> Peace with God through the blood of Christ is one thing, and peace in our minds through a holy frame is another. The former is communicated to us by an immediate act of the Holy Spirit dwelling in us [Rom 10:5], the latter is an effect of our minds, begun and gradually carried on by [holy] duties. The immediate actings of the Holy Spirit, in sealing us, witnessing to our adoption, and being an earnest of glory, are required for the former; our own sedulity and diligence in duties, and in the exercise of all grace, are required for the latter.[59]

Unlike his antinomian opponents, Owen conceived of the necessity of both the grant of divine gifts and the diligent pursuit of Christian duties for assurance and sanctification to bear fruit in holy and useful Christian living. He closed his treatise by stating that the main way spiritual-mindedness produces a holy frame of heart and mind is by helping the Christian cherish a sense of God's love.[60]

---

[58] *Works*, 7:476.
[59] *Works*, 7:490.
[60] Ibid.

Summary

Mainstream Puritan theology retained the strong distinctive emphasis placed by Calvin on the indissoluble link between justification and sanctification and thereby erected a considerable bulwark against Seventeenth-Century antinomians who considered sanctification a *fait accompli* and not continuously threatened by conflict with indwelling sin. Owen's burden to maintain the practical link between justification and sanctification is reflected in his *The Grace and Duty of Being Spiritually Minded* (1681) where he concerned himself mainly with two kinds of people: nominal Christians and true Christians who content themselves with resting in "low measures of grace." According to Owen, in direct contradiction of his antinomian adversaries, even the latter will lack assurance of salvation unless they pursue the "highest degree of being spiritually minded."[61] Rejecting the sort of notional faith hawked by antinomian preachers, Owen expressed his greatest fear that those seeking God would rest short of true salvation in temporary convictions, temporary faith, or mere doctrinal orthodoxy.

Owen thought spiritual-mindedness the most certain evidence of genuine regeneration. Though the great resemblance between temporary and saving faith and the operation of gifts and graces makes self-deception a distinct danger, Owen recommended the efficacy of fervent prayer that the Holy Spirit would reveal one's spiritual state through the application of Scripture. Scripture gives several telltale marks of regeneration: (1) a hunger for prayer that nourishes, humbles, and equips for service and obedience; (2) continued meditation on God's law; (3) a willingness to seek out the sins causing chastisement; and (4) heavenly-mindedness cultivated by true apprehension of glory, comparison of heaven and hell, and concerted meditation on God's attributes. The second and third marks of regeneration given by Owen would not have pleased his antinomian adversaries who considered the Mosaic law superseded and the sins of God's elect invisible to God.

Owen declared, in a direct rebuff to the immediatism espoused by Seventeenth-Century English antinomian writers, that inner peace with God depends on both "an immediate act of the Holy Spirit dwelling in us" testifying to our adoption and to "our own diligence in duties and in the exercise of all grace."[62] Unlike his antinomian opponents, Owen believed in the dual necessity of both receiving divine gifts and performing Christian duties for assurance and sanctification to bear fruit in holy and useful Christian living.

[61] *Works*, 7:274.
[62] *Works*, 7:490.

11

Preparation for Glory: Conflict Against Sin

The first proof of the reality of regeneration, according to Owen, is spiritual-mindedness, and the second proof is unceasing conflict against sin. Owen once likened the unbeliever to a man who never recognizes how strong the current is because he is swimming with the tide of sin. Only the Christian knows how fiercely the current rages because he alone is swimming against the tide. Owen's regimen for the ruin of sin involves lifelong commitment and full use of the means of grace. His approach to conflict with sin stands in stark contrast to the "program" put forward by Eaton, the "grand heresiarch"[1] of English antinomianism. Eaton, as quoted in chapter 2, taught that God neither sees nor chastises the sins of the redeemed and that Christian obedience to the "spiritual" meaning of the moral law flows rather effortlessly from the joy of justification. As one Puritan scholar well observes:

> Eaton construed justification as the portal to moral adulthood. Leaving all tutelage [of the moral law] behind, [they] can be trusted fully to steer themselves. [Though] sometimes their obedience might slacken, now the saints simply 'cannot chuse but to' perform good works. In a way unimagined in Puritan quarters, *the less they worried and strained, the more their power for good would increase*, and works would flow of their own accord. In this vision of effortless discipline, or duties 'voluntarily flowing' from relief and joy, we find at once the core of Eaton's (and of much antino-

[1] Como, Blown by the Spirit, 177.

mian) ethics: Christian morality is virtually automatic. Ethical behavior flows so readily, indeed so 'infallibly' from the saints–and with all its imperfection removed from God's gaze and concern–as to exempt them outright from the law.[2]

Eaton's lax approach is par for the course, as antinomianism is characterized generally by a deficient doctrine and sense of sin.[3] In *The Nature and Causes of Apostasy* (1676), Owen argued that a policy of appeasement toward sin leads to moral and eternal destruction.

> The holiness which the gospel requires will not be kept up or maintained, either in the hearts of lives of men, without a *continual conflict*, warring, contending; and that with all care, diligence, watchfulness and perseverance. To suppose [otherwise] is to deny the Scriptures and [Christian] experience. Satan, sin and the world are continually assaulting and seeking to ruin us. Nothing so promotes the interest of hell and destruction in the world as a presumption that a lazy, slothful performance of some duties and abstinence from some sins, is what God will accept as our obedience. Crucifying of sin, mortifying our inordinate affections, contesting against the world, Satan and the flesh in inward actings of grace and outward duties is what is required of us.[4]

Owen's key treatises treating the Christian's conflict against sin are *Of the Mortification of Sin in Believers* (1656), *Of Temptation* (1658), *The Nature, Power, Deceit, and Prevalency of the Remainders of Indwelling Sin in Believers* (1668), and *On the Dominion of Sin and Grace* (1688). This chapter will treat the last three of these treatises in depth.

Of Temptation

In *Of Temptation* (1658), Owen defines temptation as any seduction toward sin.[5] According to him, God tests Christians by imposing great duties above human strength, great sufferings, or providential occasions to sin, in order to demonstrate human grace or corruption and His restraining or converting grace.[6] Owen believed that every Christian had a "great duty" to prepare for the inevitable hour of temptation when the mind has become entangled through long and frequent solicitations to sin.[7] Chris-

---

[2] Bozeman, *The Precisianist Strain*, 195 (emphasis his).
[3] Packer, *Redemption and Restoration*, 369–70.
[4] *Works*, 7:171–72 (emphasis his).
[5] *Works*, 6:96.
[6] *Works*, 6:93–94.
[7] *Works*, 6:98–99.

tians should seek to avoid temptation through prayer, mortification, and watchfulness.[8]

Owen's treatise was occasioned, in part, by the "spirit of error, giddiness and delusion" and moral "abominations" abounding in the land.[9] Though his theological opponents cannot be clearly identified, Owen was probably answering several antinomian objections against resisting temptation. These seem to be antinomian objections because they are explicable only on the presupposition of essentialism: since regeneration purportedly leaves fallen human faculties untouched, the outbreak of indwelling sin, to the antinomian way of thinking, is inevitable and irresistible.

The first objection is a foolish wresting of James 1:2 to mean that one should not avoid temptations since they are to be counted "all joy." Owen replied that James is discussing providential afflictions sent to test faith, not temptations caused by spiritual negligence.[10] The second objection is drawn from Christ's example of not avoiding temptations. Owen replied that Christ's "temptations are reckoned among the evils that befell him in the days of his flesh," and more importantly, that the level of risk was not comparable because Christ (being sinless) never entered into defilement or entanglement through temptation.[11] A third objection relies on God's promises of deliverance (e.g., 1 Corinthians 10:13 and 2 Peter 2:9) as a safe harbor. Owen skewers this objection by pointing out that the promise is conditional; it is limited to the godly as they walk with God, not as they foolishly put themselves in harm's way:

> The promise is made to them whom temptations befall in their way… not them that willfully fall into them, that run out of their way to meet them. And therefore the devil (as is usually observed), when he tempted our Savior, left out that expression [of Psalm 92] 'all thy ways.'[12]

A fourth objection similarly counts on the doctrine of perseverance. With the Puritan gift for using illustrations from everyday life, Owen considered it shameless presumption to risk temptation merely on account of eternal security: "Is it not madness, for a man willingly to suffer the ship in which he is a passenger to be split on a rock, destroying his cargo, merely because he supposes he shall swim safely to shore on a plank?"[13]

---

[8] *Works*, 6:105–109.
[9] *Works*, 6:89–90.
[10] *Works*, 6:114–15.
[11] *Works*, 6:115–16.
[12] *Works*, 6:116–17.
[13] *Works*, 6:117.

In expounding upon Jesus' admonition to watch and pray, Owen gave five general directions to prevent entry into temptation. The first general direction is to ponder the great danger associated with temptation since temptation and sin are hard to keep apart.[14] Owen warned that otherwise "grief of the Spirit of God, disquietude, loss of peace, and hazard of eternal welfare, lie at the door. Temptation despised will conquer." [15] Lest he appear to attribute success over temptation to human agency, Owen quickly mentioned a second general direction, the necessity of prayer, because only the "power of God" (1 Peter 1:5; John 17:15) can preserve one from temptation. The Christian's vulnerable and overmatched position makes prayer all the more urgent:

> The ways of our temptation are so many, various and imperceptible—the means of it so efficacious and powerful, the entrances of it so deceitful, subtle, insensible and plausible, our weakness, our [heedlessness] so unspeakable—that we cannot in the least keep or preserve ourselves from it. We fail both in wisdom and power for the work.[16]

In the Puritan tradition of 'preaching to oneself,' Owen gave a soliloquy encouraging the saint's conscientious, daily attendance at the throne of grace. Prayer engages God's grace and compassion, kindles faith in God's promises of deliverance, and cultivates a train of graces. Both a prayerful frame of heart and answers to prayer serve as means of preservation.[17]

Owen's third general direction is to watch out for seasons of temptation. He mentioned prosperity, religious formality, self-confidence and "mountaintop" experiences. Regarding the last, Owen comments "A man would think this was the securest condition in the world. But yet very frequently some bitter temptation is now at hand."[18] The fourth general direction is to watch the heart. Owen considered self-knowledge crucial as constitutional traits lend themselves to certain darling sins.[19] A Christian should beware of any occasions of sin. But more is required than a purely defensive posture. Owen recommends storing a sense of God's love in Christ to withstand a concerted assault of temptation:

> But store the heart with a sense of the love of God in Christ, with the eternal design of his grace, with a taste of the blood of Christ, and his

[14] *Works*, 6:123.
[15] *Works*, 6:124.
[16] *Works*, 6:125
[17] *Works*, 6:125–26.
[18] *Works*, 6:129.
[19] *Works*, 6:131–32.

love in shedding it; get a relish of the privileges that we have – our adoption, our justification, acceptation with God; fill your heart with thoughts of the beauty of holiness... and you will have great peace and security from the disturbance of temptations.[20]

If surprised into temptation, one should control his thoughts, expect help from Christ through prayer, "act faith" on God's promises of deliverance, and close the breach as quickly as possible.[21]

Owen observed that graces work in opposition to sin, and the fruit of the Spirit, to the works of the flesh. Every direction for resisting temptation should "itself lie in direct opposition to all the ways and means that temptation can make use of to approach our souls."[22] Spying out the very first approach of temptation is essential so Owen furnished directions for this espionage. First, make an early discovery of temptation's approach. Secondly, ponder that the goal of the temptation is your "utter ruin." Thirdly, take the shield of faith to quench Satan's fiery darts and do not get drawn into argument: "Entertain no parley, no dispute with it, if you would not enter into it."[23]

For the Christian who finds himself even further entangled, Owen gave three specific directions for disentanglement. To begin with, pray expectantly to Christ who is uniquely equipped to help: "Lie down at his feet, make your complaint known to him, beg his assistance, and it will not be in vain."[24] Next, look to God's faithfulness in performing His promises of deliverance and His many resources to that end such as affliction, providence, thwarting of Satan, fresh supplies of grace or removal of the temptation. Then figure out how the temptation entered and "with all speed make up the breach."[25]

The fifth general direction for resisting temptation is to "keep the word of Christ's patience."[26] Universal gospel obedience, for several reasons, is the best preventative against temptation. For one thing, it "will keep the heart in such [an obedient] frame [by exercising graces that] no prevalent temptation can seize it."[27] Universal obedience not only mortifies indwelling sin but also fills the heart with wonderful gospel treasure. Owen mentions "pardon of sin, fruits of holiness, hope of glory, peace with God, joy

[20] *Works*, 6:134.
[21] *Works*, 6:131–34.
[22] *Works*, 6:134.
[23] *Works*, 6:135–36.
[24] *Works*, 6:136.
[25] *Works*, 6:137.
[26] *Works*, 6:138.
[27] *Works*, 6:142.

in the Holy Ghost, and dominion over sin," such that a Christian experiences a "holy contempt" of temptation.[28] Secondly, the universally obedient Christian has "preserving considerations." One is the need to acquit oneself honorably in time of trial *coram Deo*. The other is the dismal prospect of losing Christ's favor and communion.[29] The Seventeenth-Century antinomian view that God neither notices nor punishes the sins of His children found no place in Owen's theology.

Thirdly, the universally obedient Christian also has "preserving principles." Principles differ from considerations in that principles work internally, whereas considerations work externally. Owen gave two examples of such "preserving principles." The first is that faith helps preserve a Christian because it not only empties him of self-reliance but also engages Christ's help.[30] The second preserving principle is a Christian's love for, and consequent desire not to stumble, other Christians.[31] Owen again warned that prayer against particular sins without a settled intention to render universal obedience is futile.[32] Again, he stresses the vital importance of pursuing the appointed means of grace:

> If you neglect the only means prescribed by the Savior, you will certainly enter into temptation and as certainly fall into sin. Do not flatter yourself. It is not any grace received, nor any experience obtained, nor any resolution improved, that will preserve you from evil unless you stand on your watch. If you neglect your duty, God may send heavy affliction or judgment. All your bones will be broken, and all your peace and strength gone in a moment.[33]

Indwelling Sin

Owen's treatise *The Nature, Power, Deceit and Prevalency of the Remainders of Indwelling Sin in Believers* (1668) continued the theme of Christian resistance to sin. The purposes of his treatise are to give Christians "a full and clear acquaintance with the power of this indwelling sin, to stir them up to watchfulness and diligence, to faith and prayer, and to call them to repentance, humility, and self-abasement."[34] Owen considered Romans 7:14–25 as a depiction of mature Christian experience, the dismaying and

---

[28] *Works*, 6:144.
[29] *Works*, 6:144–45.
[30] *Works*, 6:145–46.
[31] *Works*, 6:146.
[32] *Works*, 6:147–48.
[33] *Works*, 6:150–51 (two quotations conflated).
[34] *Works*, 6:156.

ongoing encounter with the "remaining power of indwelling sin."[35] The
first rule of warfare, it has been said, is to know your enemy. Although the
whole course of Christian obedience hinges on the conquest of indwelling sin, Owen found few Christians who study the plague of their own
hearts.[36]

Owen warned of the great efficacy possessed by indwelling sin as a
law. Owen defined "law" less technically as "an operative effective principle, which seems to have the force of a law."[37] As such its fearsome battle
strength derives from eight cumulative factors. First, it seeks to usurp the
dominion of grace at every turn.[38] Secondly, as an internal law or principle,
this traitor lurks in the Christian's very breast. "Men little consider what
a dangerous companion is always at home with them."[39] Thirdly, it is has
power to dispense rewards (i.e., the pleasures of sin) and punishments (i.e.,
self-denial). Its rewards elicit sins of commission; its punishments, sins
of omission.[40] Fourthly, it is meddlesome beyond all reckoning and never
more so than when a Christian earnestly pursues Christian obedience.[41]
Fifthly, it easily manipulates our naturally depraved faculties. Owen spends
so much time belaboring the strength of indwelling sin precisely because
nothing but a full-orbed discovery of its formidable power will prevent
disaster:

> The more they [Christians] find its power, the less they will feel its effects.
> Proportionate also to their discovery will be their earnestness for grace,
> nor will it rise higher. All watchfulness and diligence in obedience will
> be answerable to it. Upon this one hinge of finding out and experiencing
> the power and efficacy of this law of sin, turns the whole course of our
> lives. Ignorance of it breeds senselessness, carelessness, sloth, security and
> pride. Eruptions into great, open, conscience-wasting sin [come] from
> want [lack] of due spiritual consideration of the law [of indwelling sin].[42]

The sixth factor is that indwelling sin is seated in the very heart. For
Owen, grace and sin are principles in the heart whose power increases with
exercise. When seemingly exhausted, grace and sin only grow stronger.
Opening Luke 6:45, Owen points out profound spiritual realities:

[35] *Works*, 6:157.
[36] *Works*, 6:162.
[37] *Works*, 6:158.
[38] *Works*, 6:163.
[39] *Works*, 6:166.
[40] *Works*, 6:164–65.
[41] *Works*, 6:167.
[42] *Works*, 6:168–69.

And it [the heart] is also called a treasure for its abundance. It will never be exhausted; it is not wasted by men's spending on it; yes, the more lavishly men draw out of this treasure, the more it grows and abounds! As men do not spend their grace, but increase it, by exercise, [likewise] do they indwelling sin. The more men exercise their grace in duties of obedience, the more it is strengthened and increased: and the more men exert and put forth the fruits of their lust, the more is that enraged and increased in them; it feeds upon itself, swallows up its own poison and grows. The more men sin, the more are they inclined to sin. It is from the deceitfulness of this law of sin that men persuade themselves that by this or that particular sin they shall so satisfy their lusts that they need sin no more. Every sin increases the *principle*, and fortifies the habit of sinning.[43]

The heart is quite dangerous because it is both unsearchable and incomparably deceitful. As a result, the need to resist and mortify sin is never-ending:

The work must be endless in this lifetime. If we give over, we shall quickly see the enemy exerting himself with new strength and vigor. Under great affliction or eminent enjoyment of communion with Christ, we may have been ready to [conclude] there was an end of sin, that it was gone and dead forever; but have we not found the contrary by experience?[44]

A seventh contributory factor is indwelling sin's implacable, universal, and constant enmity against God. Its enmity is implacable because it cannot be reconciled to Him. Nothing but continual fighting can be expected: "Here lies no small part of its power—it can admit of no terms of peace."[45] Its enmity is universal because it is directed against God's grace, holiness, and authority. Its enmity is constant because its opposition is relentless.[46]

An eighth contributory factor is its two-pronged assault on grace. The first prong of attack is to give the Christian a secret aversion to holy duties, with the holier the duty, the greater the aversion. Owen noticed this especially in private prayer.

A secret striving will be in [the heart] about close and cordial dealing with God, unless the hand of God in His Spirit is high and strong on his soul. Even when convictions, sense of duty, dear and real esteem of God and communion with Him have carried the soul into the closet, yet if the vigor and power of spiritual life is not constantly at work, there will be

---

[43] *Works*, 6:170.
[44] *Works*, 6:175.
[45] *Works*, 6:177.
[46] *Works*, 6:180–81.

a secret loathness [aversion] to duty; yes, sometimes a violent contrary inclination so strong that the soul would rather do anything else.[47]

Owen furnished five directions for counteracting the secret aversion to Christian duty which he regarded as a slippery slope toward backsliding and even apostasy.[48]

1. The great means to prevent this aversion is the constant keeping of the soul in a universally holy frame. A universal respect to all God's commandments is the only preservation from shame.

2. Make sure grace precedes aversion in every duty. Prevent indwelling sin from parleying [reasoning, disputing] with the soul by vigorous, holy, violent stirring up of the graces peculiarly required in that duty.

3. Never allow indwelling sin a conquest.

4. Let this aversion to spiritual duties keep you humble.

5. Work to delight your mind in the spiritual beauty of obedience and communion with God.[49]

A second prong of indwelling sin's attack is to wage war by force and deceit. Owen marks out four progressive steps in its use of force. The first degree lies in a "hidden, habitual propensity" to embrace every proffered temptation.[50] Indwelling sin is so potent that it sometimes turns mortification on its head: "Yes, to manifest its power, [even] when the soul is seriously engaged in the mortification of any sin, it will lead it away into a dalliance with that very sin whose ruin it is seeking."[51] The second forceful step is its vigorous pursuit of sin. Indwelling sin rebels against universal obedience by diverting the Christian's mind from his Christian duties.[52] Owen asks, What could be more humbling?

> There is nothing so suited as to bring us to self-abasement and to teach us to walk humbly and mournfully before God. It is no small evidence of grace when one is willing to search out the secret corruption of the heart as readily as the doctrines of God's grace and pardon of sin. Breaking up the fallow ground of their hearts is no less necessary than the other

[47] *Works*, 6:183–84.
[48] *Works*, 6:184–85.
[49] *Works*, 6:185–88.
[50] *Works*, 6:189–95.
[51] *Works*, 6:192.
[52] *Works*, 6:195–98.

and will produce due reverence of God and an unwillingness to censure others.[53]

The third step of violence is that of taking the Christian captive. Owen comments, "Success is the greatest evidence of power, and leading captive in war is the height of success."[54] Though the renewed will may consent to the sin that causes captivity, it does not consent to the captivity itself. That indwelling sin can lead the Christian captive for a season despite the opposition of his renewed will is further proof of great power:[55]

> Sometimes one thinks or hopes that he may through grace be utterly freed from this troublesome inmate. Upon sweet enjoyment of God, full supply of grace, return from wandering, deep affliction, or thorough humiliation, he begins to hope that he shall now be freed from the law of sin; but after a while it perceives that [the situation] is quite otherwise. Sin acts again, makes good its old station; and he finds that whether he will or not, he must bear its yoke. This makes him sigh and cry out for deliverance.[56]

The fourth and final act of violence is enragement. Owen likened sin unleashed in the heart to a wild runaway horse, who casts offs his rider, ignores every obstacle in his path, and bolts away.[57] With sin so prone to career out of control, Owen counsels nip-it-in-the-bud defense:

> The great wisdom and security in dealing with indwelling sin is to put a violent stop to its beginnings, its first motions and actions. Venture all on the first attempt. Die rather than yield one step to it. You never would have experienced the fury of sin unless you had been content to dally with it.[58]

Owen believed that indwelling sin's stealth campaign has even greater effectiveness because it proceeds by degrees in entangling the mind, so that the other faculties play follow-the-leader:

> The ground of this efficacy is that sin deceives the mind. When sin attempts any other way of entrance into the soul, as by the affections, the mind, retaining sovereignty, is able to check and control them. But when

---

[53] *Works*, 6:200–201.
[54] *Works*, 6:202.
[55] *Works*, 6:205.
[56] *Works*, 6:204.
[57] *Works*, 6:208, 210.
[58] *Works*, 6:208.

the mind or understanding, the leading faculty of the soul, is tainted, whatever it seizes on, the will and affections rush after.[59]

James 1:14–15 describes the five stages of the deceitfulness of sin: distraction, enticement, conception, accomplishment, and death. Owen focused on the first three stages since for true believers, God usually prevents the fourth and always prevents the last.[60] Christians should be thankful that God providentially hinders sin[61] and permits it only insofar as necessary to exercise Christian graces, but never so far as to "disannul the covenant relationship."[62]

Indwelling sin distracts the mind in two basic ways. First, it makes light of sin. It infers, from the assurance of pardon for sin, heedlessness rather than holiness.[63] Secondly, it preoccupies the mind with worldly matters.[64] The Christian becomes especially distracted from prayer. Meditation and prayer, both designed to weaken and subdue sin, discover the secret workings of sin, present sin in its horrid visage, and serve as means of obtaining grace to help in time of need.[65] Indwelling sin counterattacks by causing weariness in prayer or by suggesting less effective—and less demanding—means of grace.[66]

The requisite standard of performance for Christian duty is nothing less than universal obedience.[67] By universal obedience, Owen meant full and complete obedience with respect to all God's commands motivated by faith and sincerity for God's glory.[68] Sin's devious strategies involve encouragement to settle for good intentions or formality in duty.[69] Under this regimen, nothing ensues but spiritual sloth and dereliction of duty.[70] The second stage in the deceitfulness of sin is enticement. Indwelling sin entices the heart through inspiring frequent evil imaginations, which cause secret delight and prompt ready excuses.[71] Indwelling sin shows the bait of sin while hiding the hook:

---

[59] *Works*, 6:213.
[60] *Works*, 6:215–16.
[61] *Works*, 6:260–78.
[62] *Works*, 7:557.
[63] *Works*, 6:218–21.
[64] *Works*, 6:222–23.
[65] *Works*, 6:225–27.
[66] *Works*, 6:229–30. He considers public and family prayer less effective.
[67] *Works*, 6:234.
[68] *Works*, 6:234–36.
[69] *Works*, 6:236–42.
[70] *Works*, 6:242–43.
[71] *Works*, 6:245–47.

Hopes of pardon shall be used to hide it; and future repentance shall hide it; and present importunity of lust shall hide it; occasions and opportunities shall hide it; surprises into sin shall hide it; extenuation of sin shall hide it; balancing of duties against it shall hide it; fixing the imagination on present objects shall hide it; desperate resolutions to venture the uttermost for the enjoyment of the lust in its pleasures and profits shall hide it.[72]

For the promotion of universal obedience, Owen recommends mortification of sin (see chapter 12), together with meditation on the "vileness, the demerit and punishment of sin as represented in the cross, the blood, the death of Christ."[73]

The third stage of the deceitfulness of sin is the conception of actual sin. Conception involves the consent of the will, though such consent by a Christian is always ambivalent in the sense that the renewed will graciously and invariably remains in loyal opposition. Owen warned that habitual consent makes for greater future readiness.[74] Indwelling sin perverts the order and method of the gospel. The gospel promises pardon with a view to universal obedience (1 John 2:1–2), whereas indwelling sin promises sin with a view to the supposed exaltation of pardoning grace.[75] Again, much of indwelling sin's power comes from its working imperceptibly and gradually:

It works the soul insensibly off from the mystery of the law of grace–to look for salvation as if we unprofitable servants had never performed any duty [by] resting on sovereign mercy through the blood of Christ; and to attend to duties with all diligence as though we looked for no mercy.[76]

Owen observes that many men in Scripture unexpectedly fell into grievous sin after long-term obedience and enjoyment of God's "great and stupendous mercies" and that many Christians and churches begin the Christian life better than they finish it.[77] Nevertheless, he insists that the covenant of grace abundantly provides for constant Christian growth through the ministry of the word, continual and inexhaustible supplies of grace, and Christ's intercession.[78] As might well be expected, the same culprits that

---

[72] *Works*, 6:249.
[73] *Works*, 6:250.
[74] *Works*, 6:252.
[75] *Works*, 6:254–55.
[76] *Works*, 6:256.
[77] *Works*, 6:279–84.
[78] *Works*, 6:284–89.

cause spiritual decay also strengthen the hand of indwelling sin: sloth, weariness, rationalizations, heedlessness, worldliness, bad Christian examples, secret sins, prayerlessness, hardening of heart, and failure to improve gospel light.[79] As for failure to improve one's gospel knowledge, Owen sounds this somber warning:

> When men have attained to a deeper and clearer discovery of evangelical truths, they will lose the power of truths previously known unless they labor to have the power of these new discoveries prevailing in their hearts. By means of such [failure] many have withered from humble, close walking with God into an empty and barren profession.[80]

Owen saw sin's total degradation of the *imago Dei* reflected particularly in the abominations of the unregenerate, such as infanticide.[81] Finally, indwelling demonstrates power by often squelching legal convictions, in other words, the convictions of sin caused through the preparatory work of the law.[82]

The Dominion of Sin and Grace

In *Indwelling Sin* (1668), Owen marshalled weighty arguments to demonstrate the formidable power and long reach of indwelling sin. His posthumously published treatise *On the Dominion of Sin and Grace* (1688) provides a salutary counterbalance to *Indwelling Sin* (1668) inasmuch as he expresses more optimism that sin, true to God's promise, will not have dominion over the Christian. Sin usurped the dominion of grace as a result of the Fall.[83] God punished man by permitting natural depravity whereby man is spiritually impotent. Every person is either under the dominion of sin or grace.[84] Because there is no middle ground, it is imperative to know which dominion one is under.[85] Owen gave three tests for proving the dominion of sin. The first is whether sin rules every faculty.[86] The second test is whether sin delights the heart so as to prevent repentance.[87] The fi-

---

[79] *Works*, 6:301.
[80] *Works*, 6:302.
[81] *Works*, 6:305.
[82] *Works*, 6:313–22.
[83] *Works*, 7:509.
[84] *Works*, 7:508.
[85] *Works*, 7:513.
[86] *Works*, 7:519.
[87] *Works*, 7:525.

nal test is whether mortification of sin suffers neglect. The indulgence of a darling sin or hardness of heart serves as a telltale sign of sin's dominion.[88]

What is most shocking about Owen's treatment of the dominion of sin is how far a Christian may proceed under the dominion of sin without committing final apostasy. Owen mentioned four fact patterns one might call rebuttable presumptions[89] of the dominion of sin. A rebuttable presumption is a highly probable assumption but one that can still be overcome by a greater weight of contrary evidence. These rebuttable presumptions of the dominion of sin over a Christian are:

1. The commission of great, actual sins does not lead to any peculiar humiliation.

2. The guilt of one sin fails to make a person watchful against others.

3. A fall into spiritual deadness and decays is found to be irrecoverable by ordinary means of grace, even that of preaching.

4. Complacency in a barren profession is unaccompanied by any profit from God's word.[90]

Owen clearly stated that a Christian under the dominion of sin cannot possibly enjoy assurance of salvation. Yet he still encouraged the backslider to pursue recovery with all his might, given several assurances from Scripture that sin will not have dominion over him. The first is that the state of regeneration (see chapter 9) not only casts out the law's power to condemn but also curtails the power of sin.[91] God uses the gospel to communicate spiritual strength (grace) to believers for dethroning sin in a way of duty:

> And sin must be really dethroned by the powerful acting of grace in us, and that in a way of duty in ourselves. We are absolved, quitted, freed from the rule of sin, as to its pretended right and title, by the promise of the gospel; for thereby are we freed and discharged from the rule of the law, wherein all the title of sin to dominion is founded, for 'the strength of the law is sin:' but we are freed from it, as to its internal power and exercise of its dominion, by internal spiritual grace and strength in its due exercise.[92]

---

[88] *Works*, 7:531–34.

[89] *Works*, 7:540. Owen does not use the term but I borrow it from legal usage because it seems fitting. He also gives ten irrebuttable presumptions (Works, 7:541).

[90] *Works*, 7:537–40.

[91] *Works*, 7:545.

[92] *Works*, 7:546–47.

Reiterating the same point, Owen declares that actual grace for the subduing of sin is communicated to believers "in a way of concurrence with
us in the discharge of our duties."[93] In this context Owen makes the very
important distinction between preparation for grace and preparation for
glory. The former, not involving human cooperation, is monergistic; the
latter is synergistic and does entail human cooperation or, more precisely,
divine concurrence in the believer's performance of spiritual duties:

> *Remember always the way and method of the operation of divine grace and
> spiritual aids.* It is true, in our first conversion to God, we are as it were
> surprised by a mighty act of sovereign grace, changing our hearts, renew-
> ing our minds, and quickening us with a principle of spiritual life. Ordi-
> narily, many things are required of us in a way of duty in order thereunto;
> and many previous operations of grace in our minds, in illumination and
> in the sense of sin [conviction of sin], do materially and passively dis-
> pose us thereunto, as wood when it is dried is disposed to firing; but the
> work itself is performed by an immediate act of divine power, without
> any active cooperation on our part. But this is not the law or rule of the
> communication or operation of actual grace for the subduing of sin. It
> is given in a way of concurrence with us in the discharge of our duties;
> and when we are sedulous in them, we may be sure we shall not fail of
> divine assistance, according to the established rule of the administra-
> tion of gospel grace. If, therefore, we complain that we find not the aids
> mentioned, and if at the same time we are not diligent in attendance on
> all the duties whereby sin may be mortified in us, we exceedingly injure
> the grace of God.[94]

The next assurance is that gracious motives do prove effective "in a way
of duty" and in all the soul's "work and duty" to ruin sin. Five such motives
are cited: the love of God and Christ, the whole work and end of Christ's
mediation, the ready assistances of the Holy Spirit, gospel promises, and
the believer's past experiences.[95] The final assurance is our union with
Christ through the gospel whereby we partake of Him and His benefits.

Recognize, however, that in Owen's theology a merely negative approach to conflict with sin, that is, mortification alone, will not suffice to
overthrow the dominion of sin. Like Calvin, Owen insisted that effective
sanctification requires both mortification and vivification.[96] The path of
duty lies in working for the ruin of sin, running directly to and through the
appointed means of grace:

[93] *Works*, 7:549.
[94] Ibid. (emphasis his).
[95] *Works*, 7:551.
[96] *Works*, 7:554.

The instrumental cause of this freedom [from sin] is the duty of believers themselves in and for the destruction of sin.... This is one of the principal ends of all our religious duties – of prayer, of fasting, of meditation, of watchfulness toward all other duties of obedience; they are all designed to prevent and ruin the interest of sin in us. We are called to fight and contend.... And certainly [what God has appointed and commanded] as the great end of lifelong and constant endeavor is to us of highest importance.[97]

This regimen for the ruin of sin involves lifelong commitment and hard work. Why didn't God just glorify the Christian at the point of regeneration? Owen sees a silver lining: "Our continued struggle with sin exercises our graces and puts a luster on our obedience, humbles us, makes us love Christ all the more, and sweetens our heavenly reward."[98]

Owen closes his treatise by giving specific directions to prevent sin from gaining the upper hand. First, nip sin in the bud before it becomes habitual by watching and practicing severe and diligent mortification. Secondly, beware lest secret sins develop into presumptuous ones. Thirdly, keep the heart tender and teachable under the word of God. Fourthly, hate false peace.[99] Fifthly, continually pray to Christ for deliverance especially when tempted. Lastly, remember that due gratitude for the gift of salvation is the most effectual motive for universal obedience and holiness."[100]

Owen insisted that conflict of sin must not be merely negative through mortification, but positive through vivification of graces. But he held equally to the converse: vivification of graces still required mortification to prove effective in the conflict against sin. In the next chapter, his view regarding the necessity and biblical methodology for mortification of sin will appear.

Summary

Owen's regimen for the ruin of sin, which requires grace to be actualized in duty, is a polar opposite to that of Eaton. Owen insisted that gospel holiness necessitated the diligent application of the means of grace and unceasing warfare against sin, while Eaton believed that Christian obe-

---

[97] Ibid.

[98] *Works*, 7:556. Here again Owen parted company with antinomians in regarding both fear of punishment and hope of rewards as legitimate Christian motives.

[99] The concept of true peace (spoken by God to the conscience) and false peace (spoken by man to himself) is delineated in chapter 12.

[100] *Works*, 7:558–60.

dience to the "spiritual" meaning of the moral law would spontaneously emerge from the joy of justification.

In his treatise *Of Temptation* (1658), Owen declared resistance to temptation an indispensable Christian duty. The applicable means of grace include prayer, mortification of sin, and watching. He dismissed as foolish several antinomian pleas against resistance to temptation, such as reliance on God's promises of deliverance or preservation of the saints. Owen stressed the vital importance of staunchly resisting the first entrances of temptation especially because they are so "deceitful, subtle, insensible and plausible." Directions included recognition of grave danger, urgent prayer in the face of human frailty, wariness of certain predictable seasons of temptation, and knowing one's darling sins. He pointed out the key principle that graces work in direct opposition to sin. Universal gospel obedience, motivated by faith and love, serves as the best preservation against temptation and will even give the Christian a "holy contempt" of sinning. Owen's prescription of obedience as the main cure for temptation parted company with the antinomian view that God neither saw nor punished the sins of His elect.

His treatise *Indwelling Sin* (1668) stressed the crucial importance for a Christian to realize the plague of his own heart. Indwelling sin derives fearsome battle strength because it is an internal law empowered to dispense rewards and punishments that gains strength through the commission of sin, easily manipulates human faculties, and expresses its hatred of God by refusing to accommodate grace. It also pursues a powerful, two-pronged attack by creating a secret distaste for holy duties, especially private prayer, and by waging a war of force and deceit. Indwelling sin makes a show of force by causing "surprisals" of sin, diverting the mind from duty, and even filling a Christian under its power with a rage to commit sin, heedless of consequences. Owen counseled nipping sin in the bud because even small beginnings are so apt to career out of control. Indwelling sin pushes the Christian through four of the five worsening stages described in James 1:14–15 (distraction from duty, enticement through the power of imagination, conception of sin through consent of the divided will, and actual commission of sin), but not to the fifth state of death (since though through the covenant of grace, the Christian is spared spiritual destruction, though not God's temporal chastisement). Owen made the profound point, which would seem to be equally applicable to the antinomian objections against resisting temptation, that indwelling sin perverts the order and method of the gospel: the gospel promises pardon with a view to universal obedience, whereas indwelling sin promises sin for the supposed exaltation of pardoning grace. Christians must struggle to keep the power of new gospel discoveries alive in their hearts.

On the Dominion of Sin and Grace (1688) serves as a counterweight to *Indwelling Sin* (1668) by expressing more optimism that God will keep His promise not to let sin have dominion over the Christian. Owen based his confidence in the dominion of grace on the efficacy of regeneration, the bond of grace and duty culminating in the dethronement of sin, potent motives such as love for God and Christ, gratitude for deliverance from sin, and the believer's union with Christ. Even so, it is shocking to read how far Owen believes a true Christian can sink into the mire of sin. He may commit great sins, experience spiritual decays and deadness, and live out a barren profession of faith. Though Owen expects his return from backsliding under the covenant of grace, conflict of sin must not be merely negative through mortification, but positive through vivification of graces. Continual conflict with sin serves God's larger purposes of exercising Christian graces like humility and love, showcasing Christian obedience, and creating a longing for heaven.

12

Preparation for Glory: The Mortification of Sin

And this is the reason why we have so many withering professors among us, decayed in their graces, fruitless in their lives, and every way conformed to the world.[1]

True evangelical mortification is almost lost amongst us.[2]

It [unmortified sin] will take away a man's usefulness in his generation. His works, his endeavors, his labors seldom receive blessing from God. If he be a preacher, God commonly blows upon his ministry, that he should labor in the fire and not be honored with any success or doing any work for God. The world is at this day full of poor withering professors. How few there are that walk in any beauty or glory! How barren, how useless are they for the most part! Many men harbor spirit-devouring lusts in their bosoms, that lie at the root of their obedience, and corrode and weaken it day by day. All graces are prejudiced and [all success blasted].[3]

The Antinomian Distaste for Mortification

Seventeenth-Century antinomian writers grossly misunderstood mortification as a needless exercise in futility. Antinomian Error 34, for instance, declares that, "We are not to pray against all sin, because the old

[1] *Works*, 3:45.
[2] *Works*, 6:14.
[3] *Works*, 6:56.

man is in us, and must be, and why should we pray against that which cannot be avoided?"[4] Similarly, Unsavoury Speech 7, compiled by the Newtown Synod, asserts, "I know I am Christ's, not because I do crucify the lusts of the flesh, but because I do not crucify them, but believe in Christ that crucified my lusts for me."[5] There were probably two reasons for these antinomian pronouncements. The first is their essentialist view of regeneration. Because they misconstrued regeneration not as the renewal of human faculties, but as the peaceful coexistence side-by-side of the old man and the divine essence, their interpretation was that indwelling sin cannot be resisted or mortified. And why should mortification matter much anyway if God cannot see their sins? The second reason for their rejection was their general disparagement of Christian duties in general and of mortification in particular. In one remarkable outburst, Eaton accused Puritans practicing mortification of "resting upon their dead faith principally by works," defined as "a preposterous sanctification, repentance, mortification, grace and graces."[6] By mortification Eaton claimed that "[the Puritans] withdraw people from Christ to hang upon their own works and doings" and "teach a false bastard sanctification."[7] These are strong fighting words that Owen, by insisting on the urgency of mortification, will meet head-on, though whether Owen had Eaton specifically in mind is anyone's guess.

Vast Importance of Mortification for Owen

The opening quotations above, from two of Owen's treatises, *Of the Mortification of Sin in Believers* (1658) and *Pneumatologia* (1674), show the great weight he placed on the grace and duty of Christian mortification. Without a constant course of mortification, of dying daily to sin and self, Owen considered a gracious Christian walk, even more a fruitful ministry, impossible. The former treatise is an extended exposition of Romans 8:13—"If you are living according to the flesh, you must die but if ye through the Spirit do mortify the deeds of the body, ye shall live." Owen dealt with both clauses of the verse. As to the first clause, he concludes that, "By this 'walking in the flesh' I understand not, at least not principally, the committing of actual sins, but a compliance with the principle or habit of sin prevailing in depraved, unsanctified nature, allowing it a predominancy in the heart and affections."[8] His interpretation of the second

---

[4] Hall, *The Antinomian Controversy*, 227.
[5] Ibid., 246.
[6] Como, *Blown by the Spirit*, 195.
[7] Ibid.
[8] *Works*, 3:543.

clause proceeded element by element. His paraphrase reads: "If [when] ye [Christian believers] through the Spirit [by means of the Holy Spirit] mortify [kill, or sap the strength of] the deeds of the body [the works of indwelling sin as set forth, for example, in Galatians 5:19], ye shall live [not only live eternally, but also experience joy, comfort and vigor in one's present spiritual life in Christ]."[9]

Owen derived three principles from his interpretation. First, mortification of indwelling sin, to prevent the eruption of sinful behavior, is the constant duty of believers.[10] Second, the "vigor, comfort and power" of one's Christian walk depends on mortification."[11] Third, in criticizing the Roman Catholic approach to mortification, Owen declares, "Mortification, from a self-strength, carried on by ways of self-invention, with the end of self-righteousness obtained, is the soul and substance of all false religion in the world."[12]

Owen assigned six reasons why mortification is the Christian's constant duty. To begin with, indwelling sin continues to be present in believers. Based upon 1 John 1:8, Owen rejected the possibility of Christian perfection.[13] In addition, indwelling sin exerts considerable power. Interpreting Romans 7:14–25 as typical of Christian experience, Owen warns that, "Just as still waters run deep, sin is usually most active when least suspected."[14] Moreover, indwelling sin is deceitful and destructive. Citing David and Solomon's fearful lapses, he argued in effect that if you give sin an inch, it will take a mile, and do so almost imperceptibly until it is too late to recover.[15] Further, because God grants regeneration to enable Christian opposition to sin and lust, the practice of mortification serves to prove one's sincerity *coram Deo*. Next, grace has to be appropriated. Owen asserts the equivalent of "use it or lose it." Grace flourishes through exercise but withers through neglect. Finally, Christians need to grow in grace. Sin, says Owen, will oppose every act of holiness and every degree of growth in grace: "Let not that man think that he makes any progress in holiness who walks not over the bellies of his lusts."[16] He also warns:

To use the blood of Christ, which is given to cleanse us, 1 Jn. 1:7, Tit. 2:14; the exaltation of Christ, which is to give us repentance, Acts 5:31;

[9] *Works*, 6:5–9.
[10] *Works*, 6:8.
[11] *Works*, 6:9.
[12] *Works*, 6:7.
[13] *Works*, 6:10.
[14] *Works*, 6:11.
[15] *Works*, 6:12.
[16] *Works*, 6:14.

the doctrine of grace, which teaches us to deny all ungodliness, Tit. 2:11–12, to countenance sin, is a rebellion that will break the bones.[17]

Dying daily to sin and self, then, is make or break for Christian growth in holiness and effectiveness in ministry.

A Divine Grace and a Christian Duty

Against Roman Catholicism and Anglican moralism, Owen stressed the necessity, sufficiency, and efficacy of the Holy Spirit in this "gift" of mortification.[18] He anticipated though an objection: How can a Christian possibly be exhorted to mortify sin if mortification is the work of the Holy Spirit alone? Although Owen indicated that the motive of his writing *Of the Mortification of Sin in Believers* (1658) was mainly to oppose self-mortification,[19] the only plausible explanation of this particular objection is that it comes from an antinomian source. Three facts support this conclusion: Antinomian Error 34 demonstrates the fatalistic view of sin that led antinomians to oppose the practice of mortification. Eaton thought the practice of mortification promoted a "false bastard sanctification." Unsavory Speech 7 evinces that antinomians denied all human agency in mortification on the theory that Christ did all the work. In reply, Owen points out from Philippians 2:13 that the Holy Spirit normally works in and through renewed human faculties for mortification of sin:

> He doth not so work our mortification in us as not to keep it still an act of our *obedience*. The Holy Ghost works in us and upon us, as we are fit to be wrought in and upon; that is, so as to preserve our liberty and free obedience. He works upon our understandings, wills, consciences, and affections, agreeably to their own natures; he works *in us* and *with us*, not *against us* or *without us*; so that his assistance is an encouragement as to the facilitating of the work, and no occasion of neglect as to the work itself.[20]

Note Owen's key point that the Holy Spirit normally promotes mortification in a Christian through his renewed faculties such that his liberty is

---

[17] *Works*, 6:15.

[18] *Works*, 6:18–19.

[19] *Works*, 6:7.

[20] *Works*, 6:20 (emphasis his). Owen discusses the various aspects of the Holy Spirit's work of mortification in believers under the categories of conviction of sin, regeneration and sanctification, purging and refinement, baptism into Christ's death, faith and hope, and intercession.

preserved, for the Holy Spirit "works *in us* and *with us*, not *against us* or *without us.*"

Owen began by defining mortification negatively. First, it is not the total destruction of the sin nature, for that will not occur until glorification. Secondly, neither does it consist in mere legal (or moral) reformation (see Chapter 7). Thirdly, improvement of one's natural temperament does not qualify. Fourthly, exchanging one type of sin for another, as when an old man pursues wealth rather than youthful lusts, does not count as mortification. Finally, mortification does not consist in occasional victories over sin, especially when motivated by a dreadful bout of sin or pressing affliction.[21]

Owen then identified the three essential elements of mortification. The first is habitual weakening of lust by the habitual strengthening of grace. Each carnal lust must be weakened by the cultivation of its gracious opposite: "By the implanting and growth of humility is pride weakened, passion by patience, uncleanness by purity of mind and conscience, and love of this world by heavenly-mindedness."[22] The second is constant warfare against sin. Owen declared that this warfare must take place promptly and vigorously through full use of the means of grace. Great spiritual wisdom consists in learning the ways, wiles, methods, advantages and occasions of sin's success. The third element is frequent victory over sin. Owen insists that effective mortification leads to unbroken peace with God:

> When lust is weakened in the root and principle, that is, motions and actions are fewer and weaker than formerly, so that they are not able to hinder his duty nor interrupt his peace, then sin is mortified in some considerable measure and, notwithstanding all its opposition, a man may have peace with God all his days.[23]

Directions to the Practice of Mortification

Owen gave both general principles and specific directions for mortification. Two general principles are the necessity of conversion and "universal" obedience:

> Without sincerity and diligence in a universality of obedience, there is no mortification of any one perplexing lust to be obtained. 2 Cor. 7:1 exhorts, 'Let us cleanse ourselves from *all* defilement of flesh and spirit, perfecting holiness in the fear of God." So, then, it is not only an intense opposition to this or that particular lust, but a universal humble frame

[21] *Works*, 6:24–27.
[22] *Works*, 6:32.
[23] Ibid.

and temper of heart, with watchfulness over every evil and for the performance of every duty, that is acceptable.[24]

Two very important implications follow from the requirement of universal
obedience. One is that mortification of a lust will not succeed if a Christian
neglects vivification, or the use of positive means of grace, such as Scripture
reading, prayer, and meditation.[25] The other implication is that mortification must be motivated by universal hatred of all sin, not merely desire to
be rid of certain sins:

> Hatred of sin as sin, not only as galling or disquieting, a sense of the love
> of Christ in the cross, lie at the bottom of all true spiritual mortification.
> If you hate sin as sin, every evil way, you will be no less watchful against
> every thing that grieves and disquiets the Spirit of God, than against that
> which grieves and disquiets your own soul.[26]

Owen's stricture rules out a "pick and choose" approach and insists on "all
or nothing."

In *Of the Mortification of Sin in Believers* (1658), Owen supplied ten
specific directions for the practice of mortification. The first direction is to
look for dangerous symptoms of a prevailing lust. He mentioned four such
symptoms: (1) The sin has long resided in the heart; (2) The individual
secretly longs to keep sinning; (3) The sin often prevails; (4) The person's
major concern is only fear of punishment. (Owen declared that when a
Christian resists sin only from fear of consequences, sin has already taken
over the will. He also noted that many gospel principles motivate Christian obedience: the death of Christ, the love of God, the detestable nature
of sin, the preciousness of communion with God, and deep-seated abhor-
rence of sin.); and (5) the person displays lack of repentance, ingratitude to
God, or resistance to divine chastisement.

The second direction is to meditate on the guilt, danger and evil of sin.
Citing Romans 6:1–2, Owen warns that indwelling sin seeks to extenuate
the guilt of actual sin, whereas grace seeks rather to aggravate one's guilt.
Four dangers emanate from sin: hardening of the heart, great judgments,
loss of peace and strength, and even total apostasy. Sin not only destroys
a Christian's fruitfulness and graces, but grieves the Holy Spirit. Owen
counsels:

> Among those who walk with God, there is no greater motive and incen-
> tive unto universal holiness, and the preserving of their hearts and spirits

[24] *Works*, 6:42 (emphasis his).
[25] *Works*, 6:41.
[26] Ibid.

in all purity and cleanness, than this, that the blessed Spirit, who hath undertaken to dwell in them as temples of God, and to preserve them meet for Him who so dwells in them, is continually considering what they give entertainment in their hearts to, and rejoices when His temple is kept undefiled.[27]

The third direction is to come willingly under conviction of sin. According to Owen, there are three sources of conviction: the law, the gospel, and God's character. Ask yourself, "Is this the return I make to the Father for his love, to the Son for his blood, to the Holy Ghost for his grace?"[28] Conviction from God's character looks at His infinite patience and forbearance and His gracious dealings in "providences, deliverances, afflictions, mercies and enjoyments."[29] The fourth direction is to long for deliverance from the rule of sin: "Longing, breathing and panting after deliverance is a grace in itself, that has a mighty power to conform the soul into the likeness of the thing longed after."[30] This practice, wrote Owen, will make one watchful and ready to exercise whatever grace has been granted for mortification. The fifth specific direction is to ascertain whether the perplexing sin lies deep in one's natural constitution. Deeprooted sins call for "extraordinary watchfulness, care and diligence," lest sin gain the upper hand.[31] Owen recommended Paul's practice of keeping his body under submission (1 Corinthians 9:27) but without making the Roman Catholic mistake of attributing efficacy to the ordinance itself.[32] The sixth direction is to avoid opportunities to sin: "He who dares to dally with occasions of sin will dare to sin. He who will venture upon temptations to wickedness will venture upon wickedness."[33] The seventh direction is to rise up against the first signs of sinning. Owen counsels using one's full strength to nip sin in the bud, since sin will otherwise wreak havoc:

> Rise up with all thy strength against it, with no less indignation than if it had fully accomplished what it aims at. Consider what an unclean thought would have; it would have thee roll thyself in folly and filth. Ask envy what it would have: murder and destruction is at the end of it.[34]

---

[27] *Works*, 6:55.
[28] *Works*, 6:58.
[29] *Works*, 6:59.
[30] Ibid.
[31] *Works*, 6:60.
[32] *Works*, 6:61.
[33] *Works*, 6:62.
[34] Ibid.

The eighth direction is to humble oneself by meditating on Scripture and considering God's excellent majesty and our infinite distance from Him. Owen argued that this frame of heart is the most important to be cultivated for the mortification of sin:[35] "Will not a due apprehension of this inconceivable greatness of God, and that infinite distance wherein we stand from Him, fill the soul with a holy and awful fear of Him, so as to keep it in a frame unsuited to the thriving or flourishing of any lust whatever?"[36] The ninth direction is to "take heed that you do not speak peace to yourself before God speaks it."[37] It is absolutely critical whether God speaks peace to someone or he merely speaks it to himself. When men speak peace to themselves, these six factors are usually present:

1. Their peace is easily disturbed.

2. They do not detest sin and self.

3. They heal their wounds slightly (Jeremiah 7:14).

4. There is usually haste rather than waiting on the Lord.

5. There is no humiliation for sin and no changed life.

6. They lack an equal respect to all of God's commandments so that other serious sin remains to be mortified.[38]

By contrast, when God in His absolute sovereignty speaks, these seven criteria are normally found:

1. Sin and self are detested.

2. The Holy Spirit gives life and power to the application of Scripture promises.

3. God usually, but not always, requires waiting on Him.

4. God restores the soul's rest.

5. There is humiliation for sin, a discovery of God's love, and a heartfelt desire not to repeat folly.

6. God speaks with irresistible power.

7. Christ speaks recognizably and His sheep know His voice (John 10:4).[39]

---

35 *Works*, 6:63.
36 *Works*, 6:70.
37 Ibid.
38 *Works*, 6:70–77.
39 *Works*, 6:70–78.

The tenth and the most important direction is to "act" faith in "Christ crucified and slain" for the killing of sin.[40] This direction requires consideration of Christ's provision to purge sin, your expectation of relief, His mercy as High Priest, and His faithfulness in keeping promises. According to Owen, an expectation of relief has two major advantages: it enlists Christ for "full and speedy assistance" and each Christian for diligent use of the means for conformity to Christ.[41]

The Holy Spirit's Work in Mortification

Does Owen's use of such detailed and elaborate directions for mortification lay him open to the charge of practicing self-mortification himself? Certainly Eaton lodged a heated protest that Puritan promotion of mortification serves only to "withdraw people from Christ to hang upon their own works and doings." To distinguish his approach from Roman Catholic self-mortification, Owen emphasizes that mortification, although a Christian duty, is also a grace carried on and accomplished by the Holy Spirit:

1. He alone clearly and fully convinces the heart of the evil and guilt and danger of the corruption, lust, or sin to be mortified.

2. The Spirit alone reveals to us the fullness of Christ for our relief.

3. The Spirit alone establishes the heart in expectation of relief from Christ.

4. The Spirit alone brings the cross of Christ into our hearts with its sin-killing power.

5. The Spirit is the author and finisher of our sanctification.

6. In all the soul's addresses to God in this condition, it has the support of the Spirit [of supplications].[42]

The Indispensable Role of Love

This tenth direction ends Owen's treatise *Of the Mortification of Sin in Believers* (1658), but it would be a serious mistake to assume that this represents his most mature reflection on mortification. Other modern studies on his view of mortification have not taken into account Owen's richer exposition in *Pneumatologia* (1674), where he discusses for the first time

---

[40] *Works*, 6:83.
[41] *Works*, 6:85.
[42] *Works*, 6:85–86.

the crucial role played by love in mortification.[43] There Owen gives an extended description of how mortification works not only by opposing the principle and operation of indwelling sin, but also by strengthening the contrary principle and operation of grace:

> The work and duty of mortification consists in a constant *taking part* with grace, in its principle, acts and fruits against the principle, acts and fruits of sin, [for] as the one is increased, strengthened and improved, the other must necessarily be weakened and decayed. Wherefore, the mortification of sin must consist in these three things:
>
> 1. The cherishing and improving of the principle of grace and holiness by all the ways and means which God has appointed;
>
> 2. Frequent actings of the principle of grace in all duties, internal and external; and
>
> 3. In a due application of the principle, power and actings of grace [in opposition to] the principle, power and actings of sin.[44]

Owen provides directions for the practice of mortification similar to those he had spelled out over a decade earlier. First, because mortification is a gradual work, it must be a continuous duty; negligence can cause spiritual decays from which one never fully recovers.[45] Secondly, constantly watch against the operations of indwelling sin in spiritual duties, work, society and various providences.[46] Thirdly, bear in mind that the goal of mortification is that one should no longer serve sin, not merely some sins, but all of them. Again, success requires not only "diligence and holy violence" but also universal obedience:

> Contests against particular sins are only to comply with light and convictions. Mortification, with a design for holiness, respects [all three aspects of indwelling sin: principle, operation and actual sins]. The first will miscarry, and the latter will be successful. And herein consists the difference between mortification motivated by legal convictions, which is always fruitless, and that motivated by the gospel. The first respects only particular sins, as the guilt of them reflects upon conscience; the latter, the whole interest of sin, as opposed to the renovation of the image of God in us.[47]

---

[43] See especially Book 4, Chapter 8, "Mortification of Sin, the Nature and Causes of it" (*Works*, 3:538–565). No extended discussion of this important chapter appears in Ferguson, *John Owen on the Christian Life* or Gleason, *John Calvin and John Owen on Mortification*.

[44] *Works*, 3:543 (emphasis his).

[45] *Works*, 3:545.

[46] *Works*, 3:546.

[47] *Works*, 3:547.

Although mortification is performed by the Holy Spirit, it remains, *contra* Eaton, a Christian duty. Owen infers from Romans 8:13 that, "As it is a work of grace, it is said to be wrought by the Spirit; and as it is our duty, we are said to work it 'through the Spirit.'"[48] Furthermore, Owen observed two principal considerations that motivate mortification, both of which center on the Holy Spirit:

> First, the life and spring of [the duty] as wrought in us by grace; secondly, the principal reason of and motive for it to be performed by us in the way of duty. Both of these, in the case of mortification, do centre in this inhabitation of the Spirit. For it is He who mortifies and subdues our corruptions [and] who quickens us to life, holiness and obedience. And the principal reason and motive [care and diligence in performing our duty] is to preserve His dwelling-place [so that we will not be destroyed for defiling it].[49]

Again, parting company with antinomians who believe that God is blind to the believer's sins, Owen warns of the destruction that can befall a believer for neglecting mortification and consequently defiling God's temple, the indwelling Holy Spirit (1 Corinthians 3:16–17 and 6:19).

Against self-mortification, Owen insisted that the Holy Spirit graciously enables the Christian to perform his duty of mortification in three ways. First, He enables the Christian to grow in holiness and abound in fruit of the Spirit. Again, mortification requires universal obedience for success, not merely the avoidance of sin:

> We mortify sin by cherishing the principle of holiness and sanctification in our souls, labouring to increase and strengthen it by growing in grace, and by a constancy and frequency of acting of it in all duties, on all occasions. Growing, thriving, and improving in universal holiness, is the great way of the mortification of sin. The more vigorous the principle of holiness, the more weak will be that of sin. The more frequent and lively the acts of sin, the more feeble and seldom will be the acts of sin. The more we abound in the 'fruit of the Spirit', the fewer shall be the 'works of the flesh'. And we deceive ourselves if we expect mortification on any other terms.[50]

Secondly, the Holy Spirit empowers the performance for the duty of mortification by communicating grace to the Christian.[51] This empowerment

---

[48] *Works*, 3:550.
[49] *Works*, 3:550–51.
[50] *Works*, 3:552.
[51] *Works*, 3:553.

requires the Christian to exercise diligence in utilizing the means of grace such as "prayer, meditation, reading, hearing of the word, and other ordinances of divine worship" and in developing graces directly contrary to besetting sins.[52] Thirdly, the Holy Spirit empowers performance by directing to the right duty in the right way at the right time. After criticizing misguided models of mortification, Owen fleshes out what he meant by the right duty at the right time.[53]

> The circumstances of our condition will direct us. Sometimes prayer and meditation will claim this place when our danger arises solely from ourselves and our own perverse inclinations, disorderly affections or unruly passions; sometimes watchfulness and abstinence, when sin takes occasion from worldly temptations or business; sometimes wisdom and circumspection, when the avoidance of temptations and opportunities of sinning is called for.[54]

Again, the Christian must practice the duty of mortification in faith by expectantly praying that Christ's death will mortify sin in him. Faith has a "peculiar efficacy" for subduing sin, for it is by beholding Christ that one is transformed into His image, and God's grace is communicated to the Christian mainly by faith.[55] More importantly, the Christian must exercise faith in fervent prayer for the success of mortification:

> By fervent prayer [for mortification] the habit, frame and inclination of the soul to universal holiness, with a detestation of all sin, are increased, cherished and strengthened. The soul of a believer is never raised unto a higher intension of spirit in the pursuit of, love unto, and delight in holiness, nor is more conformed to it or cast into the mold of it, than in prayer. And frequency in prayer is a principal means to consolidate holiness.[56]

The most dramatic improvement on Owen's earlier treatment of mortification is his newly added discussion of the crucial role played by love. Finally, and most importantly, the Christian must practice mortification in love. He should bestir himself to love Christ by considering His grace, love, patience, condescension, and obedience, and the end and design of His death. With great profundity and brevity, Owen pointed out that all true love has two effects. The first is adherence: true love knits one soul to

---

[52] *Works*, 3:554.
[53] *Works*, 3:555–57.
[54] *Works*, 3:558.
[55] *Works*, 3:562–63.
[56] *Works*, 3:560.

another, so the Christian will cleave in love to Christ. The second is conformity: Love begets a likeness between the lover and the Beloved so that a mind filled with the love of Christ as crucified will be changed into His image from one degree of glory to the next:

> Love... begets a likeness between the mind loving and the object beloved. A mind filled with the love of Christ as crucified will be changed into his image by the effectual mortification of sin through deriving power and grace from thence for that purpose.[57]

Summary

Although Seventeenth-Century English antinomians like Eaton dismissed the necessity or functionality of the practice of mortification, Owen considered the cause of spiritual barrenness, whether in the pulpit or pew, to be the loss of true evangelical mortification among professing Christians. Though a constant duty of believers, mortification must be performed in the power of the Holy Spirit, who works in and through renewed human faculties to accomplish these purposes: of the blood of Christ to cleanse, the exaltation of Christ to grant repentance, and the doctrine of grace to teach godly living. To mortify sin, it is not enough simply to avoid sinning. Every carnal lust must be weakened by the cultivation of its gracious opposite: pride by humility, anger by patience and so forth. The good news is that a substantial degree of mortification can give a man "peace with God all his days."

Mortification is both a grace and a duty. Contrary to Eaton's claim that mortification withdraws a Christian from Christ or the Catholic claim that mortification can be self-generated, the Holy Spirit accomplishes mortification in the Christian by convicting him of sin, revealing Christ as Savior, and inspiring fervent prayer for relief. Yet Owen, consistent with his theology that grace gives rise to corresponding duty (because God ordains means as well as ends), gave the Christian three very important directions for success in mortification: (1) the need to pursue universal obedience, not merely the forsaking of particular sins; (2) the importance of placing faith in Christ crucified as faithful High Priest; and (3) the appreciation of the power of love for Christ to transform the Christian into the selfsame image of God.

---

[57] *Works*, 3:564.

13

Preparation for Glory: Prayer and Meditation on the Glory of Christ

True Faith: Not Notional but Transformative

A convenient starting point for evaluating Owen's treatment of prayer and meditation is Packer's trenchant observation that the purely notional concept of faith espoused by Seventeenth-Century antinomians produces a spirituality entirely devoid of prayer and communion with Christ:

> [T]he antinomian concept of faith itself is viciously intellectualistic.... For it is a matter of knowing rather than doing; of ascertaining, as distinct from apprehending; of receiving a truth, rather of receiving a Savior. It begins and ends in the mind.... The antinomian never "comes to Christ" at all.... Man's part is simply to believe himself a justified child of God, whatever conscience may say. We need not wonder that union and communion with Christ are Puritan rather than antinomian themes. Antinomianism requires faith *about* Christ, but does not insist that this must become faith *in* Christ.[1]

By contrast, Owen, like other mainstream Puritans, stressed not simply spiritual information, but also spiritual transformation, and viewed prayer and meditation as a means to the latter. According to Owen in his extended treatment of this theme in *The Glory of Christ* (1684), mere notional knowledge about God and Christ is deficient because it is not

---

[1] Packer, *Redemption and Restoration*, 370 (emphasis his).

transformative.[2] A full orbed faith, which receives Christ in all His offices
as Prophet,[3] Priest,[4] and King,[5] and meditates deeply on His person and
work as culminating in his glory as Mediator is critical to spiritual transformation. Christ's kingly power equips the Christian for duty, Christ's infallible prophetic authority helps the Christian to acquiesce in duties dis-
pleasing to the flesh like mortification and self-denial, and Christ's priestly
mediation secures grace for the Christian's obedience as well as for God's
acceptance of his duties performed through faith in Christ.[6] Meditation
on the person of Christ "generates humility, faith, delight and assurance."[7]
Owen waxes eloquent about the transformative power of faith derived
from contemplating the glory of Christ:

> The faith of this mystery [Christ's hypostatic union] ennobles the mind–
> rendering it spiritual and heavenly, transforming it into the image of
> God. Herein consists the excellence of faith above all other powers and
> acts of the soul–that it receives, assents unto, and rests in, things in their
> nature absolutely incomprehensible. The more sublime and glorious–the
> more inaccessible unto sense and reason–the things which we believe;
> the more are we changed into the image of God, in the exercise of faith
> upon them. Hence we find this most glorious effect of faith, or the trans-
> formation of the mind into the likeness of God, no less real, evident and
> eminent in many, whose rationally comprehensive abilities are weak and
> contemptible...than in those of the highest natural sagacity, enjoying the
> best improvements of reason.[8]

> There is a peculiar ground of the spiritual efficacy of this representation
> of God... not only because there is a more full and extensive revelation
> of God, his counsel and his will, in Christ and the gospel than in all the
> works of creation and providence; but because this revelation and repre-
> sentation of God is received by *faith* alone, the other by *reason* only; and
> it is faith that is the principle of spiritual life and light in us.[9]

Yet faith, to bring about fuller conformity to the image of Christ, cannot operate in a vacuum; it must work by love.[10] Accordingly, a Christian
should make it his life study to collect and improve motives for love to

[2] *Works*, 1:23.
[3] *Works*, 1:94.
[4] *Works*, 1:133.
[5] *Works*, 1:98–99.
[6] *Works*, 1:137, 148.
[7] *Works*, 1:96.
[8] *Works*, 1:50.
[9] *Works*, 1:76–77 (emphasis his).
[10] *Works*, 1:169.

Christ.[11] For love to God, which involves a desire for union, complacency, benevolence, and friendship brings about assimilation to His character:[12]

> Love… stirs up constant endeavors after assimilation unto [God], and hath a principal efficacy unto that end…. In our renovation into the image of God, the transforming power is radically seated in faith, but acts itself in love. Love proceeding from faith gradually changes the soul into the likeness of God; and the more it is in exercise, the more is that change effected.[13]

> Seeing and admiring the glory of Christ prepares us to press after conformity to him. We labor for this conformity in opposing all sin [mortification], in duly improving and continually growing in every grace [vivification] and in following Christ's example.[14]

Owen pointed out in the context of mortification that all true love has two effects: adherence and conformity (see chapter 12).[15]

Owen's Responses to Antinomian Errors

A good barometer for gauging the attitude of Seventeenth-Century antinomians may well be the "catalogue of errors" drawn up by Winthrop during the New England Antinomian Controversy. At least six of the 82 errors alleged by Winthrop bore directly on the practice of prayer. Antinomian Error 23 asserts that, "We must not pray for gifts and graces, but only for Christ."[16] Owen refuted this Error directly in his treatise *Pneumatologia* (1674) where he points out that prayer for the Holy Spirit should be the "great subject matter" of Christian prayer so that a believer's gifts and graces will increase.[17] He notes, moreover, a continuing Christian duty to pray for completion of one's sanctification because "the same work is to be preserved and carried on by the same means and the same grace wherewith it was begun."[18] Owen then declares that the Holy Spirit works in prayer

---

[11] *Works*, 1:163–64.

[12] *Works*, 1:154.

[13] Ibid.

[14] *Works*, 1:174–75.

[15] *Works*, 3:564.

[16] Hall, *The Antinomian Controversy*, 225. I have omitted discussion of Antinomian Error 82, which deals with the supposed necessity of "naming names" whenever a minister prays or preaches against theological error, though technically it qualifies.

[17] *Works*, 3:155.

[18] *Works*, 3:325.

secretly (though without immediate inspiration, contrary to the illuminist presupposition of antinomians) in three ways:

1. By giving spiritual insight into the promises of God and the grace of the covenant, whereby we know what to ask [for];

2. By giving a deep sense of our needs and a [corresponding] desire for relief;

3. By creating and stirring up desires for [spiritual growth].[19]

As one might expect from chapter 4, the Holy Spirit's gracious guidance in prayer gives rise to corresponding Christian duties to seek further grace. Owen accordingly rejects Antinomian Error 51, which states, "The soul need not go out to Christ for fresh supplies, but is acted by the Spirit inhabiting."[20] He observes that "although our sanctification and growth in holiness be a work of the Holy Spirit, as the efficient cause thereof, yet is it our own work in a way of duty."[21] He includes in this context two primary duties: the one of mortifying sin and the other of making full use of all appointed means and ordinances for spiritual growth.[22] This need for diligence is imperative:

> It is required of us that we give all diligence to the increase of grace (2 Ptr. 1:5–7), and that we abound therein (2 Cor. 8:7), and not only so, but that we 'show the same diligence unto the end' (Heb. 6:11). If we get slack or give over as to our duty, the work of sanctification will not be carried on in a way of grace.[23]

Owen also insists, in direct opposition to Antinomian Error 51, that fresh supplies of grace are necessary, even in those already regenerate:

> The inquiry is, what believers themselves who have received this principle of spiritual life and are habitually sanctified, can do as to actual duties by virtue thereof, without a new and immediate assistance and working of the Holy Spirit in them; and I say, they can no more do anything spiritually good without the particular concurrence and assistance of the grace of God, than a man can act or move in absolute independence of God's power and providence.[24]

[19] Works, 3:398–99.
[20] Hall, A Documentary History, 233.
[21] Works, 3:404.
[22] Works, 3:404–5.
[23] Works, 3:405.
[24] Works, 3:530.

Owen turns to the specific question of how a Christian may pray for further grace. His answer is that a Christian must pray for further grace, not on the ground of any inherent righteousness, but on the basis of God's faithfulness and righteousness as engaged in his promises, and out of a sense of weakness.[25] He declares, in view of 1 Corinthians 12:31, that a Christian may lawfully pray for the enhancement of his spiritual gifts, provided that the purposes of such prayer fulfill God's specific will for the edification of others and His glory.[26]

Antinomian Error 34 declares that, "We are not to pray against all sin, because the old man is in us, and must be, and why should we pray against that which cannot be avoided?"[27] This error betrays the essentialist presupposition of Seventeenth-Century antinomians, who construed regeneration not as involving the renewal of human faculties, but the side-by-side coexistence of the old man and the divine essence. According to their reading, indwelling sin cannot be effectively mortified or prayed against. Owen rejects this piece of folly, declaring that prayer against sin is essential because "it is that only single duty wherein every grace is acted, every sin opposed... and the whole of our obedience concerned."[28] Moreover, he contends that a Christian may not properly plead God's promises in prayer unless he truly means to part company with his sins:

> By pleading them in Christ; and by pleading them for the end of the promise, not to spend on our lusts. When we ask for pardon of sin with secret reserves in our hearts to continue in sin, we ask the choicest mercy of the covenant, to spend it on our lusts. The end of the promise the apostle tells us [in] 2 Cor. 7:1, "Having these promises, let us cleanse ourselves from all pollution of the flesh and spirit, perfecting holiness in the fear of God.[29]

Antinomian Error 64 has a similar thrust to Antinomian Error 34. It contends that, "A man must take no notice of his sin, nor of his repentance for his sin."[30] Again, Owen will brook no nonsense. Arguing that far from ignoring his continuing sinfulness, a Christian should pray for illumination by the Holy Spirit into the depths of the plague of his own heart.[31] He even questions whether a person so heedless of indwelling sin and the way it mars communion with God can even know what sanctification is:

[25] *Works*, 3:410–11.
[26] *Works*, 3:411–12.
[27] Hall, *The Antinomian Controversy*, 227.
[28] *Works*, 4:318.
[29] *Works*, 2:124.
[30] Hall, *The Antinomian Controversy*, 236.
[31] *Works*, 3:451–52.

He who has no experience of spiritual shame and self-abhorrence [on account of natural depravity] is a great stranger to sanctification. Who is [a Christian but] can recount the unsteadiness of his mind in holy meditation, his low and unbecoming conceptions of God's excellences, his proneness to foolish and unprofitable imaginations and vanities and sensuality, and his aversion to spirituality in duty and fixedness in communion with God.[32]

Since sanctification flows from justification in Reformed theology, Owen's observation raises the question whether such a person is saved at all.

Finally, carelessness about sin ignores the very real problem of how a defiled sinner can enjoy communion with an infinitely holy God. Owen, like other mainstream Puritans, saw an ongoing need for the believer to keep short accounts with God by continual prayer for Christ's blood to purge his defilement.[33] Despite the antinomian antipathy toward "conditions," Owen discovers conditions of communion with God under the covenant of grace:

Where the means of purification are duly used, no defilement ensues, on any sin that believers fall into, which does or can totally obstruct communion with Christ, according to the tenor of the covenant. Three things are required: (1) Constant, humble acknowledgment of sin. (2) Daily cleansing from sins, especially secret ones. (3) Preservation from 'presumptuous sin' or willful sins committed with a high hand.[34]

Antinomian Error 49 affirms that, "We are not bound to keep up a constant course of prayer in our families, or privately, unless the Spirit stirs us up thereunto."[35] In his treatise *A Discourse of Spiritual Gifts* (1693, posthumously), Owen rejects this error because God gives spiritual gifts to those who need them and such gifts must be exercised for the recipient—as well as for those under their charge—to grow in grace.

These gifts are a great means and help to excite and exercise grace, without which it will be lifeless and apt to decay. Men grow in grace by the due exercise of their own gifts in duties. Wherefore, every individual person on his account needs them to exercise and improve grace. Most men, such as those who have families to provide for, have a duty to instruct others that they cannot discharge without the special aid of the Holy Spirit.[36]

---

[32] *Works*, 3:437.
[33] *Works*, 3:463–64.
[34] *Works*, 3:465–66.
[35] Hall, *The Antinomian Controversy*, 232.
[36] *Works*, 4:517.

Finally, Error 70 claims that, "Frequency or length of holy duties or trouble of conscience for neglect thereof, are all signs of one under a covenant of works."[37] As mentioned in chapter 5, Owen took great pains to prove that the means of grace are inextricably bound to the ongoing administration of the covenant of grace. In *A Brief Instruction in the Worship of God and Discipline of the Churches of the New Testament* (1667), Owen refuted the antinomian chimera that the necessity of the means of grace has for the most part ceased under the covenant of grace.

Q.6.   May not such an estate of faith and perfection in obedience be attained in this life, as wherein believers may be freed from all obligation for the observation of gospel institutions?

A.6.   No; for the ordinances and institutions of the gospel being inseparably annexed to the evangelical administration of the gospel of grace, they may not be left unobserved, disused, or omitted, whilst we are to walk before God in the covenant, without contempt of the covenant itself, as also of the wisdom and authority of Jesus Christ.[38]

Owen's attitude toward observance of Christian worship calls to mind the warning in Hebrews for Christians not to forsake their assembling together.

Christ's Glory

So much, then, for Owen's reply to Seventeenth-Century antinomians. He had much more to convey about the importance of meditation and prayer. His theology of meditation is somewhat unusual in the sense that he stressed meditation on the glory of Christ more than meditation on Scripture *per se*. He saw such meditation as a panacea for many ills: it frees the Christian from earthly-mindedness,[39] prepares him to receive communications of God's love,[40] produces steadfast faith and settled assurance,[41] gives comfort and victory in conflict with sin,[42] and even prepares one for faithfulness and self-denial,[43] death,[44] and heaven.[45] Christ-centered

---

[37] Hall, *The Antinomian Controversy*, 238.

[38] *Works*, 15:454.

[39] *Works*, 1:222.

[40] *Works*, 1:279.

[41] *Works*, 1:222.

[42] *Works*, 1:277.

[43] *Works*, 1:332.

[44] *Works*, 1:280–84. Owen discusses the familiar Puritan theme of dying well.

[45] *Works*, 1:291–92.

meditation is especially effective for recovering a Christian from spiritual lethargy and decay. So wrote Owen in his posthumously published treatise, *The Glory of Christ Applied to Unbelievers and Saints Under Spiritual Decays* (1691). Again insistent that such meditation is transformative, Owen cites five benefits:

1. Virtue [power] will proceed from [Christ] to repair all our decays, to renew a right spirit in us, and to cause us to abound in all duties of obedience;

2. It will fix the soul on Christ, who is alone able to give it delight, complacency and satisfaction.

3. Heavenly-mindedness will preclude earthly-mindedness.

4. This duty will stir up every grace to its due exercise.

5. It will keep one on constant watch against entry into temptation or surprisal into sin.[46]

Owen prescribes a regimen for Christ-centered meditation. Preparation involves laying aside worldly cares and concerns, forming biblical concepts of Christ's love, and taking relish in Jesus Christ.[47] He recommends pertinent biblical themes or topics: His active and passive obedience,[48] His exaltation,[49] Old Testament types and preincarnate appearances and prophecies,[50] His headship of the church,[51] His communication to believers,[52] and the recapitulation of all things in Him.[53]

Owen insists that the imitation of Christ practiced in Roman Catholic spirituality will not produce Christ-like character; in God's appointment of means of grace, only fervent prayer and meditation will suffice.[54] Consistent with his belief in the indissoluble bond of grace and duty, he gives seven directions for meditating on the glory of Christ. First, realize that He is the most noble and beneficial object of our thoughts and affections.[55] Secondly, search the Scriptures to collect fit matter for meditation

[46] *Works*, 1:460–61.
[47] *Works*, 1:338–39.
[48] *Works*, 1:338–42.
[49] *Works*, 1:342–47.
[50] *Works*, 1:348–52.
[51] *Works*, 1:352–59.
[52] *Works*, 1:360–67.
[53] *Works*, 1:367–74.
[54] *Works*, 1:304–6.
[55] *Works*, 1:312–14.

on Christ's glory.[56] Thirdly, meditate frequently to retain the full benefit of the practice.[57] Fourthly, use every occasion to engage in holy meditation on Christ.[58] Fifthly, meditation should proceed with a heart attitude of "admiration, adoration and thanksgiving."[59] Sixthly, endeavor to be transformed by the truth apprehended by faith.[60] Seventhly, cultivate heavenly-mindedness.

Communion with God

Owen's treatise *On Communion with God* (1657) is typical of mainstream Puritan divinity in taking the Canticles as an allegory for communion between Christ and the church.[61] Yet it is atypical in conceiving of *distinct* communion between the Christian and each of the three persons of the Trinity.[62] Owen has been criticized in this regard for straying beyond the bounds of biblical precedent.[63] Owen assumed distinct communion with each person because 1 Corinthians 12:4–6 ascribes communication of grace to each person individually as well as jointly.[64] This distinct communion with one person does not exclude, however, communion with the other persons of the Trinity.[65]

Owen begins by marveling that sinners can have fellowship at all with "an infinitely holy God."[66] He defines communion as "his [God's] communication with himself to us, with our return to him of what he requires and accepts [through] our union with Christ."[67] Each person of the Trinity is to receive a specialized return from the Christian: for the Father, the return should be faith, love, and obedience.[68] Owen directs the Christian in prayer to "eye the Father as love; look by faith on him as one more

[56] *Works*, 1:314–16.
[57] *Works*, 1:317.
[58] *Works*, 1:317–20.
[59] *Works*, 1:320.
[60] *Works*, 1:321.
[61] See e.g., *Works*, 2:128–31.
[62] *Works*, 2:4.
[63] *Works*, 1:lxxii. Biographer Andrew Thomson mentions the criticism somewhat approvingly.
[64] *Works*, 2:16. See Ferguson, *John Owen on the Christian Life*, 75, for handling of relevant texts.
[65] *Works*, 2:18.
[66] *Works*, 2:7.
[67] *Works*, 2:8–9.
[68] *Works*, 2:11

kind and tender, with everlasting thoughts of kindness towards us."[69] Such prayer, says Owen, will "endear your soul to God, cause you to delight in him, and make your abode with him."[70] Christ should be viewed as having "a fitness to save [through] pity and power, fullness to save [through his purchase] of redemption and sanctification, and suitability to save through furnishing continual supplies of grace."[71] Christ's excellencies underlie the efficacy of gospel promises and His penal substitutionary atonement gives the greatest luster to God's attributes, especially His justice, forbearance, wisdom, and all-sufficiency.[72] Friendship with Christ prompts the saint to unburden all his secrets to Him.[73] Christ's specialized return should be faith, love, and hope expressed in worship and obedience.[74]

Owen emphasizes that believers and unbelievers alike are to pray for the gift of the Holy Spirit.[75] It is the Holy Spirit who assists prayer by revealing true needs, interceding for unspoken and misspoken prayer requests, and helping the saint pray according to the promises through pleading them in Christ with a genuine willingness to part with sin.[76] The believer's response to the Holy Spirit should be threefold. First, the saint should not grieve, quench or resist Him.[77] He should neither grieve His person by lapsing into sin, nor quench His motions in stirring up grace or giving new supplies of grace,[78] nor resist Him by despising the preached word.[79] Second, he should return praise and glory to Him.[80] Third, a Christian should be duly humbled by his miscarriages.[81]

The Holy Spirit's Work in Prayer

Owen's *A Discourse of the Work of the Holy Spirit in Prayer* (1682) is a full-scale assault on set prayers and liturgies in favor of extemporaneous prayer. Though Owen believed set prayers and liturgies were guilty of

---

[69] *Works*, 2:32.
[70] *Works*, 2:35.
[71] *Works*, 2:52, 199.
[72] *Works*, 2:75, 83–90.
[73] *Works*, 2:119–21.
[74] *Works*, 2:14.
[75] *Works*, 2:229.
[76] *Works*, 2:121–24.
[77] *Works*, 2:266.
[78] *Works*, 2:266–67.
[79] *Works*, 2:268.
[80] *Works*, 2:271.
[81] *Works*, 2:272.

introducing idolatrous worship and causing the cessation of ministerial gifts, especially in Roman Catholicism, he stops short of advocating their outright abolition.[82] He deems prayer to be one of the most important Christian duties because it is how "we exercise toward [God] all the grace received from Him, and render him an acceptable acknowledgment of homage and revenue of glory."[83]

This treatise is an extended treatment of Zechariah 12:10, which refers to the Holy Spirit as "the Spirit of grace and of supplications" given by God to believers. Owen, once more, connects the indissoluble bond of grace and duty in the matter of prayer:

> Whereas God has graciously promised his Holy Spirit, as a Spirit of grace and supplication, enabling them to pray according to his mind and will, in all their circumstances and capacities, present and future, it is the duty of all Christians to expect those promised aids and assistances to their prayers, and to pray according to the ability so given.[84]

According to Owen, the Holy Spirit acts as a Spirit of supplication by working in believers giftedness and delight in prayer, despite their secret aversion to immediate communion with God.[85] Given the more plentiful effusion of grace under the gospel, believers would be remiss not to pursue prayer more often and more fervently.[86] He understands Romans 8:15 as though both the Holy Spirit (as the Spirit of adoption) and the believer concur in crying "Abba, Father" and regards such concurrence as further evidence that prayer is both a grace and a duty.[87]

Owen defines prayer as "a gift, ability or spiritual faculty of exercising faith, love, reverence, fear, delight and other graces by vocal requests, supplications and praises to God."[88] The Holy Spirit guides the petitions of prayer, especially the longing prompted by the saint's continued experience of indwelling sin for the "inward sanctification of all our faculties,"[89] inspires prayer in faith in dependence on God's promises, and furnishes an understanding of the wisdom and suitability of God's answers.[90] He also guides the manner of prayer by granting delight in God and by giving a

[82] *Works*, 4:237–49.
[83] *Works*, 4:252.
[84] *Works*, 4:239.
[85] *Works*, 4:258–60.
[86] *Works*, 4:264, 316.
[87] *Works*, 4:268.
[88] *Works*, 4:271.
[89] *Works*, 4:274.
[90] *Works*, 4:271–76.

holy desire for union with Christ, who is spotlighted in His preeminence as Mediator.[91]

Owen likens those using nothing but set forms of prayer to a learner who never learns to swim because he always enters the water wearing an inner tube.[92] His unmistakable implication is that they never learn to pray. Owen declares that the "constant and unvaried use of set forms of prayers may greatly quench the Spirit and [stifle] all growth in gifts and graces."[93] The Holy Spirit will give both ministers and ordinary saints spiritual ability in prayer if they improve the means of grace given by God to that end, including self-examination, the study of Scripture, and memorization.[94]

Chapter 9 of this treatise goes to the heart of the matter by prescribing the Christian duties involved in prayer. Owen gives one general duty and six particular ones. The general duty is to glorify God constantly for the "treasury of mercies" enfolded within the privilege of gospel prayer. No Christian seriously interested in his own spiritual welfare should willingly neglect opportunities for prayer after reading Owen's stirring summary of its practical benefits:

> It is that only single duty wherein every grace is acted, every sin opposed, every good thing obtained, and the whole of our obedience [everywhere] concerned. What difficulties, what discouragements, what aversion, what distractions and weariness are apt to oppose prayer! Yet on prayer depends the blessedness of our present and future condition. Prayer is given to relieve us against all those [impediments], to give us freedom, liberty and confidence in approaching the throne of grace, to [grant us the spirit of adoption]. Who can express how great a folly it is not to engage in constant prayer? How can we grieve the Holy Spirit and endanger our souls more than this?[95]

Six specific directions to stir up the gift of prayer follow: The first direction is to engage in continual self-examination. Through prayer informed by impartial self-examination, a Christian "may know the beginnings of temptation, the deceitful [workings] of indwelling sin, the risings of particular corruptions, supplies of grace and ways of deliverance."[96] The second direction is to search the Scriptures, which reveal all our needs and all God's supplies of grace and mercy. Owen recommends turning Scripture

---

[91] *Works*, 4:287–97.
[92] *Works*, 4:301. Owen uses the phrase "flags and bladders."
[93] *Works*, ibid.
[94] *Works*, 4:301–15.
[95] *Works*, 4:318.
[96] *Works*, 4:321.

into prayer and praise.[97] The third direction is meditation on God's glorious attributes to engender reverence and godly fear, holy boldness, and faith.[98] The fourth is to meditate on the glory of Christ in His incarnation, mediation and intercession, a theme already elaborated fully in *The Glory of Christ* (1684).[99] The fifth direction advises frequent prayer, which strengthens the gift, both through exercise and God's blessing.[100] The sixth direction is that fervent prayer promotes personal holiness through the process of assimilation.[101] Owen mentions the seeming anomaly of those whose assimilation outpaces their doctrinal grasp.

> [Through petitionary prayer] the Holy Spirit does so [strongly] represent and exhibit the truth, reality, power and efficacy of spiritual things to a believer that he mixes faith with [them, and they are made real to him] even though he cannot explain these spiritual [operations] with proper doctrine. Thus we often see a man low and weak in doctrinal apprehension, yet in his prayers led into communion with god in the highest and holiest mysteries of His grace.[102]

Though never willing to dilute the claims of Christian duty or minimize the importance of orthodox doctrine, Owen always stood ready to magnify the glories of God's grace.

Summary

As Packer observes, the Seventeenth-Century antinomian had a "viciously intellectualistic" concept of faith that resulted in neglecting prayer and communion with Christ. Owen viewed true faith as transformative, not merely informative. His wholistic concept of faith involved receiving Christ as Prophet, Priest, and King, meditation on the glory of Christ, and earnest seeking after greater Christlikeness.

Owen refuted a number of theological errors about the practice of prayer, which Winthrop attributed to New England antinomians. Against their dispensation of the necessity of prayer, Owen reiterated the rectitude of prayer for both the enhancement of spiritual gifts and the invigoration of graces in the already regenerate. Just as the Holy Spirit works in prayer to create and enliven desires for spiritual growth, so the Christian should

---

[97] *Works*, 4:321–22.
[98] *Works*, 4:322.
[99] *Works*, 4:322–23.
[100] *Works*, 4:323–24.
[101] *Works*, 4:324–25.
[102] *Works*, 4:439–40.

make diligent and constant use of all appointed means for spiritual growth. Though the Holy Spirit empowers sanctification, which is effectuated in the Christian in a way of concurrence, "the work of [sanctification] will not be carried on in a way of grace if the Christian [slackens] in duty."[103]

Owen also rejected the antinomian notion, which was based on an essentialist misunderstanding of regeneration, that the Christian should neither pray against nor mourn over the remaining power of indwelling sin. Owen pointed out that prayer presupposes a willingness to part with sin and opposes sin at every turn. Because eruptions of indwelling sin serve to bar communion with God, Owen considered daily repentance and confession a necessary means of purging defilement. Also against antinomian laxity, Owen advocated regular private and family prayer inasmuch as gifts exercise graces, not to mention the vast importance of answered prayers. He further affirmed, over against the antinomians, that the means of grace remain important in the covenant of grace, especially since "the same work [sanctification] is to be preserved and carried by the same means, the same power, the same grace wherewith it was begun."[104]

In *The Glory of Christ* (1684), Owen made the case that Christ-centered meditation, drawn from biblical themes, is particularly beneficial. By focusing on the glory and all-sufficiency of Christ, grace and heavenly-mindedness are strengthened, greatly weakening sin and earthly-mindedness. Frequent meditation is the way to transformation.

His treatise *On Communion with God* (1657) stressed distinct communion with, and a specific return to, each member of the Trinity. Generally speaking, communion centers on the role played by each in the covenant of redemption: the Father in election and adoption, the Son in redemption through His penal substitutionary atonement, and the Holy Spirit in the application of redemption.

A Discourse of the Work of the Holy Spirit in Prayer (1682) upholds liberty in prayer over against set forms. Owen expected a mature Christian, in reliance on gospel promises of a more plentiful effusion of the Holy Spirit, to develop his gift of prayer through the appointed means of self-examination, biblical study, and meditation, and the exercise of the gift of prayer itself. Prayer, contrary to the antinomian posture, is absolutely indispensable to spiritual growth and perseverance because it exercises every grace, opposes every sin, gives freedom and holy boldness in petitionary prayer, and promotes personal holiness through love and assimilation.

---

[103] *Works*, 3:405.
[104] *Works*, 3:325.

14

Preparation for Glory: Obedience

Owen parted company with antinomian theology in his great emphasis on the importance and indispensable necessity of sanctification and obedience. Contrasts abound between Owen and Seventeenth-Century antinomians:

- Antinomians denied that the covenant of grace is conditional whereas Owen held that faith and repentance were necessary for conversion and obedience for sanctification.

- Whereas antinomians deemed the Mosaic law to have been superseded,[1] Owen insisted on the continuing validity of the moral law.

- Antinomians thought God could not see the sins of the saints, whilst Owen, falling in with the mainstream Puritan view spelled out in the Westminster Confession,[2] contended that God chastised his saints for their disobedience.

---

[1] Como, *Blown by the Spirit*, 34.

[2] Westminster Confession, Chapter 11, Section 5 declares that, "God doth continue to forgive the sins of those that are justified: and although they can never fall from the state of justification, yet they may by their sins fall under God's fatherly displeasure, and not have the light of his countenance restored unto them, until they humble themselves, confess their sins, beg pardon and renew their faith and repentance.

- Though antinomians considered sanctification instantaneous,[3] Owen argued that it was gradual and progressive.

- Unlike antinomians, who placed their trust in assurance through the direct witness of the Holy Spirit, Owen considered obedience to have evidential value in establishing assurance of salvation.

- Though antinomians tended to disparage the means of grace, Owen even viewed obedience as a means of grace.

- Though antinomians regarded obedience as relatively effortless, Owen considered its attainment difficult and accordingly gave motives for obedience and even directions for avoiding apostasy.

- Ironically, Owen was compelled to defend justification by faith through the imputed righteousness of Christ from the specious Socinian claim that it promotes antinomianism.

Given the numerous points of direct contact–and opposition–between his soteriology and antinomian theology, it is far-fetched to believe that Owen did not have Seventeenth-Century antinomians largely in view.

Obedience as a Condition of the Covenant of Grace

Owen defines sanctification as "the immediate work of God by his Spirit upon our whole nature, proceeding from the peace made for us by Jesus Christ, whereby being changed into his likeness, we are kept entirely in peace with God, and are preserved, or in a state of gracious acceptation with him, according to the terms of the covenant to the end."[4] Sanctification has two aspects: dedication to God, and the real and internal communication of a principle of grace to human nature that produces "acts and duties of holy obedience to God."[5]

As John Flavel noted,[6] antinomian writers denied the conditionality of the covenant of grace. Owen for his part listed three conditions of the covenant of grace: faith, repentance, and obedience. He writes, "The gospel proposes life and salvation by Jesus Christ to all who shall believe, repent and yield obedience to Him."[7] Though Owen observed many Christians

---

[3] Ibid., 207–208, 308.

[4] *Works*, 3:369.

[5] *Works*, 3:370.

[6] See chapter 2 quotation; for specific examples, see Stoever, *'A Faire and Easye Way to Heaven'*, 143–44 (Tobias Crisp) and 147 (Eaton and Traske).

[7] *Works*, 3:595.

neglecting the pursuit of holiness,[8] he insists that "God requires holiness indispensably in all believers."[9] Owen declares that "The whole that God requires of us in a way of gospel duty is that we should be holy, and abide in the use of [those] means of grace [designed for] its attainment and improvement."[10] In fact, holiness is the Christian's "principal duty."[11]

More specifically, under the terms of the covenant of grace, God requires "sincere and universal" obedience from the Christian.[12] Questions 5, 6, and 7 of Owen's *Greater Catechism* (1645) reflect his settled judgment:

Q.5.   What is that holiness which is required of us?

A.5.   That universal, sincere obedience to the whole will of God, in our hearts, minds, wills and actions, whereby we are made in some measure conformable to Christ our head.

Q.6.   Is this holiness or obedience in us perfect?

A.6.   Yes, in respect to the parts of it, but not in respect of the degrees wherein God requires it.

Q.7.   Will God accept of that obedience which falls so short of what requires?

A.7.   Yes, from them whose persons he accepts and justifies freely in Christ Jesus.[13]

For obedience to be acceptable to God under the covenant of grace, two requirements must be satisfied. First, obedience must be wrought by faith in Christ. Owen asserts:

For there is no duty of [evangelical moral obedience], but we are obliged to perform it in faith through Christ, on the motives of the love of God in him, of the benefits of his mediation, and the grace we receive by him; whatever is otherwise done by us is not acceptable unto God.[14]

Secondly, obedience must be sincere and universal (though not perfect). Does Owen contradict himself here? How can obedience be universal, yet not perfect? The key to resolving this apparent contradiction is his defini-

---

[8] *Works*, 3:373.
[9] *Works*, 3:376.
[10] *Works*, 3:377.
[11] *Works*, 3:370.
[12] *Works*, 3:381.
[13] *Works*, 3:488.
[14] *Works*, 1:137, 148.

tion of universality. By "universal" is meant that the "whole will of God" is honored; Owen equated "universal sincerity" with equal respect to all of God's commands.[15] Owen stresses that this standard of sincere and universal obedience under the covenant of grace is much more demanding than easy-going antinomianism would allow. It excludes two things. To begin with, this standard rules out living habitually and impenitently in any known sin:

> Men may please God and be accepted with Him, notwithstanding many mistakes, errors, and misconceptions of their mind about spiritual things; but that anyone should live habitually or die impenitently in any known sin, without striving against it, laboring for repentance and endeavoring for mortification, would overthrow the Christian religion.[16]

In addition, this standard of obedience precludes habitual dereliction of any known Christian duty or the cherishing of any darling sin: "This evangelical holiness will not allow of the constant, habitual omission of any one duty, or the cherishing of any one sin."[17] If Owen's standard seems incapable of attainment, his countervailing emphasis on God's power to work holiness in the Christian should be considered. Though the Christian's personal holiness is often "weak, infirm and imperceptible," Owen praises God's preservation of the saint who is engulfed by a sea of corruption and temptation:

> Among all the glorious works of God, next to that of redemption by Jesus Christ, my soul most admires this of the Spirit in preserving the seed and principle of holiness in us, as a spark of living fire in the midst of the ocean, against all corruptions and temptations.[18]

Owen gives six cogent reasons why sincere and universal obedience is a necessary condition of the covenant of grace. First, it glorifies God by prevailing with men through gospel truth and God's promises to renounce their sins and carnal expectations, and place their faith in Christ for salvation.[19] Secondly, God's "fiery holiness in Christ" should inspire personal holiness for unbroken communion with God and preparation for eternal life.[20] Thirdly, God's decree of election plays a vital role. Appealing to

---

[15] *Works*, 3:607.
[16] *Works*, 7:159–60.
[17] *Works*, 7:176.
[18] *Works*, 3:397–98.
[19] *Works*, 3:377.
[20] *Works*, 3:573–76.

2 Thessalonians 2:13, Owen points out that "holiness [is] proposed as God's design in election as the indispensable means for attaining salvation and glory."[21]

Fourthly, obedience involves respect to the commandments of God on several grounds. The first is God's authority as sovereign lawgiver.[22] The second is His power to mete out eternal rewards and punishment.[23] Owen expressly rejects the antinomian claim put forward in *The Marrow of Modern Divinity* (1645) that fear of punishment and hope of reward are illegitimate motives for Christian obedience.

> Some, perhaps, will say that to yield holy obedience to God [on account of] rewards and punishments is servile and unbecoming to the free spirit of the children of God. But these are vain imaginations; a due respect to God's promises and threats is a principal part of our duty.[24]

A third ground is that obedience serves one's best interests.[25] Owen recommends full use of the means to render obedience "equal, easy and pleasant."[26] According to Owen, power to fulfill God's command comes from grace, both habitual and actual, administered under the new covenant:[27] "The first work of grace [habitual grace communicated by regeneration] is merely *upon* us. But this latter work of grace [actual grace communicated for sanctification] is *in* us and *by* us, [so that our strength, though coming from God, is still our own]."[28] Again, Owen confirms his distinction

---

[21] *Works*, 3:392.

[22] *Works*, 3:610.

[23] *Works*, 3:612.

[24] *Works*, 3:613–14. Owen explained this concept more fully in *The Glory of Christ in His Person, Office and Grace* (1684). "Slaves take liberty from duty; children have liberty in duty. There is not a greater mistake in the world, than that the liberty of the sons in the house of God consists in [choosing whether to serve to obey]. The liberty of sons in the inward spiritual freedom of sons is in the inward spiritual freedom of their hearts, naturally and kindly going out in their hearts in all the ways and worship of God. When they find themselves straitened and shut up in them, they wrestle with God for enlargement, and are never contented with the doing of a duty, unless it be done as in Christ, with free, genuine and enlarged hearts" (*Works*, 2:214 and also see *Works*, 7:166 where Owen denied the presence of legal fear in Christian liberty).

[25] *Works*, 3:616.

[26] *Works*, 3:619.

[27] *Works*, 3:622.

[28] *Works*, 3:620 (emphasis his). Owen also discussed the role played by each member of the Trinity in the communication of grace under the covenant of grace (*Works*, 3:291–92).

between monergistic preparation for grace and synergistic preparation for glory.

Fifthly, Christ's mission as Prophet, Priest, and King, is designed to engender personal holiness. As High Priest Christ purified a peculiar people zealous for good works and through his intercession keeps them holy through having purchased all necessary further supplies of grace.[29] As Prophet he declared the "inward spiritual nature of the law" and the "true sense of its commands" and taught that obedience must be cordial and extensive.[30] As King He concerns himself mainly with "making and preserving [Christians] holy."[31] His example of obedience is supreme, and though beyond reach, worthy of emulation.[32] Stubborn disobedience to God's commands casts serious doubt on the reality of regeneration and dishonors both Christ and the gospel.[33] Sixthly, personal holiness is the only cure for the human condition. Owen spotted a silver lining in the cloud of natural depravity: "The greatest hardships to which sin reduces a believer only cause him to exercise those graces and duties, such as repentance, humiliation, and prayer, that will give him great peace and satisfaction."[34]

Continuing Validity of the Moral Law

Owen took issue with the antinomian belief in supersession of the moral law.[35] Citing new covenant promises in Jeremiah 31:33 and Ezekiel 36:26–27, Owen defined holiness as a restored conformity not only to the image of God but also to the law:[36]

> The whole of our sanctification and holiness is comprised in these promises. To be cleansed from the defilements of sin, to have a heart inclined to fear the Lord always, and to walk in all his ways and statutes accordingly, with an internal habitual conformity of the whole soul to the law of God, is to be sanctified or to be holy.[37]

---

[29] *Works*, 3:630–31.
[30] *Works*, 3:632–33.
[31] *Works*, 3:637.
[32] *Works*, 1:339–40.
[33] *Works*, 3:638.
[34] *Works*, 3:645.
[35] *Works*, 3:374.
[36] *Works*, 7:382.
[37] *Works*, 3:383.

As discussed in chapter 2, although imputative antinomians held in theory, if not in practice to the continuing validity of the moral law, perfectionist antinomians tended to jettison the moral law in favor of a more amorphous "law of love."[38] By contrast, Owen insists that the commandments of God have to be obeyed wholeheartedly with one's conscience impressed with God's authority, one's mind grasping the "reasonableness, equity and advantage" of [them], and one's heart filled with "love and delight [in them] because [they are] holy, just and good."[39]

The Progressive Nature of Sanctification

Book 4, chapter 2 of *Pneumatologia* (1674) defends the proposition that sanctification is gradual and progressive. Antinomians, owing to their illuminist, essentialist, and hyper-supernaturalist presuppositions, typically viewed sanctification as an instantaneous work not dependent on continued use of the means (other than meditation on "free" justification) and as already accomplished at regeneration by the infusion into the believer of the divine essence. David Como's description of the Eatonist position captures this thrust well:

> The Eatonists argued that everything necessary for salvation had already been accomplished. Accordingly, the primary 'means' was to pray and meditate upon the power of free justification. This violated the traditional Puritan understanding of the necessity of the means of grace, and such illuminism violated God's commandment to his saints to work out their salvation in fear and trembling. From this perspective, no 'growth in grace' was necessary, for God had already granted all the 'unsearchable treasures of His grace" in Christ's death. Mainstream Puritans saw the godly life as a progressive process of maturation, in which God responded to his saints' diligent use of the means of grace by granting them further gifts of grace.[40]

Owen declares that although regeneration is instantaneous, sanctification is gradual and progressive.[41] Citing passages such as 2 Peter 1:5–6 and 3:18 that urge growth in grace (a phrase disliked by John Cotton), Owen proposes that the Holy Spirit exercises the Christian's graces in several ways. First, He set forth suitable objects of faith and love (e.g., God in

[38] "This intangible 'something' was often taken as Love, which was juxtaposed over and against the [Moral] Law by a number of antinomian propagandists" (Como, *Blown by the Spirit*, 36).

[39] *Works*, 3:384–85.

[40] Como, *Blown by the Spirit*, 208–9.

[41] *Works*, 3:387.

Christ and covenant promises) through ordinances of worship, especially preaching. Sitting under preaching is much more than mere memorization:

> We are greatly mistaken if we suppose that we [gain] no benefit [from preaching] beyond what we retain in our memories, though we should labor for that also. Our chief advantage lies in the excitement to proper [spiritual] exercise thereby given our faith and love; this [excitement] keeps these graces, which would otherwise decay and wither, alive.[42]

Secondly, He supplies Christians with gracious experiences of the truth. Thirdly, through trials and afflictions He cultivates the growth of Christian graces like faith and patience.[43]

Owen abundantly refuted the antinomian objection to the necessity of "painstaking" growth in grace. His first argument is that Scripture clearly posits "a consistency between God's effectual grace and our diligent obedience."[44] His second reply is that Christian growth is portrayed in Scripture as gradual and progressive by frequent comparison to the natural growth of trees and plants.[45] The third argument derives from the Christian's prayer life. Owen contends that the Holy Spirit incites prayers primarily for subduing sin and strengthening grace for universal obedience.[46] A fourth consideration is that the sheer number of gospel promises respecting holiness should encourage pursuit based on God's faithfulness.[47] A fifth and related argument is that grace and duty work in complementary tandem to accomplish holiness in the believer. Owen writes:

> Although our sanctification and growth in holiness is a work of the Holy Spirit as the efficient cause, yet it is our own work in a way of duty. On our diligence [in constant use of all appointed ordinances and means of grace] depends our growth and thriving. If we slack or give over as to our duty, the work of sanctification will not be carried on in a way of grace.[48]

As if he had not already completely skewered this objection, Owen ascribes the widespread antinomian neglect of sanctification to two of their "foolish" beliefs. The first was their groundless presumption of perfection;

---

[42] *Works*, 3:389.
[43] *Works*, 3:393.
[44] *Works*, 3:394–95.
[45] *Works*, 3:395.
[46] *Works*, 3:399.
[47] *Works*, 3:401.
[48] *Works*, 3:404–5.

the second, their exaltation of "free" justification at the expense of sanctification.[49] Of the antinomian position Owen complains:

> They will not admit that there can be a consistency between the unchangeableness of God's decrees and the freedom of our wills; that justification by the blood of Christ does not render our obedience needless; that the efficacy of God's grace and the necessity of our duty are reconcilable.[50]

In other words, Owen's antinomian opponents were consistent in their belief that God's method of grace was characterized by inconsistency.

Obedience as Positive Evidence to Confirm Assurance

Seventeenth-Century English and American antinomians rejected the use of the "practical syllogism" in confirming assurance of salvation. Speaking of the axis of antinomianism represented by Tobias Crisp, John Traske, and John Eaton, William Stoever notices their shared belief in immediate, direct assurance:

> The affirmation of Reformed divines that assurance of salvation may be obtained by practical reasoning from the effects of grace inherent in oneself appeared to them to be erroneous. As a result, they were forced to seek [assurance] in works of divine immediacy.[51]

Insisting that God's decree of election required personal holiness, to the contrary Owen declares that assurance of salvation is impossible without evidence of universal obedience:

> We can have no evidence of our interest in God's decree of election without holiness effectually wrought in us. The apostle says, 'Let everyone who names the name of Christ depart from iniquity.' There is no way to come to evidence thereof but by universal obedience. So the apostle Peter directs us to 'give all diligence to make our election sure.'[52]

Of course, by "universal," Owen does not mean perfect, but sincere with equal respect to all of God's commands.

---

[49] *Works*, 3:405–6.
[50] *Works*, 7:133.
[51] Stoever, '*A Faire and Easye Way to Heaven*', 147.
[52] *Works*, 3:593.

Christian Obedience as a Means of Grace

Discussing the strong emphasis placed by mainstream Puritans on full use of the means, Como writes, "In some of the more exuberant presentations of this doctrine, godly ministers flirted with the idea that good works were a means of grace."[53] While denying that obedience is meritorious, Owen nevertheless stressed that just as sin encourages sin, so obedience strengthens grace. This viewpoint emerges clearly in his handling of Luke 6:45, which he interpreted as teaching two principles. The first principle is that "the more men sin, the more they are inclined to sin."[54] The second principle, obverse to the first, also holds true. The more a Christian obeys, the more he is inclined to obey further: "Men do not spend their grace, but increase it by exercise. The more men exercise their grace in duties of obedience, the more it is strengthened and increased."[55]

The Arduous Path of Obedience

Though Owen believed that obedience could prove "easy and pleasant,"[56] the overall thrust of Owen's soteriology stresses that ongoing conflict with sin necessitates strenuous exertion. Against those, including perfectionist antinomians, who "pretend perfection," Owen insists that the holiness required under the covenant of grace involves ceaseless warfare: "The holiness required by the gospel will not be kept up or maintained, either in the lives or hearts of men, without a *continual conflict*, warring, contending; and that with all care, diligence, watchfulness, and perseverance."[57] In addition, obedience can be achieved only if Christian duties are taken seriously. As Como noted, seventeenth-century antinomians like Eaton "sought to undermine reliance on duties."[58] On the contrary, Owen affirms the reconciliation of command and promise, grace and duty and the consequent necessity of duties:

> Some would separate the command and the promise, or duty and grace, as inconsistent. A command they suppose leaves no room for a promise, at least not such a[n] absolute promise that God takes on Himself to work in us what the command requires of us. A promise they think takes

[53] Como, *Blown by the Spirit*, 124.
[54] *Works*, 6:170.
[55] Ibid.
[56] *Works*, 3:619.
[57] *Works*, 7:171 (emphasis his).
[58] Como, *Blown by the Spirit*, 208. Strictly speaking, mainstream Puritans did not believe in "trusting in" duties *per se* either.

off all the influential authority of the command. Although our works and grace are opposed in the matter of justification, our duty and God's grace are nowhere opposed in sanctification: yes, the one absolutely presupposes the other. Neither can we perform our [Christian] duty without the grace of God; nor does God give grace except that we rightly perform our duty.[59]

In fact, Owen did not consider the performance of Christian duty barren legalism. On the contrary, he saw faithful performance of Christian duty as the glory and honor of the Christian life:

The glory and honor of the Christian religion principally consists in the glorious internal operations of the Holy Spirit, renewing our nature, transforming us into the image and likeness of God, with the fruits of His grace in righteousness and true holiness, in a meek, humble, gracious conversation, and the performance of all duties according to the rule.[60]

A higher view of Christian duty, and its importance for personal holiness, can scarcely be imagined.

Clearing Justification by Faith from the Charge of Antinomianism

Ironically, mainstream Puritan Reformed theologians, though championing the continuing validity of the moral law, had to fight a rearguard action against the baselessly repeated Socinian charge that the doctrine of justification by faith by the imputed righteousness of Christ promotes antinomian neglect of obedience and good works. Owen, though denying good works as a condition of justification, still insists on the necessity of good works. He proposes five major motives for rendering gospel obedience. The first motive is thoroughly theocentric: "universal holiness and good works" are indispensably necessary to obey God and exalt His glory in salvation.[61] The second motive is purely anthropocentric. Holiness gives a Christian honor, peace, and usefulness: honor by renewing the *imago Dei*, peace by restoring the joy of fellowship with God, and usefulness by making him fruitful in good works.[62] The third motive is predominantly altruistic. Holiness is indispensably necessary for other people in three ways. It stops the mouths of God's enemies here and hereafter, promotes the conversion of observers, and benefits everyone, partly by restraining God's

---

[59] *Works*, 3:406.
[60] *Works*, 7:208–9.
[61] *Works*, 3:316.
[62] *Works*, 3:318.

judgments and partly by doing good works.[63] The fourth major motive follows from the nature of both justification and sanctification. Because a justified person is accepted and befriended by a holy God too pure to behold iniquity, the former should strive for personal holiness so as not to defile communion. Because a sanctified person is a new creature, he should recognize that "this new creature is fed, cherished, nourished, [and] kept alive by the fruits of holiness."[64] Serving a threefold purpose, the fifth motive derives from the "proper place of holiness in the new covenant."[65] It serves a threefold purpose. To begin with, "though neither the cause or condition of justification, [personal holiness] is the way to obtain salvation appointed by God. Therefore, he who has hope of eternal life purifies himself, even as God is pure, for without holiness it is impossible to see God."[66] In addition, holiness proves itself a testimony of adoption when the Christian bears family likeness to God. Finally, holiness serves as full expression of Christian gratitude to God for the gift of salvation. As Owen declares in *The Grace and Duty of Being Spiritually Minded* (1681), "A due sense of [gratitude for] deliverance from the dominion of sin is the most effectual motive for universal obedience and holiness."[67] Regarding the nature of the new creature Owen maintains:

> The new creature is the principle and spiritual ability, produced in believers by the power and grace of the Holy Ghost enabling them to walk in newness of life and holiness of conversation [behavior]. And this principle being bestowed on us, wrought in us, for that very end, it is necessary for us, unless we will neglect and despise the grace which we have received, that we walk in holiness.[68]

Personal holiness, then, is an ultimate purpose of God's recreation of the new creature in Christ.

Directions for Avoiding Apostasy

Owen did not consider these previously enumerated motives to personal holiness, though important, totally sufficient. Therefore, Owen supplemented them with five particular directions for avoiding apostasy in his treatise *The Nature and Causes of Apostasy* (1676). His first direction is

[63] *Works*, 3:318–19.
[64] *Works*, 3:319.
[65] *Works*, 3:319.
[66] *Works*, 3:320.
[67] *Works*, 7:560.
[68] *Works*, 3:323.

total commitment to realize God's glory here and now. This duty has three requirements: secretly mourning the sins of the Christian church, constant prayer for its revival, and maintaining a strong Christian testimony in both life and doctrine.[69] The second direction is to guard the heart against sinful compliances and carnal frames through continual prayer.[70] The third direction is to eschew formalism, which can be accomplished—contrary to antinomian counse—only through divine worship.

> There is not anything in the whole course of our obedience more indispensably required to become a spiritually thriving Christian than the due improvement of gospel privileges and ordinances, especially since worship is the only ordinary outward means of spiritual intercourse between Christ and us whereby He communicates His grace to us and we return love, praise, thanks and obedience to Him. This is what our growth depends on.[71]

The fourth direction is to avoid the contagion of national vices. The fifth direction for avoiding apostasy is to keep from stumbling others through schism, lovelessness, barrenness, and spiritual pride. Owen paints a lovely picture of what he would consider fetching in a Christian:

> Love to the saints without dissimulation; readiness to bear in meekness with different [doctrinal] apprehensions and palpable misapprehensions, so long as they do not entrench on foundation[al Christian truths]; freedom from imposing your sentiments on those who cannot receive them, and from judging supposed failures rashly; and readiness for universal communion in all religious duties with all that 'love the Lord Jesus Christ in sincerity.'[72]

These were character traits largely missing among antinomians who often lambasted Puritan pastors as "priests of Antichrist" and as stunted legalists still preaching a covenant of works. That deficiency was probably something to be expected since the antinomians considered the pursuit of holiness not as an ongoing priority, but as a "done deal." Owen felt still deeper grief that these character traits comprising the beauty of holiness had not been more prevalent among his Puritan brethren. He laments, "And there is nothing of a more ominous presage that things are yet wax-

[69] *Works*, 7:243–45.
[70] *Works*, 7:245–49.
[71] *Works*, 7:250.
[72] *Works*, 7:259.

ing worse, than that general regardless [apathy] about [the degeneracy of contemporary Christianity] among the best of us."[73]

Summary

Owen and Seventeenth-Century antinomians shared no common ground whatsoever on the issue of the importance of Christian obedience. First, though antinomian writers denied the conditionality of the covenant of grace, Owen insisted on the necessity of faith and repentance for conversion and of personal holiness for sanctification. His view of sanctification was that it involves the real and internal communication of a principle of grace whereby the saint performs obedience to God. For Owen, the standard is "sincere and universal" obedience. In other words, it must be wrought by faith in Christ and have equal respect to all of God's commands. Though Owen rigorously maintained that universal obedience precludes habitual impenitence or dereliction of duty, he emphasized God's preservation of the saint's "seed and principle of holiness" against all odds.

This standard of obedience is required, according to Owen, for a number of reasons: the design of the gospel, God's holiness and the purpose of election, and respect to God's sovereignty and Christ's mediatorial office. Owen expressly rejected the *Marrow* notion that fear of punishment and hope of rewards bastardized Christian obedience since "due respect to God's promises and threats is a principal part of our duty." Secondly, unlike the antinomians, who trumpeted an amorphous "law of love," Owen declared that holiness involved a restored conformity not only to the image of God but to the law as well. Owen believed that God's commandments had to be both understood and obeyed wholeheartedly as an expression of his holiness, justice, and goodness. Thirdly, whereas antinomians viewed sanctification as instantaneously accomplished through regeneration by the infusion of the divine essence, Owen noted several biblical injunctions that command growth in grace and rejected the antinomian exaltation of "free justification" at the expense of sanctification. Fourthly, whereas antinomians believed assurance to be immediate from the direct witness of the Holy Spirit, Owen distrusted assurance obtained without evidence of personal holiness. Fifthly, while antinomians disparaged obedience, Owen saw obedience functioning as a means of grace in the sense that "The more men exercise their grace in duties of obedience, the more it [obedience] is strengthened and increased."[74] Sixthly, while antinomians considered obe-

---

[73] *Works*, 7:244.
[74] *Works*, 6:170.

dience a spontaneous overflow from the joy of justification, Owen stressed the importance of strenuous exertion in ongoing conflict with sin.

Finally, Owen had to clear justification from faith from the Socinian slander, and one for which antinomian teaching lent fuel to the flames, that it promoted moral laxity. Though denying good works as a condition of justification, he still insisted that sanctification must evidence the reality of justification. In the covenant of grace, holiness serves a threefold purpose: it provides the holiness without which it is impossible to see God, establishes the testimony of adoption by proving family likeness between God and his children, and fully expresses gratitude for salvation. Owen's treatise on apostasy showed how highly Owen regarded personal holiness. He strongly recommended worship as a means of Christian growth and sketched a picture of Christian graciousness that eluded the antinomians. He lamented that so few of his contemporary Puritan brethren (as Puritanism began to degenerate in the generation following the Restoration) shared his white-hot zeal for the beauty of holiness.

15

Conclusions and
Contemporary Observations

Conclusions

A threefold cord of evidence has been presented to demonstrate the thesis that Owen deliberately battled a theological opponent largely unnoticed by earlier Owen scholars, Seventeenth-Century antinomians. The first strand of evidence consists of his contemporary observations, expressed in several treatises, bemoaning widespread prevalence of doctrinal and practical antinomianism (libertinism) in the church. In his treatise *On Indwelling Sin* (1658), Owen, having witnessed "dreadful" moral lapses, complains that the antinomian ruse of excusing sin works "by a horrible abuse of gospel grace."[1] "From the doctrine of the assured pardon of sin, it insinuates a regardlessness [heedlessness] of sin."[2] In *The Glory of Christ Applied to Unconverted Sinners and Saints under Spiritual Decays* (1692, published posthumously), he blames a period of "public apostasy," marked by "notorious" neglect of public worship and private devotion,[3] on the false coupling of alleged Christian perfection with moral laxity: "Cursed be the man who encourages you to come to Christ with hopes of indulgence for even one sin. I do not speak this as though you could at once absolutely and perfectly leave all sin, in the roots and branches of it."[4] Owen seems

---

[1] *Works*, 6:218.
[2] *Works*, 6:219.
[3] *Works*, 1:455.
[4] *Works*, 1:431.

to be addressing perfectionist antinomians (see chapter 2) and echoing Rutherford's statement: "Antinomians will have the justified to be so quiet in spirit, as if Christ had removed sin root and branch."[5]

The second and most conclusive strand of evidence is his express identification in *Pneumatologia* (1674) of a major theological opponent called "enthusiasm," a term broad enough to include the peculiarities of antinomian thought.[6] There Owen pointed out two distinctives of antinomian theology: willingness to accept divine guidance from irrational impulses and belief in new and direct revelation. Owen, while not naming names when refuting antinomian authors, probably to deny them "the oxygen of publicity,"[7] mentions "antinomianism" by name twice in *The Doctrine of Justification by Faith* (1677).

The third strand of evidence comes from reconstructing the identity of Owen's theological adversaries by analyzing the coherence of his arguments given his opponents' theological divergence and convergence. Clear theological divergence was reflected in their varied approaches to the role of reason. Owen straddled a tightrope between them by insisting on the necessity of divine illumination for conversion while eschewing the extremes of antinomian irrationalism and Socinian and moralistic rationalism. Similarly, contemporary antinomians rejected the role of legal reformation in prompting conversion through inducing self-despair, whereas Socinians saw legal reformation falling short of regeneration as the terminus of the Christian life. Owen had to explain *legal* reformation to the former and *evangelical* reformation to the latter, whom he accused of raising the roof of morality before laying the foundation of regeneration.

Theological convergence was shared, however, in his opponents' misunderstanding of the Holy Spirit's work in regeneration: Socinians denied His divine person, Anglican moralists His work, and antinomians, any intersection between grace and nature. It hardly seems coincidental that the key chapter in this study, "The Bond of Grace and Duty," draws most heavily on *Pneumatologia* (1674), quoting it no fewer than sixteen times to rebut antinomian concepts. Owen's soteriology, with its tightly reasoned and comprehensive presentation of the bond of grace and duty covering as it does the warp and woof of the Christian life could not have developed so fully without studied interaction with antinomian thought. In fact, Owen marshalled a whole series of arguments against antinomian opponents: the necessity of preparation for grace and the preparatory work of the law; the abiding validity of God's moral law; the legitimate condi-

[5] Rutherford, *The Trial and Triumph of Faith*, 245.
[6] *Works*, 3:13 and see Packer, *Redemption and Restoration*, 325.
[7] See statement of Robert W. Oliver on back cover.

tionality of the covenant of grace, given the distinction and interaction between absolute (Bunyan's "big-bellied") promises and conditional ones, with the former guaranteeing the believer's acceptable fulfillment of the latter; the continuing importance of a believer's improvement of the means of grace; divine discipline; justification in time (not from eternity); divine preservation through perseverance; obedience as a means of grace; the vital role played by regenerate human faculties in Christian devotion and maturation; the necessity of mortification of sin and vivification of graces; the ongoing pattern in the Christian life of conviction, faith and repentance; the Holy Spirit working in, by and through the word of God; the necessity of spiritual illumination for conversion; spiritual-mindedness and ceaseless conflict with sin as true marks of regeneration; and the vital role played by prayer and meditation in spiritual transformation.

Owen's strategy to rebut antinomianism was to single out antinomian presuppositions for attack whenever opportunities arose. I have argued that five presuppositions comprise the "deep structure" of antinomian theology: illuminism, immediatism, irrationalism, essentialism and hyper-supernaturalism. As already seen in the case of irrationalism, Owen let none of these presuppositions pass unchallenged. Against antinomianism, Owen asserted not only the continuing validity of the moral law as a rule of life for the Christian[8] but also the importance of preaching the law to promote conversion and meditating on it to produce Christ-like character.[9] Against *illuminism*, he castigated the "empty pretense" of "*enthusiastical*"[10] claims to the gift of prophecy and emphasized the sufficiency of Scripture.[11] Against *irrationalism*, he insisted that regeneration, far from bypassing the intellect, renewed reason and drew it out to its proper use. Against *immediatism*, Owen maintained that full assurance apart from vigorously exercised gifts and graces is a sheer impossibility, the seal of the Spirit notwithstanding.[12] Against *essentialism*, Owen made light work of their flawed view of imputation, which rendered Christ sinful and the sinner perfect.[13] Against *hyper-supernaturalism*, Owen urged that only full use of "gospel privileges and ordinances" guarantees Christian perseverance.[14]

Had Owen stopped here, he would have already done the Christian church signal service. But Owen apparently realized that attacking an-

---

[8] *Works*, 3:383.
[9] *Works*, 4:96.
[10] *Works*, 4:472 (emphasis his).
[11] *Works*, 3:13.
[12] *Works*, 5:439.
[13] *Works*, 3:83.
[14] *Works*, 7:250.

tinomian errors and even its overarching presuppositions would not be nearly enough to stem the floodtide of antinomianism, so he undertook to eliminate it "root and branch." Erupting in London in the latter half of the 1620's, antinomianism had spread to New England in the 1630's, come to a head among radical sectaries in the Puritan Commonwealth in the 1640's and 1650's, and midwifed the birth of Quakerism. Antinomianism, with a fairly extensive theology of its own, cried out for systematic rebuttal, and Owen answered by erecting the bond of grace and duty as a massive bulwark defending Biblical truth. His theological genius is displayed in his architectonic erection of this edifice, an unbroken and unending bond of grace and duty that commences monergistically in the unbeliever's seeking God for salvation and continues synergistically in the Christian's worship of God and lifelong pursuit of personal holiness.

To grasp the broader implications of Owen's approach, consider two seekers, one influenced by antinomian theology, the other by mainstream Puritan theology, and the strikingly divergent paths they trod. Although both seekers probably heard a gospel presentation outlining the demands of the moral law, even here their paths would begin to part. The antinomian seeker would be encouraged not to seek God's face diligently through the means of grace, but simply to accept God's gift of free justification without further ado. The Puritan seeker, urged to "be up and doing," sought God's gift of faith and repentance brokered through his self-despair resulting from his impotence to keep the moral law and part with his deep-seated sins. The antinomian seeker expected instantaneous conversion; the Puritan seeker anticipated a more drawn-out affair usually involving sequenced steps. The antinomian seeker, counseled to await conversion passively, presumably took it easy. The Puritan seeker, heeding Owen's mainstream Puritan counsel, discovered three duties preparatory to regeneration: "outward attendance" on the means of grace, "diligent intension [intensity]" to understand and receive God's self-revelation and plan of salvation,[15] and fervent prayer for the gift of the Holy Spirit.[16]

The paths of the antinomian "convert" and the Puritan convert diverged even further when it came to the *continued* use of the means of grace. The antinomian thought their importance was primarily a thing of the past whereas the Puritan stress lay on their use in the future. Because regeneration supposedly infused the divine essence and made him really or apparently perfect, the importance of the means subsided for the antinomian. The Puritan, by contrast, considered the means of grace vital for

[15] *Works*, 3:229–30.
[16] *Works*, 3:109.

growth in grace and perseverance. Owen, for his part, declared that gospel "ordinances and institutions may not be left unobserved, disused, or omitted [under the covenant of grace] without contempt of the covenant itself, and of the wisdom and authority of Jesus Christ."[17]

Did the antinomian, as certain writers seem to suggest, have a happier lot than the Puritan because the latter, striving to keep intact the bond of grace and duty, strenuously pursued sanctification as his great life's work? What these writers uniformly overlook is the spiritually stultifying position occupied by the antinomian. A serious pastoral problem reared its ugly head because the antinomian convert was led to expect perfection. In seeming recognition of this problem, Eaton counseled fellow antinomians, whenever convictions troubled them, to take their perfection before God "by faith."[18] The Puritan convert would instead embrace, not repress, convictions of sin as integral to spiritual refinement. Owen regarded strong convictions as beneficial because they destroyed the notional faith and self-righteousness of nominal Christians, including antinomians, and he also taught that ongoing conviction and confession of sin facilitated recovery from backsliding.[19]

The antinomian's spiritual position was further compromised, in the mainstream Puritan view shared by Owen, because he could not reasonably hope to experience genuine assurance of salvation in low- or no-growth mode. Whereas the antinomian believed it sinful even to question the fact of his salvation, the Puritan convert was encouraged to examine himself and his life for marks of grace. Owen advocated self-examination by two indispensable proofs that regeneration has indeed taken place. One essential proof was spiritual-mindedness, a God-centered and heavenly-minded thought life, which served as a foil to notional faith. Spiritual-mindedness involved "not [merely] to have the notion and knowledge of spiritual things in the mind, [but] to have our minds really exercised with delight about heavenly things, especially [the risen and exalted] Christ."[20] The other essential proof was ceaseless conflict against sin, involving self-abhorrence, self-suspicion, and hatred of sin as sin.[21] The antinomian was far more likely than the Puritan to fall into conscience-searing or soul-destroying sins because the antinomian thought it futile to resist sin's seductive siren call. After all, regeneration had left his fallen faculties untouched. Again, the antinomian, approaching Christian obedience on automatic pi-

[17] *Works*, 15:454.
[18] Eaton, *Honeycombe*, 25.
[19] *Works*, 1:456.
[20] *Works*, 7:348.
[21] *Works*, 3:437.

lot, resigned himself to slow or no spiritual growth. The Puritan convert, made aware that God works through created gifts and graces capable of nurture and growth, worked out his salvation with fear and trembling, and pursued that holiness without which it is impossible to see God. The antinomian convert lacked the deep hatred and fear of sin exhibited by the Puritan convert. Owen taught that a heart fired with God's love in Christ manifested a "holy contempt" of sin and dreaded God's chastisement.[22] The antinomian heard that God winked at the sins of His children and that such forgiveness exalted the gospel of free justification. The Puritan convert, cognizant that sinning dishonors God and grieves the Holy Spirit, would seek the ruin of sin through mortification. Finally, the "viciously intellectualistic" concept of faith held by the antinomian and his denial of any need for fresh supplies of grace would vitiate prayer and communion with Christ.[23] The Puritan convert believed that prayer enhanced spiritual gifts and invigorated graces and that he should pray "without ceasing," not merely when "moved by the Spirit." Because he did not believe that God saw his sins, the antinomian would take lightly Owen's insistence on daily confession and repentance to clear the way for communion with God and transformation into greater Christlikeness.

An Objection Answered

One major objection likely to be raised against reinstituting the Puritan model of evangelism is that Puritan evangelism works only where the preacher has a captive audience, as in Great Britain or New England with mandatory church-attendance laws, and that this model will never work in entertainment-oriented American churches. While major adjustments would have to be made if a sea change in the prevailing model of evangelism took place, Owen makes a fascinating observation: *Convictions of sin, the kind invariably produced by faithful gospel preaching, are not voluntary but involuntary*: Owen insists that, "Convictions put a kind of force upon the mind, or an impression that causes it to act contrary to its own habitual disposition and inclination."[24] If a congregation comes under true conviction of sin, it will be much easier to direct them willingly into the way of salvation, even if their original motive in coming to church was entertainment. As Owen points out from his reading of Acts, men "cut to the heart" do one of two things: they either repent (Acts 2:37) or kill the messenger

---

[22] *Works*, 6:144.
[23] Packer, *Redemption and Restoration*, 370.
[24] *Works*, 7:280.

(Acts 7:54). The church in Acts lifted ongoing prayer to God for holy boldness in preaching and witness, and the timorous preacher would do well to follow suit.

Contemporary Observations

Much as Dietrich Bonhoeffer in *The Cost of Discipleship* (1937) exposed the soft antinomian underbelly of modern German Lutheranism, the so-called Lordship controversy, which erupted in the United States in the decade of the 1980's, uncovered a similar weakness in modern American evangelicalism, particularly among the segment of churches strongly influenced by dispensational theology and its "viciously intellectualist" antinomian concepts of notional faith and of a divided Savior. Several prominent professors from dispensational seminaries, including the editor of a best-selling study Bible, insisted that mere intellectual belief in the gospel *sans* repentance qualifies as saving faith and further that Jesus could be accepted as Saviour without submitting to him as Lord. (The latter claim violates Calvin's insight that Christ's offices as Prophet, Priest and King cannot be divided.) Both movements have left little impact in the church at large because of their lethal combination of pietism and antinomianism.

The dominant revivalistic method of evangelism in the United States has made matters worse. Inherited from evangelicals like Charles Finney who exalted pragmatism in search of results, this technique-oriented approach insists on instantaneous conversion and rules out preparation for grace, preaching based on a morphology of conversion, or patient waiting on the unfolding process of conversion. Modern evangelicals spellbound by revivalism and its doctrinal indifferentism serve an imprecise God who they think turns a blind eye to theological error and blesses truth mixed with falsehood.

Reformed pastors in the United States typically fall into two camps; both are clueless about the importance of preparation for grace in evangelism. The first camp, more or less unconsciously, as a creature of modern evangelical culture, adopts the revivalistic model of evangelism even though it is clearly inspired by Arminian theology. They seem oblivious to the theological implications of their decisionism. How do sinners "dead in sins and trespasses" (Ephesians 2:1) have power to make the Holy Spirit blow where they want, contrary to the clear teaching of John 3:8, simply by mouthing the words of a sinner's prayer when the evangelist beckons? Edwards declared that his sermons most visited with conversions during the Great Awakening were those insisting on God's sovereignty in granting—or withholding—salvation. Vast damage has been done to the evangelical church by revivalistic evangelism. How about the multiplication of false conversions, and the weakening of Christian testimony to a lost world? Revivalism has wrought many suspect converts who flunk Owen's two tests of true regeneration: spiritual-mindedness and ceaseless conflict against sin.

The second camp of Reformed pastors has understandably recoiled from accommodation to revivalism yet gone to the other extreme by becoming, in common parlance, the "frozen chosen." This group contents itself with doctrinal triumphalism. Packer commented in the 1950's regarding widespread uncertainty about the evangelistic implications of the Reformed faith. Despite the valuable contribution made to clearing up much muddled thinking by *Evangelism and the Sovereignty of God* (1963), this widespread uncertainty has stubbornly persisted. The late John Gerstner testified that his lectures to Reformed pastors on the vital topic of Edwardsean preparation for grace always fell on deaf ears. To the second camp, Dwight Moody's retort to his Reformed critics still rings—and stings—true: "I prefer the evangelism I do," said he, "to the evangelism you don't!"

But the problem in Reformed church circles runs much deeper. Reformed pastors in the United States, though abundantly aware of the antinomian theology often encountered in dispensational quarters, remain strangely blind to doctrinal and practical antinomianism in their own camp. Lest this charge be thought exaggerated, consider these particulars:

- Abraham Kuyper's influential embrace of the presumptive regeneration of covenant children. Though an admirer of Kuyper, Joel R. Beeke feels understandably compelled to point out the mischief caused by his stance among his followers:

  By his doctrine of presumptive regeneration, Kuyper taught that the covenant of grace warrants the presumption that children of believers are regenerated and hence possess saving grace from earliest infancy and are baptized on the basis of that presumption, even though those baptized may later reject the covenant and prove that presumption to be wrong. This led some to conclude that baptism assured salvation, or at least that covenant children need not be told that they need to be born again. Many children grew up thinking that sound doctrinal knowledge and biblical ethical conduct was sufficient for salvation without experiencing conviction of sin and conversion, or any need for self-examination with regard to the marks of grace. The net result was that, over time, Reformed experiential religion became deemed largely superfluous.[25]

[25] Joel R. Beeke, "The Life and Vision of Abraham Kuyper," *Christianity & Society* 14 (2004): 30–31.

- The reckless movement toward paedo-communion, where children who have not made a profession of faith or undergone examination for church communion are allowed to partake of the Lord's Supper as full communicant members, has been spreading in some Presbyterian churches.

- The influence of Norman Shepherd who repudiates historical Reformed evangelism and its focus on regeneration of the lost has been unfortunate. Shepherd's view is that the unregenerate can do nothing to put themselves in the way of salvation.

- A plethora of books on Christian revival stresses it as a panacea for all the church's ills while often neglecting the less glamorous and more difficult labor of reforming the church though the diligent and well-conceived use of biblical means. The Puritans did not merely pray for revival and then sit on their hands. Several generations of godly Puritan pastors built, as it were, an "infrastructure" for revival to take place through emphasis on pastoral calling and diligence, Christian literature and education, "Sabbath" observance, the development of the Westminster confessional standards, examination of ministerial candidates, catechism, family devotion, visitation, preaching seminars known as "prophesyings," and (not least) concerted prayer for intergenerational revival.

- Redemptive-historical preaching often magnifies the acts of God on behalf of his people but largely to the exclusion of the *ordo salutis*. The indicative of Christ's great accomplishment of salvation through His perfect obedience and penal substitutionary atonement, soul thrilling as those biblical truths are, is unfortunately allowed to drown out the imperative need for personal appropriation of that wondrous salvation through faith and repentance.

- Contemporary Reformed preaching lacks balance and is often one-sided. Preachers influenced by Marrow theology, as W. G. Blaikie observed in his day, often stressed the summons to faith to the exclusion of the summons to repentance (and obedience). Their belief is that the "right kind of faith" will take care of everything else, so they magnify the grace of God yet tend to deny the importance of preparation for grace (which is sometimes disparaged as nothing more than "splendid sins").

- Though Reformed preachers generally expound and apply God's moral law more effectively than their counterparts in broad evangelicalism, very few are wielding the "preparatory" sword of the law to flay open the conscience smitten by sin and induce salutary self-despair, to wound before they heal with the balm of the gospel. Far too many are what Richard Sibbes and Robert Bolton called "gospel-daubers," preachers who spill the medicine before the boil has even been lanced. Gospel warnings are seldom sounded out to the unbeliever, much less to the believer, who needs to hear them as well.

- Few Reformed Christians seem to grasp that salvation is to be worked out with fear and trembling and that the basic pattern of conversion, including conviction and confession of sin, illumination, and faith and repentance, occurs repeatedly and in an ever-deepening way in one's Christian pilgrimage. Nor do they recognize that sacrificial obedience gives God the full revenue of the His glory and paves the way for even deeper devotion. Seldom is self-denial or mortification given more than a passing thought, or sanctification realistically recognized as a no-holds-barred, lifelong war between the Christian and indwelling sin in which the Christian, striving to keep intact the bond of grace and duty, must employ holy violence to ruin sin by "walking over the belly of his lusts," thereby avoiding the dangerous and deadly shoals of backsliding and apostasy.

The recovery of full-orbed Reformed theology that began in the 1950's has been exciting and wonderful to behold. But the movement, marred and disfigured by serious antinomian errors and a failure to match zeal for Biblical truth with compassion for the lost and theologically underprivileged, will come to little or naught unless its pastors grasp the full implications of Reformed theology for evangelism and sanctification and repent of spiritual pride and lovelessness. Owen's supremely balanced and incisive soteriology with its carefully forged and unbreakable linkage between grace and duty, its exaltation of glorifying God through arduous devotion and obedience, and its resolute insistence on seeking God constantly and loving and serving Him with all the might of one's regeneration-renewed faculties points the way forward to the true happy medium between the extremes of indifferentism and triumphalism—to experiential Calvinism where the glorious truths of God's grace are lived out through faith working by love. Jonathan Edwards exclaimed during the Great Awakening that his congregation did not need to have their heads stored with knowledge so much as their hearts fired with love. Owen's greatest personal sorrow, besides losing 10 of his 11 children to stillbirth and early death, was the great declension in truth, love, and spiritual power that he witnessed during his own lifetime among Reformed churches throughout Europe. It is to be deeply lamented that, despite their very promising beginning, this same phenomenon of spiritual decline seems poised to repeat itself in the Reformed churches of our era.

Bibliography

Augustine, Aurelius. *Confessions*. Translated by R. S. Pine-Coffin. New York: Penguin Books, 1961.

Baxter, Richard. "A Treatise of Self-Denial." *In The Practical Works of Richard Baxter*. Volume 3. Ligonier, Pa.: Soli Deo Gloria, 1990 reprint.

Beeke, Joel R. *Assurance of Faith: Calvin, English Puritanism, and the Dutch Second Reformation*. New York: Peter Lang, 1991.

_____. "The Life and Vision of Abraham Kuyper." *Christianity & Society* 14 (2004): 24–32.

Blaikie, W. G. *The Preachers of Scotland*. Glasgow: T. & T. Clark, 1888.

Boersma, Hans. *A Hot Pepper Corn: Richard Baxter's Doctrine of Justification in Its Seventeenth-Century Context of Controversy*. Uitgeverij: Boekencentrum Zoetermeer, 1993.

Bozeman, Theodore Dwight. *The Precisianist Strain: Disciplinary Religion and Antinomian Backlash in Puritanism to 1638*. Chapel Hill: University of North Carolina Press, 2004.

Bunyan, John. *The Works of John Bunyan*. Edited by George Offor. Glasgow: W. G. Blackie, 1854.

Bush, Sargent, Jr. *The Writings of Thomas Hooker: Spiritual Adventure in Two Worlds*. Madison: University of Wisconsin Press, 1980.

Caldwell, Patricia A. *The Puritan Conversion Narrative: The Beginnings of American Expression*. London: Cambridge University Press, 1983.

Calvin, John. *Institutes of the Christian Religion*. Edited by John T. McNeill and translated by Ford Lewis Battles. Philadelphia: Westminster, 1960.

————. *The Bondage and Liberation of the Will: A Defense of the Orthodox Doctrine of Human Choice against Pighius*. Edited by A. N. S. Lane and translated by G. I. Davies. Grand Rapids: Baker, 1996.

Como, David R. *Blown by the Spirit: Puritanism and the Emergence of an Antinomian Underground in Pre-Civil-War England*. Stanford, Calif.: Stanford University Press, 2004.

Cotton, John. *The Covenant of God's Free Grace*. London: n.p., 1645.

Craig. Philip A. "'And Prophecy Shall Cease': Jonathan Edwards on the Cessation of Prophecy." *Westminster Theological Journal* 64 (2002): 163–84.

Dever, Mark E. *Richard Sibbes: Puritanism and Calvinism in Late Elizabethan and Early Stuart England*. Macon, GA.: Mercer University Press, 2000.

Eaton, John. *The Honeycombe of Free Justification by Christ Alone*. London: Robert Lancaster, 1642.

Edwards, Jonathan. *Works of Jonathan Edwards*. The Great Awakening, Vol. 4. Edited by C. C. Goen. New Haven: Yale University Press, 1972.

————. *Works of Jonathan Edwards*. The Religious Affections, Vol. 2. Edited by John E. Smith. New Haven: Yale University Press, 1959.

Ferguson, Sinclair B. *John Owen on the Christian Life*. Edinburgh: Banner of Truth, 1987.

Flavel, John. *Works of John Flavel*. Edinburgh: Banner of Truth, 1982 reprint.

Gerstner, John H., and John N. Gerstner. "Edwardsean Preparation for Salvation." *Westminster Theological Journal* 42 (1979): 5–71.

Gleason, Randall G. *John Calvin and John Owen on Mortification: A Comparative Study in Reformed Spirituality*. New York: Peter Lang, 1995.

Guthrie, William. *The Christian's Great Interest*. Edinburgh: Banner of Truth, 1982.

Hall, David D., ed. *The Antinomian Controversy, 1636–1638: A Documentary History*. 2d ed. Durham: Duke University Press, 1990.

_____. "On Common Ground: The Coherence of American Puritan Studies." *William and Mary Quarterly* 44 (1987): 193–229.

_____. *Puritans in the New World: A Critical Anthology*. Princeton: Princeton University Press, 2004.

Hambrick-Stowe, Charles. *The Practice of Piety: Puritan Devotional Disciplines in Seventeenth-Century New England*. Chapel Hill: University of North Carolina Press, 1982.

Helm, Paul. *Calvin and Calvinism*. Edinburgh: Banner of Truth, 1982.

Huehns, Gertrude. *Antinomianism in English History: With Special Reference to the Period, 1640–1660*. London: Cresset Press, 1951.

Kendall, R. T. *Calvin and English Calvinism to 1649*. Oxford: Oxford University Press, 1979.

Knight, Janice. *Orthodoxies in Massachusetts: Rereading the American Puritans*. Cambridge, Mass.: Harvard University Press, 1994.

Kuyper, Abraham. *The Work of the Holy Spirit*. Translated by Henri De Vries. New York: Funk and Wagnalls Company, 1900.

Letham, Robert, and Donald Macleod. "Is Evangelicalism Christian?" *Evangelical Quarterly* 67 (1995): 3–33.

Logan, Samuel T. "Jonathan Edwards and the Northampton Awakening." In *Preaching and Revival*. London: Westminster Conference, 1984.

Luther, Martin. *The Bondage of the Will*. Translated by James I. Packer and O. R. Johnston. Old Tappan, N.J.: Revell, 1957.

M'Crie, Thomas. *The Story of the Scottish Church*. Glasgow: Bell and Bain, 1874.

McGowan, A. T. B. "Thomas Boston." In *New Dictionary of Theology*. Edited by Sinclair B. Ferguson and David F. Wright, 108–109. Downers Grove: InterVarsity Press, 1988.

McGrath, Gavin J. "Puritans and the Human Will: Voluntarism within Mid-Seventeenth Century English Puritanism in Richard Baxter and John Owen." Doctoral thesis, University of Durham, 1989.

_____. *Grace and Duty in Puritan Spirituality*. Nottingham, England: Grove Books, 1991.

McMullen, Michael. *God's Polished Arrow: William Chalmers Burns*. Ross-shire, UK: Christian Focus Publications, 2000.

Miller, Perry. *The New England Mind*. Boston: Beacon Press, 1961.

_____. "'Preparation for Salvation' in Seventeenth-Century New England." *Journal of the History of Ideas* 4 (1943): 253–86.

Muller, Richard A. *Dictionary of Latin and Greek Theological Terms*. Grand Rapids: Baker, 1985.

Murray, Iain H. "Antinomian: New England's First Controversy." *Banner of Truth* 179–180 (August 1978): 7–75.

Nuttall, Geoffrey F. *The Holy Spirit in Puritan Faith and Experience*. Chicago: University of Chicago Press, 1946.

Ozment, Steven. *The Age of Reform: 1250–1550*. New Haven: Yale University Press, 1980.

Owen, John. *The Works of John Owen*. Vol. 1, Meditations and Discourses on the Glory of Christ. Edited by William H. Goold. Edinburgh: Banner of Truth, 1850; reprint, 1967.

_____. *The Works of John Owen*. Vol. 2, On Communion with God. Edited by William H. Goold. Edinburgh: Banner of Truth, 1850; reprint, 1967.

_____. *The Works of John Owen*. Vol. 3, Discourse on the Holy Spirit. Edited by William H. Goold. Edinburgh: Banner of Truth, 1850; reprint, 1967.

_____. *The Works of John Owen*. Vol. 4, The Reason of Faith. Edited by William H. Goold. Edinburgh: Banner of Truth, 1850; reprint, 1967.

_____. *The Works of John Owen*. Vol. 4, Causes, Ways and Means of Understanding the Mind of God. Edited by William H. Goold. Edinburgh: Banner of Truth, 1850; reprint, 1967.

_____. *The Works of John Owen*. Vol. 4, A Discourse of the Work of the Holy Spirit in Prayer. Edited by William H. Goold. Edinburgh: Banner of Truth, 1850; reprint, 1967.

_____. *The Works of John Owen*. Vol. 4, Of the Holy Spirit and His Work as a Comforter and as the Author of Spiritual Gifts. Edited by William H. Goold. Edinburgh: Banner of Truth, 1850; reprint, 1967.

_____. *The Works of John Owen*. Vol. 5, The Doctrine of Justification by Faith. Edited by William H. Goold. Edinburgh: Banner of Truth, 1850; reprint, 1967.

_____. *The Works of John Owen*. Vol. 5, Evidences of the Faith of God's Elect. Edited by William H. Goold. Edinburgh: Banner of Truth, 1850; reprint, 1967.

_____. *The Works of John Owen*. Vol. 6, Of the Mortification of Sin in Believers. Edited by William H. Goold. Edinburgh: Banner of Truth, 1850; reprint, 1967.

_____. *The Works of John Owen*. Vol. 6, On Temptation. Edited by William H. Goold. Edinburgh: Banner of Truth, 1850; reprint, 1967.

_____. *The Works of John Owen*. Vol. 6, On Indwelling Sin in Believers. Edited by William H. Goold. Edinburgh: Banner of Truth, 1850; reprint, 1967.

_____. *The Works of John Owen*. Vol. 6, Exposition of Psalm 130. Edited by William H. Goold. Edinburgh: Banner of Truth, 1850; reprint, 1967.

_____. *The Works of John Owen*. Vol. 7, The Nature and Causes of Apostasy. Edited by William H. Goold. Edinburgh: Banner of Truth, 1850; reprint, 1967.

_____. *The Works of John Owen*. Vol. 7, On Spiritual-Mindedness. Edited by William H. Goold. Edinburgh: Banner of Truth, 1850; reprint, 1967.

_____. *The Works of John Owen*. Vol. 7, On the Dominion of Sin and Grace. Edited by William H. Goold. Edinburgh: Banner of Truth, 1850; reprint, 1967.

_____. *The Works of John Owen*. Vol. 8, Sermons. Edited by William H. Goold. Edinburgh: Banner of Truth, 1850; reprint, 1967.

_____. *The Works of John Owen*. Vol. 10, The Death of Death in the Death of Christ. Edited by William H. Goold. Edinburgh: Banner of Truth, 1850; reprint, 1967.

_____. *The Works of John Owen*. Vol. 11, The Doctrine of the Saints' Perseverance Explained and Confirmed. Edited by William H. Goold. Edinburgh: Banner of Truth, 1850; reprint, 1967.

_____. *The Works of John Owen*. Vol. 18–23, Concerning the Epistle to the Hebrews. Edited by William H. Goold. Edinburgh: Banner of Truth, 1850; reprint, 1967.

Packer, J. I. *Keep in Step with the Spirit*. Old Tappan, N.J.: Revell, 1994.

_____. "Regeneration." In *Evangelical Dictionary of Theology*. Edited by Walter A. Elwell, 924–26. Grand Rapids: Baker, 1984.

_____. *A Quest for Godliness: The Puritan Vision of the Christian Life*. Westchester, IL.: Crossway Books, 1990.

_____. *The Redemption and Restoration of Man in the Thought of Richard Baxter*. Vancouver, B.C.: Regent University Press, 2003 reprint.

Pelikan, Jaroslav. *The Christian Tradition: Reformation of Church and Dogma (1300–1700)*. Chicago: University of Chicago Press, 1984.

Pettit, Norman. *The Heart Prepared: Grace and Conversion in Puritan Spiritual Life*. New Haven: Yale University Press, 1966.

Primus, John H. *Richard Greenham: The Portrait of an Elizabethan Pastor*. Macon, GA.: Mercer University Press, 1998.

Rehnman, Sebastian. *Divine Discourse: The Theological Methodology of John Owen*. Grand Rapids: Baker, 2002.

Rutherford, Samuel. *The Trial and Triumph of Faith*. Edinburgh: Banner of Truth, 2001.

Schmidt, Leigh Eric. "A Second and Glorious Reformation: The New Light Extremism of Andrew Croswell." *William and Mary Quarterly* 43 (1986): 214–44.

Shepherd, Norman. *The Call of Grace: How the Covenant Illuminates Salvation and Evangelism*. Phillipsburg, N.J.: Presbyterian and Reformed, 2000.

Steinmetz, David C. "Hermeneutic and Old Testament Interpretation in Staupitz and the Young Martin Luther." *Archiv für Reformationge-schichte* 70 (1979): 24–58.

Stoddard, *Solomon. A Guide to Christ.* Ligonier, PA.: Soli Deo Gloria, 1993 reprint.

Stoever, William K. B. *'A Faire and Easye Way to Heaven': Covenant Theology and Antinomianism in Early Massachusetts.* Middleton, CT: Wesleyan University Press, 1978.

_____. "The Godly Will's Discerning." In *Jonathan Edwards' Writings: Text, Context, Interpretation.* Edited by Stephen J. Stein, 85–99. Bloomington: Indiana University Press, 1996.

Taylor, Richard. "Causation." In *The Encyclopedia of Philosophy.* Vol. 1. Edited by Paul Edwards. New York: MacMillan, 1967.

Toon, Peter. *God's Statesman: The Life and Work of John Owen.* Grand Rapids: Zondervan, 1973.

Trueman, Carl R. *The Claims of Truth: John Owen's Trinitarian Theology.* Carlisle, UK: Paternoster, 2002.

Underwood, T. L. *Primitivism, Radicalism and the Lamb's War: The Baptist-Quaker Conflict in Seventeenth-Century England.* Oxford: Oxford University Press, 1997.

Warfield, B. B. *Calvin and Augustine.* Philadelphia: Presbyterian and Reformed, 1956 reprint.

Waters, Guy Prentiss. *Justification and the New Perspective on Paul.* Phillipsburg, NJ: Presbyterian and Reformed, 2004.

Watson, Thomas. *The Doctrine of Repentance.* Edinburgh: Banner of Truth, 1987.

_____. *Select Works of Thomas Watson.* Morgantown, PA.: Soli Deo Gloria, 1990 reprint.

Westminster Confession of Faith. Glasgow: Free Presbyterian Publications, 1958 reprint.

Winship, Michael P. *Making Heretics: Militant Protestantism and Free Grace in Massachusetts, 1636–1641.* Princeton: Princeton University Press, 2002.

Ziff, Larzer. *Puritanism in America*. New York: Viking, 1973.

Indices

Index of Scripture References

Old Testament

New Testament

Index of Names and Subjects